CONVERSATIONS IN HYPERREALITY
and Other Thoughts Umberto Eco
and Dave Barry Never Had

9 780985 462376

BLUE ROOM BOOKS
DECATUR, GA

Conversations in Hyperreality and Other Thoughts Umberto Eco and Dave Barry Never Had

By
Angela K. Durden

TABLE DES MATIÈRES

"Do not despise small beginnings."[1]

Two male writers (guys) provided the spark for this book. The first guy, Umberto Eco, found his inspiration in both obscure and uncomplicated ancient Greek and Latin texts housed in dark monasteries from which he teased out meanings from weird signage and connected those to historical events ancient, modern, and post-modern. The second guy, Dave Barry, found his inspiration in having to write something funny that would sell so his paymasters wouldn't fire him; he had a family to feed and, furthermore, he's a fortunate smart-aleck who found a paying job he could do that allowed him to work within his talent set.

It is amazing where I find inspiration for my writings. I mean, can you imagine Umberto and Dave even being in the same place at the same time and having anything to talk about? But filtering their conversation through the mind of the Autodidact Polymath Magnificently Methodical Southern Woman and The Most Brilliant Woman In The World would make the two men best buddies. Yes, I could translate Umberto's thoughts so even Dave[2] could understand them.

But I get inspiration from other sources, too. For instance, my memoir[3] was inspired by a horrible childhood but one in which God was watching over me though it wasn't until decades later I would know it. And then there are the stories in my series of humor books inspired by the superb headlines from some of the best writers of spin on the planet who work

---

[1] A paraphrased Scripture from somewhere in the Old Testament, maybe Zechariah? You'll have to look it up.

[2] And possibly pussy-hat wearing men, too.

[3] *Twinkle, a memoir* is available wherever books are sold and on The Internet.

for the likes of <u>The Washington Post</u>, <u>The New York Times</u>, <u>HuffingtonPost.com</u>, <u>Pravda</u>, and <u>China Daily</u>, among others.

But Conversations in Hyperreality and Other Thoughts Umberto Eco and Dave Barry Never Had? Oh my! This book takes my genius with words to a higher level than ever before. Why, it's a sure bet to become a best seller after I kick the bucket. Original copies will fetch a handsome price in rare book stores across the globe and possibly other planets, too. Conversations like the following happen all the time.

Fan: Angela, how is it you know so much?

Angela: I was born with this knowledge, just as you are.

Fan: But, Angela, I don't know everything you do.

Angela: [Giving gentle smile] I disagree, grasshopper. You do. But you have a bigger problem.

Fan: [Leaning in close and whispering] What?

Angela: Simple. You are constipated.

Fan: But I am not constipated.

Angela: I speak not of the physical binding of waste —

Fan: The what?

Angela: [Sigh]

And so, my point is made even if they do miss it themselves and I have to take yet another hour out of my life to explain these concepts onesy-twosey while I tell them if they would only buy a book and take it home we would both save a lot of time and be more benefited. Mine is a heavy burden to bear, but just like Eco and Barry carried their burdens by shedding light in the dark corners by begging people to buy their books, so do I. And gladly because isn't that what life is all about: Making it better for others even at the expense of your own soul, financial stability, and sanity?

Of course it is. Everybody loves a martyr, right?[4] The departure from the subject here is superfluous and meant only to add word count to the book so it might accrue certain bragging rights among writer acquaintances of the author. Those conversations go like this:

Fellow Writer: Hello, Angela. Boy am I ever tired.

Angela: [Seeing the setup a mile away and ready for it] Oh, really? Are you ill?

Fellow Writer: [In an exaggerated fashion assuring not] Oh, no, no, no. No! Not at all. But, boy, am I ever tired from, whew, you know, working on my newest book.

Angela: Really? You've started another book?

Fellow Writer: [With deprecatingly small wave of the hand] Yeah. I know, right? Whew. This one just sort of…you know…hahahaha…popped out. I had no idea I was going to write it but then…boom…one week later I've got 650,000 words ready to go. All of them keepers. Yes, indeed.

Angela: Wow. All of the words are keepers? You didn't have to change not one?

Fellow Writer: That's right. It was like they were just…inspired…you know…from God.

Angela: Yes, indeed. God does like a joke.

Fellow Writer: Excuse me?

---

[4] This is not true. Martyrs may be loved, but they are not universally loved by all. For instance, Jesus. Jesus, the Son of the Almighty God, was a martyr and yet there are a bunch of folks who have never heard of Him so how can they love Him? They cannot. Then there are the martyrs that hate Jesus and The Great Satan who strap bombs on themselves and kill people to prove that hate. Who loves them? Nobody. The mother of the martyr is only happy to get the Martyr Dividend promised her each month for sacrificing her child.

Angela: Nothing. Just blabbering. Soooo…anyway. You're tired?

Fellow Writer: Oh. Oh. Yes, yes, yes, so tired.

Angela: Say, did you ever finish those other books you started?

Fellow Writer: Oh, hahahahaha! Yes. Oh, the life of a writer is simply paralyzing, but what can one do when one must write, right?

Angela: [Reaching for her truncheon] Right.

Fellow Writer: Say, you ever finish that little story you were working on? I think you were around word count… what? 15K maybe? What was it about, by the way? Something about…no…no…wait. Let me think.

Angela: [Watching them think]

Fellow Writer: [Shrugging] You'll have to tell me, dear.

Angela: Oh, yeah! I'll tell you this: Do not despise small beginnings, you! [Swinging her truncheon and claiming insanity when the police show up]

You may think it is easy to add word count to a book, but let me tell you from the start, it is not. Being a writer is the hardest job in the world for several reasons, but I shall only mention two here. One: Writers do it alone. And, two: Writers are alone when they do it.

Unlike other jobs where, when no matter how you do your job, a boss[5] will come around and berate you for not working fast enough, writers have no one but themselves to berate them[6]. It's a hard job, too, taking a lot of effort to

---

[5] And often fellow employees with aspirations of management positions, too.

[6] Until one has lunch with a writer wannabe who (it is obvious) has not read the author's works and has to hear how the author could have written

document that the berating of self was not harassment so no lawsuit will result from it. It takes a huge amount of external fortitude, internal fortitude, guts, psyllium husk fiber, a surplus of determination, true grit, fake grit, resolve, wavering, backbone, strength of character, lack of character, motivation, depression, drive, spirit, willpower, and horsepower[7] to be both boss and employee and still get to the end of writing a book.

You people out there have no idea how draining it is to sit around all day and use your brain. I have to schedule naps. That's right! I must carve out of my day one, sometimes two, hours of rest right in the middle of my most productive writing time, which is to say, in the afternoon. If the writing has been especially grueling, both mid-morning and afternoon naps are required.

Do you know how it makes me feel to have to admit this? I feel you are judging me harshly as if I were lazy but, **damn it**, I **swear** I am **not** lazy. I'm not. You must believe me. As proof of this oath of mine, just read the titles in this book. I mean, could a lazy person have come up with titles like "Explaining a Theme Park to Future Archeologists and Anthropologists"? Or-or-or "How not to rob a convenience store"? An'-an'-and how about "The Art of the Snappy Comeback: That's my name. Don't wear it out."? Huh? Can a lazy person do that? I think not. So, please read on and see the results of all my hard work. You will not be sorry.[8]

---

the book better if only they had thought of [fill in helpful suggestion here]...or they worked for the <u>Miami Herald</u>.

[7] The author wants the potential writer to note the helpful use of the thesaurus and other official listings of words in adding to the word count.

[8] This opening added 1600+ words to the total word count of the book. See? The author told you she worked hard, and she did it all for you, reader, *all for you*.

Conversations in Hyperreality, or
The Polymaths Amongst Us
and the New Renaissance

A friend recently gave me a copy of Umberto Eco's *Travels in Hyperreality*. "Angela!" he gushed. "Seeing as how you are a writer and deep thinker, you might very well enjoy this."

He then went on and on, loudly repeating himself about what he knew about the Italian novelist, literary critic, philosopher, semiotician, and professor as if I had not heard him the first time. Or else he had forgotten he told me five minutes before.

In any case, my friend does love to hear himself talk. So much so he will ask a question and before I've gotten three words out in answer he will have zeroed in on one of those words and will attempt to fashion a joke or witticism around it. Then he will repeat it until I react with a smile after which he will say, "I just knew you would find it [insert rotating descriptions of reaction type here (see choices below)]."

Hilarious. Funny. Witty. Smart. Reminding one of….

In other words, whatever reaction he needs, he implies it from my smile, though "patiently waiting for his mouth to stop running" is never one of his descriptors. Then, and only then, will he again ask his question and wait for my three-word partial answer before he interrupts with another thought suggested by one of my words.

Thank goodness our time has a forced limit and I have a polite way of sending him on his way — even as he's backing down the sidewalk and still carrying on his oration as I'm waving goodbye and walking the other direction. Before you ask: Yes, he believes I tear myself away from him.

At this point you may believe I am changing the subject. I am not. Please bear with.

I had been tasked by my Aunt Virginia to read the 1956 book *Miracle in the Mountains: The Inspiring Story of Martha Berry's Crusade for the Mountain People of the South* by Harnett T. Kane and Inez Henry. A book she gave me because she herself, one of those mountain people, had just celebrated her 55th reunion of the '63C class of Berry College in Rome, Georgia. The story was fascinating, and I had determined not to start another book until I finished it.

In any case, I took Eco's book home and moved it up in queue to be read after I finished the Martha Berry story. And so, five days after my friend gave me Umberto's book, I cried when Martha died on or near her seventy-fifth birthday as Atlanta experienced its first wartime blackout; I vowed to live my life with more gusto and gumption. On day six, I eagerly cracked the spine of Eco's 1973 paperback *Travels in Hyperreality.*

And was promptly bored out of my gourd.

Not because his writing was terrible, but because he repeated his brilliant bits over and over. No wonder my friend liked him so much. If a point could be made, Eco would damn straight make sure you knew it from every point of view there was, translated through the eyes of each epoch of mankind's history. Which is not a bad idea.

Talk about beating a dead horse. Which probably will happen in Eco's debut novel…after The Girl does something with a chicken a la *Equus*. You may remember a movie called *The Name of the Rose*. It was based on Eco's novel featuring a murder mystery in a monastery that, if I read correctly, Eco based on some old notes by a real monk from the period. *The period* being the Middle Ages, of course. The movie starred a very young Christian Slater, helper to the investigator and a monk in training, who furtively watches The Girl have sex with a chicken against every natural law but boy, oh boy, is he repulsed and turned on and conflicted and bi-curious and she is too, and guilt fairly oozes out of him. Top billing went to a grittily handsome Sean Connery playing the monkish type of person sent to solve the grisly murder.

Hang in there, y'all. You'll thank me later.

While the movie was dark and weird and there is The Chicken Incident, it was a pretty good murder mystery and the helper monk chooses the path of God and all's well that ends well as they ride off into the gloom on a horse and donkey. I bought the book with the clear intent of reading it after *Travels in Hyperreality* was finished. I believe the read will begin on Day Seven after *Travels* receivership because I cannot bear to waste any more time on such tedium.

I'm glad Umberto is now dead so he won't have to read my opinion. Still, I am sure, should he and I have found ourselves together and had a conversation about my opinion of his opinions, we would have invented a new form of tête-à-tête called Conversations in Hyperreality. It would not include my friend because nobody would get a word in edgewise nor complete a thought.

I believe Umberto and I would have enjoyed conversation with the other as it would have proved to be lively. Further, I would have had someone who could possibly keep up with me and, this is more important, he would have had someone who could magnificently and methodically test his logic; after all, nobody can test a man's logic like a Magnificently Methodical Southern Woman. I am a Magnificently Methodical Southern Woman and not the first. Martha Berry was lauded around the world as being the same. She got Henry Ford to pony up much money, time, and advice over the years when nobody else could.

Lest you think I've got the big head about myself in this matter, I'll be frank: Ain't bragging if it's a fact. But enough about you. Let's talk polymaths, of which Eco was one.

A polymath is someone who has a deep learning about a wide variety of subjects. No, polymaths are not know-it-alls. A know-it-all is one of those people who, at the drop of any topic whatsoever, will opine ad infinitum whether or not they really know anything about it. These are the people who put the yawn in party and they are most definitively not a polymath, but more like a person such as my friend who gave me the book.

Granted, polymaths can be boring, but that is so rare the following statement is almost always 100% true: All polymaths are not boring, and all know-it-alls are not polymaths.

In fact, a true polymath has more questions than answers. A polymath will readily admit they hold Opinion A and will recite marshaled Arguments A-Plenty to let listeners know why they reached said opinion.

A know-it-all states baldly, then insults you if any proof set is asked for.

Unlike know-it-alls who form an opinion and never change it come Hell or high water, polymaths hold an opinion and pray and hope somebody will shed light on the dark corners about it, dark corners they know can exist. In fact, they are notorious for questioning themselves to the point that weeks — sometimes years — later they will change Opinion A to Opinion A-2.X and will apologize for not having known the clarifying facts and/or taken so long to uncover those.

Know-it-alls are rigid and never change their minds. They live in the world of definitives: Black and white are clearly delineated and never intersect.

Polymaths are flexible and readily change their minds when there is logical reason to do so. They live in the land of the rough draft: Where black and white exist along with every spectrum of gray.

Know-it-alls, while universally hated, are universally lauded when they come in the form of a politician or preacher who is willing to tickle the ears of their audiences.

Polymaths, while universally lauded, are universally hated because they ask others to think and confirm for themselves. Polymaths never tickle ears by telling a mob what they want to hear more of, like false promises of a chicken in every bed…errrr…I mean pot and a smartphone in every pocket, and they tick off a lot of folks.

Which explains why I tick off a lot of folks. I am a polymath. And let me be the first to tell you, in case you've never met another polymath, such a life is hard to lead. A life, by the by, one cannot choose not to live because one's brain simply works that way.

My nickname growing up was "Angie…Aaahhhh!" It came about because all conversations with me never failed to end with "Angie…*Aaahhh!*"

The "Aaahhhhs" were not of the admiring variety like were hurled toward the Girl from Ipanema. No, my "Aaahhhs" were of the exasperated type hurled by vexed folks who could not answer my questions or hold up their end of a damn conversation or defend their absolute statement.

Relatives, teachers, possible business associates, now-ex-husband, my children, and a lot of men these last few years have all said, "Angie…Aaahhhh!" Some have followed with invectives, a few quietly muttered, others bursting forth in censured tirade, one or two or ten with a wave of a disgusted hand, and a surfeit of men backing away as if a bullet would be seeking their back.

Being a polymath sounds sexy, I grant you. And as you began this most profound essay, you were saying to yourself, "My God! Why can't I, too, be a polymath?" Let me assure you this is not an easy life.

You see, firstly, getting and keeping a job is difficult. You can't specialize in anything because your mind not only sees it all, it sees connections between it all where others do not. These connections make sense, but next thing you know somebody says to you, "Stop trying to figure out a better way….Just do what I tell you, okay?....Because we've *always* done it like that….YOU'RE FIRED!"

Secondly, if you have a spouse with an ego, said spouse will always accuse you of being a know-it-all because they cannot see the difference between asking questions to learn from a bad situation and asking questions to point out their shortcomings. Polymaths must have mates with thick skins and lots of love for their cuddly widdle polymath.

So, no. I would not wish upon anyone the brain of a polymath. And yet...

We seem to be in a new renaissance — or as the Brits and the rest of Europe say: ree-NAY-saunce — of polymaths. Much like the Middle Ages heralded massive social change after a thousand or so years of out-of-control barbarians at the gates, we are seeing a reawakening of wide-ranging thought at a faster pace than ever before in human history.

It's because we have the Internet.

True, the Internet has become a free and public forum for know-it-alls who used to have to chase friends and strangers down at the coffee shop and in the grocery store aisle to opine. And this is where the polymath makes a connection: Have you ever noticed with the rise of the Internet, nobody talks at the grocery store or coffee shop anymore? We can whip in and out, never making but the merest human connection at all.

You see? Polymaths think of these things.

Of course, like all good things, institutions of higher learning want to find a way to co-opt the title — for a fee, of course. There are degrees in polymath now being offered to turn you into a polymathtician. There are three tracks you can choose, but you just wait, there will be more. And who will teach these courses? You can bet your sweet, chapped cheeks it won't be true polymaths. Universities' strengths are in turning out know-it-alls, thus making this a true statement: Know-it-alls will teach the polymath courses and polymaths will never teach Polymath 101 or any other number.

Further, being a polymath is dependent on a brain pattern naturally occurring in a population and is not dependent on schooling. In fact, the polymath who does not get higher learning from an official institution of advanced studies usually has more imagination than a polymath who has to fight prevailing wisdom upon which his job is dependent.

For instance, take me, the polymath you know. I did not go to college. And yet, I have been in the company of inventors and industry-recognized thought leaders as they walk me through their newest project and of whom I have asked one simple question. It usually goes like this:

"Right. Wow. That…just…looks good! But…*what* is *that thing* right there?" I cannot tell you how many times they've been stopped cold. Their answers are:

"Huh. I do not know." (Then turning to project leader who frantically says —)

"Holy crap! *That* should not be there." (Desperately dialing a phone; ripping somebody a new you-know-what as he dashes off to handle "that thing right there".)

Now, if I had received a bunch of higher learning, I would have been so sufficiently awed by what they knew I would not have thought to question something which didn't seem to fit. I would have been useless to them and when failure ensued they would not have known why.

Only recently have I come to understand I am a polymath. The realization came when People Who Matter in the tech sector and the music industry told me, "Angela, you are a Thought Leader and an Industry Disruptor." They said this because I was able to explain to them the concepts of protection of intellectual property. A subject they, who make a living from the public dissemination of their thoughts, should have understood but did not.

They did not understand how it is I knew all this. You see, they knew everybody who was somebody, schools attended, majors, and in what they specialized; and here I was, going deeper than they had ever thought to go with a sweetly simple solution to a huge problem, yet they couldn't find out anything about me. But they took it from me because, you see, I am a Magnificently Methodical Southern Woman.

And, as men quickly find out, a Magnificently Methodical Southern Woman gets their attention. Hmmmm…might there be a higher concentration of polymaths in the South?

See?

Connections where others do not see them.

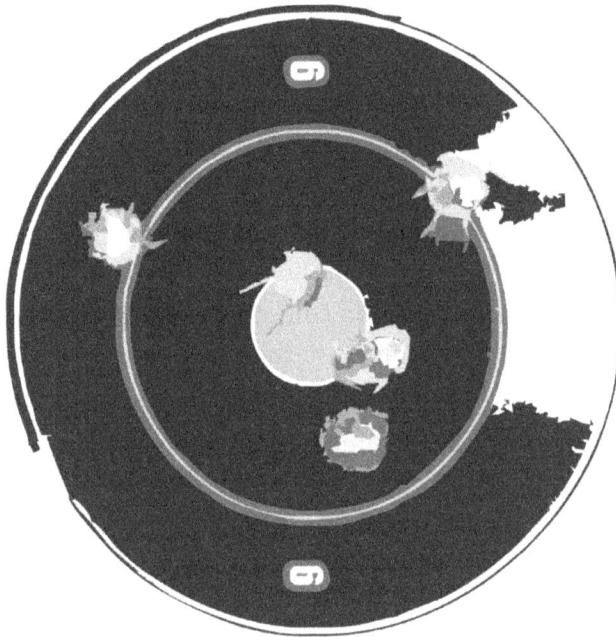

Cats throughout history, or
How I almost threw up.

I inherited my word association skills from my mother. Let me be clear, for I shall not be accused of misrepresenting those abilities: I did not say the skills were convenient or reliable, though I could fairly say I have taken those skills to a new low even Mother has never visited.

Mother could meet Lily and later call her Rose. On the face of it, seems logical. After all, both are flowers, and a Lily by any other name brings to the party a covered dish just as delicious. But I could meet Lily and end up embarrassing myself by calling her Zihuatanejo. [Say-whatta-NAY-oh.]

I told you. I'm much worse at this than Mother. Here's how the above example would work. Trust me when I tell you this is a very simple example of how my mind operates when it comes to associating:

[When you see this symbol ≅ you will read it like this: Is Approximately Equal To.]

Lily ≅ Flower ≅ Rose ≅ Umberto Eco's novel *The Name of the Rose* ≅ Monk detectives in a monastery ≅ Sean Connery ≅ Christian Slater ≅ Who battled a flood in *Hard Rain* with bad guy Morgan Freeman ≅ Who is doing prison time at Shawshank with ≅ Innocent man who escapes and sends a postcard to his friend saying "Come visit me in Zihuatanejo."

Sure, when I lay it all out for you in this linear fashion, you totally get it and it makes sense, even causing me to have something humorous to write and making you laugh.

But it doesn't help me remember the five items I need to get at the grocery store when I've forgotten my list. You would be surprised what I come home with and that makes perfect sense…when you connect the dots after going around the world, but I still need buttermilk for the biscuits and so another trip ensues.

I once met a man who was an expert — an expert, mind you, he made money from corporations paying him for this skill — in teaching people how to use word association to enhance memory of names. He swore up and down it was simple and said he could teach me in five minutes a skill I would never lose. "I've never met anybody I could not teach this skill to," he boasted. He'd been an expert for many years in this. As with all experts who meet me, The Most Brilliant Woman In The World, their experience with me is always an outlier, their confidence is greatly shaken, and my name isn't even Cecilia.

Thirty minutes later he's throwing his hands in the air and saying, "I don't know how you got that. How did you get that?"

I had to take him for a walk around the world and, sure enough, he saw it was quite logical. Anyway, his methods did not work for me. But I'm glad he did not fix my mental condition because with it I obviously see connections others do not and this has been a boon to myself and others throughout the years. If only I could figure out how to make it work on command, I would be a rich woman.

The reason I am telling you this is because recently I found myself the proud recipient of several issues of <u>MIT Technology Review</u>. I waited until I had a bunch of junk…errr…I mean paying work…off my desk so I could settle in and just loll around to my heart's content in all the technical lingo.

I came upon an article by Will Knight wherein he delved into quantum computers and how there is hope they will "supercharge artificial intelligence by crunching through data more efficiently". The question finally asked was, "What, if anything, will quantum computers be good for?"

The article tried to answer the question, but I had the answer before the question was barely asked. Listen, I'm an autodidact and a polymath in addition to being The Most Brilliant Woman In The World, so it stands to reason I would come up with the answer before them. How did I come up with the answer? Two ways. First, I thought of the term *common denominator*. Then I went around the world with my word association which, logically, led to universal worship of cats. From the misty mists of historical history, to the first posts in caves featuring cats, to fetish groups featuring "fun things to do with cats of every persuasion" I shall not enumerate here, I will point out there are more cat pictures on the Internet than there are insulting references to 45[9] and his friends and relatives, and that is a hell of a lot. There would be more cat pictures except, thank God, there are a lot of people who still do not have a computer or smartphone and there are some countries where cat is a delicacy and they have the recipes to prove it so you would be hard-pressed to identify a cat in those pictures and frankly I got hungry looking at those plated presentations. Fabulous cooks we have around the world, let me tell you.

In any case, as I often do when writing a story in the simplest fashion possible in order not to confuse those who are not as brilliant as moi, I wanted to find some research and boil it down to its most pure essence. But I couldn't in this case because as soon as the online search results came back, and I clicked Images, I almost threw up.

The images of cats simply did not end, and I hate cats and cats hate me. I have documented this hatred in a column entitled "Of Cats, and Girlfriends, and Queens" included in one of my books of humor. If I was being helpful to you, I could mention which volume it was in, but I am being sneaky and teasing you so you will go out and buy all my humor books.

Even autodidactic polymaths need a new bathing suit.

---

[9] This is a reference to Donald Trump who is the 45th president of the United States and who is, at the time of this writing, the most reviled president the fake-news spewing #CrunkNewsNetwork has ever had the pleasure of attacking.

What do Marxists, Russians, and Pussy-Hat Wearing Liberal Democrat RINO Socialist Fascist Commies all have in common? *They love money.*

Goldman Sachs Group Inc. in London had a meeting with John McDonnel, whose main interest, according to Bloomberg Businessweek, is "fomenting the overthrow of capitalism". Funny thing is, McDonnel doesn't even get the paradox.

However, he is not alone in missing the big pointing arrow. A woman on social media just told me I was wrong and did not know a thing about history if I thought Russians were or had ever been the Big C: Communists.

Someone pointed out, technically, Russian Communism ended around 1991 and now the government was an authoritarian regime with an oligarchy middle class running the country and making the lives of all the other people miserable.

His point was missed by me because I could not tell the difference between the two, especially as Vladimir Putin is KGB to the core and you know those guys never change their stripes. So, tomato-tomahtoh.

What was my point?

Oh. Right.

The loony Democrats did an expensive and huge focus group study and concluded their best marketing slogan to go against Donald Trump's MAGA, or Make America Great Again, was "For the People".

For the People.

For the love of God and all that is holy:

For the People?

They could have saved their money and just stolen the tagline from Morgan & Morgan Attorneys-at-Law[10].

But no.

They spent a lot of money to come up with it, and it was money spent badly. Which brings us back to the title of this article and why I say (come on, say it with me!)

BOOM
Shakalaka

---

[10] COATs, LOATs, and even some NOATs [these acronyms will be made clear in full later in the book] had fun at their expense by claiming they did too steal the tagline from Morgan & Morgan Attorneys-at-Law.

The Most Brilliant Woman In The World nailed it a long time ago.

The January 22, 2018, issue of Bloomberg Businessweek had a big article quoting very smart people who, I swear, had to have overheard me one day in the coffee shop years ago when I was talking to my dear friend and fellow crime novelist Linda Sands[11] because everything in the article is what I've been saying for decades, namely, unless you've got a really good reason to go, college is useless and a waste of money and time.

After all, if everybody is certified smart, then where is the advantage, right? Well, it comes when you enhance your advantage and pay more money for a master's or a doctorate and so on and so on.[12]

Just ask Alexandria Ocasio-Cortez, the pretty girl in New York who ran for Congress in 2018 as a Socialist and won her primary and who then was touted as — oh, Lord, I chuckled — the new face[13] of the Democratic Party. Anyway, seems Alexandria Ocasio-Cortez went to Boston University and got a degree in Economics. Sounds impressive, but hang on.

I capitalized Economics because Alexandria Ocasio-Cortez, graduating cum laude, paid a lot of money for that big-ass degree. Around my house, we just call it economics with a lower-case *"e"* because we either have enough money

---

[11] These same thoughts have been shared by the author in coffee shops across the Southeast, in certain places in Reno and Tahoe, and on Sunset Boulevard as she went about meeting folks for reasons that are none of your business. Linda Sands is merely one of those instances. She wanted to give her dear friend and fellow crime novelist another shout-out.

[12] The author asserts this is a pyramid scheme designed to keep Socialist/Communist professors in power and cocktail money.

[13] As if it were new. Oh, the author chuckles.

for Del Taco on Friday night or we don't. But the 28-year-old gets her degree, wins the primary, then with all the confidence of those things under her belt proceeds to go on *Firing Line* and promptly cannot answer a softball question from an admiring show host who could not save her if she was on fire and his spit was a fire hose.

After the farce interview, <u>The National Review</u> pulled no punches in upbraiding that institution of *higher learning*[14] for giving out degrees in stupid. Ocasio-Cortez, also known as Neiman Marxist, got a degree that cost four years of her life and three hundred thousand quid, yet she couldn't answer one basic question about the subject in which she majored?

However, Ocasio-Cortez did get a degree in "signaling". This has come in handy as she makes the rounds of all the liberal news shows and gets interviewed by NOATs because, even after her disaster, Ocasio-Cortez is still able to look a camera in the face with no embarrassment whatsoever and continue to spout poppycockish claptrap.

But let's get back to the question: What is "signaling"? "Signaling" has nothing to do with ability, brainpower, or proficiency in the subject of the paid-for major. I can attest to this as I have dealt with far too many who have Associate, Bachelor, Master, and el Dŏctŏrâté[15] degrees, yet who could not get my order correct at Ted's Montana Grill, Starbucks, or Del Taco.

But they knew the signals, see; those signals told others trained in the same signaling how to fit in.

One executive with Randstad North America, Linda Galipeau, must have been at the coffee shop when I was talking to my dear friend and fellow crime novelist Linda Sands because Galipeau said the same thing I've been saying

---

[14] The jokes just write themselves, folks.

[15] Yes, the author knows this is not how to spell it, but this is a book of humor and she is having her fun.

for years. Now everybody is forced to first apply for a job with an algorithm, an algorithm ill-equipped to do anything but make sure certain boxes are checked and specified language is mentioned.

Look, you don't need a damn college degree to do most of the jobs out there. Part of our unemployment problem isn't that there are no jobs. There are too many ignorant[16] people with degrees and everybody applies through the faceless online HR Department.[17]

The solution? Stop it with all the higher education crap. While "college isn't for everyone" is used as a subtle slur, it is also the truth. Not every job needs to have a degreed person to get it done.

For instance, take me. I have no college degree, though I have a GED. If you want to know the details, read *Twinkle, a memoir*[18] to get the 4-1-1. Yet lack of a degree has not stopped me from being The Most Brilliant Woman In The World and, to top it all off, an autodidact and polymath.

Also, it has been this uncredentialed person whose words you now read who has found herself teaching a credentialed-and-passed-the-bar waitress how to read the damn menu so she can make sure what I ordered is what I actually get.

See my point?

---

[16] The author does not apologize for the use of this adjective. If you, the reader, object to it and believe the author is talking about you, she reminds you of one simple phrase: If the shoe fits...
Further, the author is reminded of another phrase: Too many chiefs and not enough Indians.

[17] This is a "damned if they do/don't" moment. Many people are "overqualified" for jobs they apply for and do not get hired, thus making them spiral even further into debt.

[18] Please go online and purchase the book. Reading it will help you understand...oh, who cares if you understand me. I just want to make a sale because Mama gotta eat!

Yet when I say such things, I am branded a heretic spouting profane dissent and sowing sacrilegious rebellion to bring down restrictive institutions.

And don't get me started on Alpha Kappa Yabba-Dabba-Doo fraternities and sororities. Talk about "signaling".[19]

---

[19] Reports this morning August 10, 2018, inform us that Delta Gamma Zeta Phi sorority is shutting down their branch on the Harvard campus because they are now being required to admit men, and since the "signaling" of males is not welcomed in the sorority, they are just quitting.

How to be a Special Rapporteur for the U.N. General Assembly

A Special Rapporteur is a person charged with investigating and reporting on various situations in whatever country the United Nations asks. Even I, The Most Brilliant Woman In The World[20], do not know everything which, of course, makes me even more brilliant since I know my limitations and deficiencies and seek to make them not so limiting or deficient.

That is why when I heard of the <u>Report of the Special Rapporteur on extreme poverty and human rights on his mission to the United States of America</u>[21], I was intrigued. When I saw the title I made a little bet with myself. "Me," said I, "what do you want to bet Mr. Alston will trash the U.S. and make its citizens out to be racist and uncaring, all blacks to be helpless, and the country itself simply, simply awfully terrible?"

"Oh, Dear I," said I to Me, "we should take that bet because we will win."

We did bet, and we did win. Here's the details. From their website[22]:

> "The mission of the Organisation for Economic Co-operation and Development (OECD) is to promote policies that will improve the economic and social well-being of people around the world. The OECD provides a forum in which governments can work

---

[20] Mark Twain and Will Rogers have called me this...well, they would have if they had known me in real life.

[21] The report's full title.

[22] British spellings are kept as they occurred in the report.

together to share experiences and seek
solutions to common problems."

Wow, sounds awesome. But upon reading the report of
Mr. Alston to the U.N., I quickly found out Mr. Alston seems
to be a Socialist and the U.N., beyond any doubt, has an
agenda of which he is aware and fashioned his report to meet
their expectations. Mr. Alston is very good at identifying
"signaling"[23] because he is a very properly learned man[24] who
graduated from various institutions of higher learning.

One after the other, paragraph upon paragraph upon
beautifully notated paragraph, the 20-page report held 117
mice-type footers filled with cross-references piling broad
indictment upon generalized denunciation of two things: The
United States in general, and President Donald Trump[25] in
particular.

It is not the intention of this essay to provide a detailed
accounting of all the ills the Special Rapporteur reported as
systemic and insidious, but rather to make certain comments
as to why he is so wrong in general.

You see, Mr. Alston's paragraphs and cited footnotes
were full of the same sorts of comments we've been hearing
from Pussy-Hat Wearing Politically Correct Liberal
Democratic RINO Socialist Fascist Commies in this and other

---

[23] For a reminder of what "signaling" the author speaks of, read the essay
in this book entitled "The Most Brilliant Woman In The World nailed it a
long time ago".

[24] The grammar check program insists the author use "learned person", but
the author ignores such PC twaddle.

[25] Contrary to popular opinion and what the reader may believe to be so,
this author is not political. Mention of President Donald Trump in a
flattering light does not mean she approves of everything he does;
therefore the author asks that you please hold your scathing
denouncements of her for something that actually matters, like...how
she uses commas.

countries since before the Cold War began, namely, The Lazy Rich are evil, the Working Class is always screwed over, Capitalism is immoral, The Poor are ignored by a Government built to serve the Ruling Elite (of which The Donald[26] is the head cheerleader these days), and only Caring Socialists and Communists have the solution.

The thing is, Mr. Alston reads a certain meaning into supplied statistics, but it is obvious he's never lived a life of want or need and therefore cannot understand the situational context. In his report to the General Assembly, he tells of communities in Alabama and West Virginia where raw sewage is pumped out onto gardens because Government refuses to help the citizenry. See here:

> 69. In Alabama and West Virginia, a high proportion of the population[27] is not served by public sewerage and water supply services. Contrary to the assumption[28] in most developed countries that such services should be extended by the government systematically and eventually comprehensively to all areas, neither state was able to provide figures as to the magnitude of the challenge or details of any planned government response.

However, I know in the U.S. public health is a serious matter. Raw sewage on a statewide level not only is not allowed, it doesn't happen. I also know not all areas are densely populated enough to affordably tie into Government-sponsored pipe systems.

---

[26] The nickname Mr. Trump's first wife gave him.

[27] From what the author could ascertain, this included only two counties.

[28] It is not made clear whose assumption this is.

Which is why septic tanks exist[29] and are still widely used for human waste in these areas. The handling of animal waste on farms is a huge topic among farmers and ever-better ways are used to handle, and monetize[30], the output.

While hinting of widespread (that is, national) lack of poo control, only two areas are cited in the Special Rapporteur's report as experiencing this type of issue. Of course, the question is why are those two areas experiencing it? I will tell you. Because these people have been forced into the mindset that they are too stupid to solve their own problems and must wait upon their Government-mandated plantation *massahs* to make it all better for them. The cycle in which they live just keeps spiraling down. Are these people in Alabama and West Virginia content to live like they do? They must be or else something would have been done about it long before now.

I remember the song by Dolly Parton called "Coat of Many Colors". Remember? Poor does not mean lazy or stupid until a systematic Socialist ideology is shoved down their throats and they are slowly, generation after generation, brainwashed to the point they finally live in a cesspool and wait for somebody else to fix it.[31]

Without looking at what really caused the problem in the first place, Mr. Alston suggests the cause of the problem is to solve it[32]; in other words, he wants to continue with the

---

[29] The market for sewage-pumping services is so robust in the U.S. that this industry can afford to regularly advertise on TV, billboards, radio, and even the Internet, and they have spiffy trucks.

[30] Selling sh!t: A completely Capitalist notion.

[31] That this is not a huge problem in the U.S. and the Special Rapporteur's report could only find two instances in the whole of the U.S. should be good news for the reader: Most people are gitterdun kind of folks who believe in fixing a problem and not waiting for Gubment.

[32] The author admits this is a confusing thought, but it is the way Socialists do things. Do not blame her.

Socialist agenda. Then he discusses the alarming rise of eradicable tropical diseases without addressing two things. One: The lack of border controls hindering entry to those who carry them, and two: Exotic Vacays indulged in by the very citizens he claims are the masses living in abject poverty, but without which all airlines would be forced to make serious cutbacks.

Further, the Special Rapporteur thanked the USHRN for devoting a full day to him at their 2017 national convention. USHRN is "The U.S. Human Rights Network composed of over 200 self-identified grassroots human rights organizations and over 700 individuals working to strengthen what they regard as the protection of human rights in the United States".[33]

As I examined the list of USHRN member organizations and individual members, mostly what I saw was more of the same P-HWPCLDRSFCs[34] we have all come to identify by their "equality for all except those we disagree with" speechifying. Mr. Alston, as his multiple degrees attest, is not a stupid man[35], therefore, that makes him a true believer who likes what he hears in the echo chamber, or he is evil and is running the echo chamber.

The Special Rapporteur's 16-day visit to the U.S. was made in accordance with the Human Rights Council resolution 35/19, a bit of information included in the very first sentence of Mr. Alston's report. Never mind there is no way to fully understand any country in 16 days — especially one as large and diverse as the U.S. and coming to an accurate

---

[33] This is taken word for word from their website.

[34] Pussy-Hat Wearing Politically Correct Liberal Democratic RINO Socialist Fascist Commies.

[35] Though the case has been made in another essay that degrees from institutions of higher learning do not necessarily imply intelligence or understanding.

understanding while talking to community activists and other apparatchiks looking to have money shoveled their way — so naturally I wanted to know what was in the resolution that could possibly send a Special Rapporteur on Human Rights to the U.S.

I looked up the U.N. resolution.

There, for all to see, in not one instance was the United States mentioned in resolution 35/19. Instead, the document was all about the "human rights situation in Palestine and other occupied Arab territories…Ensuring accountability and justice for all violations of international law in the Occupied Palestinian Territory, including East Jerusalem."

So, since the U.S. is not in the Middle East, is Mr. Alston saying the U.S. is one of the "other occupied Arab territories"? If such is the case, then he should have spent more time on the topic because the U.S. would have a bigger problem than whether two small areas in two small counties have a problem managing their poo.

Mr. Alston also makes the following points: Massive quantities of U.S. citizens are living on less than $2/day *and* the U.S. has the highest rate of fat people in the developed world.

$2 per day? He must be including children in those numbers — and pets and forest creatures.

Highest rate of fat people in the developed world? That begs the questions: Does this mean an undeveloped country has a higher rate? And how can so many people get fat on two damn bucks a day? Does the U.S. population's DNA somehow duplicate caloric intake? In other words, when a U.S. body eats one Twinkie, does the body see it as four?

I am not being smart-alecky. I am seriously asking because the Special Rapporteur makes the point "vast numbers of Americans" exist in "squalor and deprivation", meaning they cannot regularly afford one Twinkie much less four.

Where did our special Special Rapporteur go to see these vast numbers?

And, if squalor and deprivation were so vast, don't you think USHRN member organizations and individuals[36] would have pictures on their websites of this vast squalor and deprivation instead of the pictures of their dues-paid members carrying lightweight banners painted with appropriately boring messaging along clean and nicely paved streets as they shout equally boring slogans, listen to speeches at their national conventions in air-conditioned halls, and congratulate themselves with beautifully designed awards presented at swanky banquets?

According to official reports from the local government itself, Skid Row in Los Angeles has around 2500 homeless living in a well-defined 0.4 sq. mile area in the city limits, with 1270 beds available for use every night in the same 0.4 sq. mile area. But our special Special Rapporteur reported: In 2016 there were 14,000 arrests on Skid Row.

However, according to the local governments, these arrests were not only on Skid Row but across the city and into the county areas as well. Further, while some of these arrests were for repeated violations of misdemeanors, most were made to solve felony crimes and stop felons from hurting again. Our special Special Rapporteur did not mention the major crime rate has fallen or the area is getting safer.

Wouldn't you think all these caring people in these social justice warrior organizations would feature first and foremost on and in their websites and literature the victims of Donald Trump and the evil oligarchs?

But they don't because they can't.[37] Instead, gullible reporters are told about their massive need to solve the

---

[36] Media commentators and other pundits often call these people "Civil Rights Whores". The author prefers to call them Civil Rights Gigolos.

[37] That's right. They cannot. Do you remember Hillary Clinton's use of a woman with Munchausen's syndrome by proxy to make the case for

problem of 14,000 women every night trying to sleep on the streets of Skid Row. But do you ever see a picture? You do not.[38]

Oh, wait. Did I just mention President Trump's name a moment ago? I did! I did! And I did it because our very own U.N.-appointed special Special Rapporteur made a point of saying how much worse things have gotten since the "dramatic change of direction in relevant United States policies" and he meant The Great Orange One, The Neon King, The Grand But Worst Combover Ever, "The Hammer", Donald Trump.

Look. I'm going to stop with the analysis of this report because you'll only accuse me of beating a dead horse. Instead, let me summarize the reasons for the report:

---

nationalized health care? Even Hillary, the smartest woman in the room when the author is not there, could not find more than one person to make her case and that woman was the one making her daughter ill.

[38] The author once saw a photo shoot where a somewhat handsome and healthy older guy with a grey beard and a head of matching hair was being made up by a special effects makeup artist and costumer to look dirty and ragged and sick. His beard and hair were teased out to look like they were rats' nests. "Dirt" was painted on and smeared just so. She stopped to watch and asked the photographer what was going on. He said a corporate client hired him for the gig, but he didn't say who or for what. Imagine her surprise a few months later when she went into a popular fast-food outlet only to have posters with that guy's face all over it accompanied by pleas to give money to help the homeless. They should have asked the Special Rapporteur for guidance on where to find an authentic dirty, ragged, sick, homeless person. Oh, wait. Never mind. Our special Special Rapporteur couldn't have found one either.

- The U.N. is pushing for a one-world government that, of course, they will run.
- The U.N. is against freedom.
- The U.N. is a big bully.
- The U.N. offers help[39] in the form of strangleholds to industriousness.
- The U.N. has been bilking[40] the U.S. on behalf of terrorists around the world.
- The U.N. has been milking[41] the U.S. cash cow[42] to pay most of their operating costs while letting other countries get far behind paying their share of those.
- The U.N. knew Donald Trump would push back against them — and he has not disappointed.
- And since we know the best defense is a good offense, the U.N. ordered their Special Rapporteur to destroy the reputation of the U.S. and all her good and honest citizens who make a difference in the communities where they stand. In other words, the U.N. hates those who actually gitterdun[43].

---

[39] Yes, the author is being facetious.

[40] This is the damn truth.

[41] The U.S. is paying the world's bills and you're wondering why you can't get ahead.

[42] The grammar check program insists the author swap out "source of income" for "cash cow", but the author says, "Where's the fun in that?"

[43] "Gitterdun" is slang for "get it done".

IMPORT-
TANT
REPORT
INSIDE.
MUST
READ
IMPORT-
ANT!

Plotting the predictable with algorithms

It is my opinion technology is responsible for horrible books. Not that horrible books didn't exist before technology, but they sure were fewer and further between, comparatively, than we have now in this 21st Century.

Writers have programs guiding them through writing songs, plays, television shows, novels, business books, and memoirs. And where something creative is systemized comes the repetition of how-to steps churning out predictable flows.

These algorithms push the software user[44] to follow what they have decided is an acceptable course for producing a book that, if truth be told, came to be because reading the minds of agents and publishers is impossible. Agents and publishers all say the same things, like these:

"We are looking for fresh voices from people we've never heard of with stories that surprise us."

This naturally makes the new writer's hopes rise.

"Please see our website or consult *The Writer's Marketplace* to find out our submission guidelines."

New writer finds submission guidelines and meticulously adheres to those when submitting. New writer waits for ages for the reply that goes something like this:

"You did not properly submit according to our guidelines. Please go to our website or consult *The Writer's Marketplace* and resubmit."

New writer reviews submission guidelines and finds they're exactly what he did, and so resubmits. He gets a reply something like this:

---

[44] Notice the author did not say "writer".

"Because you did not follow our submission guidelines, we can tell you are not a fit for our agency/house. Please go away and die."

New writer tears out his hair and gnashes his teeth. So he calls the agency/house and tells them according to their website and *The Writer's Marketplace,* he has done exactly as asked and gets this reply in that special uptick tone designed to put one in one's place:

"Oh, yeah. Well, we've changED ALL thAT? And you should've KNOWN thAT? BeSIDES, you are a no-OOBOdy from no-OOWHERE? And we only work with esTABLISHED authors? Sooooo…you can just DIE? Good LUCK?"

New writer screams invectives and pulls out remaining hair and gnashes remaining teeth.

Thoroughly discouraged, next thing you know his inbox is filled with offers to buy a new writing assistance program. Email subject line says "Are you too stupid to come up with your own plots? Then you need *Help Me Plot!*"

The body of the email says, "Yes, *Help Me Plot* got [Author You Never Heard Of] a **SIX-FIGURE PUBLISHING DEAL** and turned him into a **NEW YORK TIMES BEST SELLING AUTHOR**. Click here to find out how *Help Me Plot* can work for you! **IT'S EASY!** Yes, you too can crank out a best seller in less time than it takes to do the dishes. Still unsure? Don't believe us? **Click here *NOW* to find out how *Help Me Plot* can work for you!**"

And so writers click the link and plunk their money and download the program and spend countless hours[45] trying to make the damn thing work as advertised. Then one of the users thinks, "Who was the guy they said got the six-figure

---

[45] The hours are not, in fact, countless, but that word is used here to make a point as to how many goddamned hours writers spend attempting to use a "software solution" while ignoring their spouses and children and friends and even God.

deal?" And a little research later finds out the only award the guy won was in his own head and he's the one who wrote the software program. But, too late, the return policy expressly states that as soon as the user activated the program and opened it the first time, the warranty expired and so don't call us for a refund.

BUT WAIT!

UPDATE COMING SOON for only $357.

So the investigative user decides to start telling the world about the rip-off program and the stupid agents and the myopic publishers and becomes a mosquito on the butt of the world of writing for profit and ends up writing a book he will sell to other new writers...

The circle is vicious, as befits the world of writing.

If one enjoys writing and wants to do it for fun, then go ahead and do it. Don't let me stop you. But if one wants to do it well enough to support a family, then I say to them, "You just let me know how it turns out, Big Boy."

Because the fact is there are very few authors[46] who even make enough to pay a few of their bills. So, one cannot really blame writers' agents and book publishers when they turn down most of what is presented to them. I'm gonna walk that statement back and say, "Why, yes, one can blame writers' agents and book publishers." And here is why:

It is because agents and publishers themselves set false expectations. They say, "We are actively seeking new voices and unknown writers."

To them I say, "Liar, liar, pants on fire."

Newbies are not wanted. They only want authors who can prove their existing marketplace share is huge. Agents and publishers go after low-hanging fruit, making them no

---

[46] Authors, songwriters, singers, actors, ceramic pot makers, painters, other artistic media makers, filmmakers, scriptwriters, and any other creative type of endeavor you can imagine is included.

better than the salesman sitting on his ass at the corner used car lot. You know what? That was a bad comparison because used car lots would never put out a sign saying, "We are actively seeking buyers", and then tell the people who walk in to go away because *they've never owned a car before*. That's right. So, to all you used car salesmen[47], I apologize for comparing you to agents and publishers.

But writing to an algorithm started long before software was available to the general public. Even "serious journalists"[48] writing for established newspapers and magazines compose to an algorithm of a sort. They have a set of rules which must be used when looking at a story. The rules are:

- Say something negative about, and make fun of, everything those little people in flyover country believe.

- Show all conservative-thinking people, no matter where they are, to be racist homophobic yahoos practicing noose-making in public parks while preening with their guns and combing their super-sweet mullets as hoochie mamas holler at the kiddies "Imma gonna git mah belt and whup yer ass iffen ya do dat a-gin!" and the daddies say, "Woman! Git me mah beer. An' make it snappy, Heifer."

- Whine they did not get sent a dud bomb like CNN did that one time.[49]

[47] And women and gender neutral and gender fluid used car salespersons.

[48] We know they are "serious" because they spent a lot of money to get a journalism degree from an institution of higher learning that is dedicated to raking in money while churning out substandard students who paid big bucks to get the fancy piece of paper and who, in order not to fail their classes, kowtowed to Commie and Socialist professors.

[49] For more on this, see the essay entitled "Playing Strip Poker Like a Boss".

- Completely ignore facts while pushing the P-HWPCLDRSFC narrative.

- Featuring pictures of self-righteously angry women and men wearing pussy hats and holding signs.

- Quote angry women and men wearing pussy hats, especially when they say, "I cannot believe he TWEETS at THREE IN THE MORNING. That is so not presidential! NOT MY PRESIDENT. *I'M FOR HER!* IMPEACH HIM! "

Oh, Lord. Edward R. Murrow must be turning over in his grave. This was said at the National Press Club in 1961 after Murrow was tapped to lead the U.S. Information Agency:

When one senator asked Murrow if he intended "to tell the bad about the United States along with the good," Murrow responded, "If the bad is significant, it is going to be reported anyway, and we must report it. We must report it honestly, otherwise it will be distorted." [President] Kennedy agreed, telling the VOA staff in 1962, "you are obliged to tell our story in a truthful way, to tell it, as Oliver Cromwell said about his portrait, 'Paint us with all our blemishes and warts.'"

Murrow also said, "American traditions and the American ethic require us to be truthful, but the most important reason is that truth is the best propaganda and lies are the worst. To be persuasive we must be believable; to be believable we must be credible; to be credible we must be truthful.

"It is as simple as that."

Blemishes and warts are anathema in a world of purchased flawlessness. If mainstream media, filled as it is with all those "serious journalists" who have studied for years and years, is doing such a good job, then why are newspaper circulations and viewership ratings down?

Even their online portals cannot attract enough eyeballs to pay the bills.[50]

Deny them as one will, these are the facts of the matter.

Established editors, reporters, journalists, and writers are let go and their jobs outsourced to people with no idea of history. Who get paid a pittance. Cannot put any meaning into what they write. Have no idea how to research. Are naive and gullible. And who don't want to hold anyone's feet to a fire that a genuine serious journalist would build.[51]

For God's sake, did Edward R. Murrow whine and cry in his Scotch when the subject of his reporting said something negative about him? He did not. He shined a bright light on whatever problems he saw. Murrow inspired a generation, maybe even two, to look at facts and ask who, what, when, where, why, and then, last but not least, how can it be made better? Murrow was balanced and brilliant in his reporting. How do we know? Because he ticked off, and his bosses got back-to-back calls from, folks on every side of every issue he reported on.[52]

---

[50] They blame the Internet for their lowering profits, but obviously the cause is deeper. It is called Spin.

[51] So-called serious journalists think because they *feel* strongly about their opinion, that somehow makes it so.

[52] The author here acknowledges her Murrow-inspired balance and brilliance because she knows she has already ticked off some readers and, if any reader this far into the book is not yet ticked off, she says to them, "Wait. I have not forgotten you."

    She warrants and guarantees you will be ticked before you get to the end of the book and says if you are not ticked off by that time, you will get your money back. [NOTE: The warranty of guarantee expires the minute the reader purchases the book or in some other fashion otherwise comes into possession of it, as through a gifting process or finding it laying in a gutter by way of example but not all inclusive of methods by which one could come into possession of the book.]

Algorithms are not good for everything. Algorithms do not improve all endeavors. Algorithms make people stupid. But algorithms sure turn decision-making into a super-easy process.

Mainstream media outlets — and might I also add: book agents and publishers — are still in business but only by a tenuous thread of their own making. And they are holding sharp scissors dangerously close to that thread.

Echo chambers are only good when you're making music.

Future anthropologists will have a difficult time explaining the last two decades of the twentieth century and the first thirty-five years of the twenty-first. How else does one explain the meteoric rise and quick fall of "Disco Duck" or boring line dancing in shiny clothes?[53]

Simple: The advent of technologies allowing for the fast spreading of new forms of, well, everything, followed by marketing companies funneling people types into silos of consumerism. Yes, Marketing understands the power of echo chambers and the need to belong to Community.

Even in small villages in the Australian outback or tiny Inuit villages where nary a NOAT can be heard, echo chambers of thought have always existed and exerted power and influence. Dictators know this and enforce echo chamber thinking with threats of authentic physical torture and/or death, the kinds making people unable to walk or see or speeding them to an early mass grave, as opposed to First-World-Problem style of torture identified as when the skinny latté takes twenty seconds longer to receive than normal and makes the caring sign carrier late for the protest photo-op.

With the deployment of Social Media Platforms[54] (SMP) wherein millions of people each day would "log in" and

---

[53] They will also have a difficult time in explaining the rise of "Rap" music, but that's another topic for another day.

[54] Notes for anthropologists: In case you did not know it, Social Media Platforms (SMPs) made it possible for humans to share (via the ancient, time-consuming, and now out-of-date method called "uploading") countless pictures of cats and babies and boobs and awesome man parts via either public postings on a digital portal or through private messaging in the ether.

"post", came the new, highly focused echo chambers of the Social Justice Warrior, the Flamer, the Helpful Sharer, the Complainer, the Old Hippie, the Young Hippie, the Wannabe [fill in the blank], the Questioner, the Apologist, the Thankful, the Praiser, the Preacher, the Radical Feminist, the Queer Guy, the Straight Guy, the Gender Neutral, the Gender Spastic, the Gender Elastic, the Patriot, the Pussy-Hat Wearer, the Author, the Singer, the Actor, the Producer, the Bass Player, the Jazz Kittens, the Autodidact Polymath Genius[55], and on and on, ad infinitum and etcetera, etcetera, etcetera.

Though *echo chamber* was not the term used, each user of the SMPs was promised a place to put opinions and thoughts and build a following in their very own special echo chamber — and that is what they did.

As a Citizen Journalist, I am happy for it because I don't have to go too far to find language used like I could never have made up in my wildest dreams. Regular readers of my columns and those who purchase[56] my books have seen these phrasings peppered throughout as I report on and often make

---

It also allowed for the bragging about vacays, also known as vacations. Vacays, now out of vogue as you read this in the future, were trips taken to places one had never been wherein one proceeded to spend massive amounts of money on overpriced umbrella-decorated alcoholic drinks in order to get drunk so one wouldn't remember the vacay in a place that was decorated to look like a theme-park version of where they were going but was in a "safe" zone. You don't know what a theme park is? Ooo-kay. The author will cover that in another essay.

[55] The Autodidact Polymath Genius is a small subsection of the SMP user base and their posts are usually held or denied because they contain language that the SMPs' Thought Police view as "fake news". Therefore the promise to "freely share with all their friends and followers" was a fake promise.

[56] The author hopes the buyer also reads the books, but she will not stop them from purchasing even if their intent is not to read it but merely get it out of circulation.

fun[57] of the echo chamber du jour messaging, so I won't bore you by repeating any of that now.

Instead, this column is about the dangers of restrictions inherent in echo chambers. Echoes sound pretty in music. Using redundant amplification, sound can build upon itself to enhance its power. Concert halls are built with this concept in mind so that the quietest sound can carry strong even as it remains quiet.

With the advent of technology, though, putting an echo effect on everything in a recording makes a song suck.[58] Those with discerning ears hear a fat muddy mess, but tin ears hail the song as pure genius and purchase more of it[59].

It is the same with messaging from religious or political entities. Not God or principles of fair governing, but religion and politics attract the largest audiences to their echo chambers. It is easier to be told what to think and do than it is to apply principles of thought and action to individual instances. Many people are lazy and/or thoughtless, therefore…[60]

Those outside the echo chambers of thought are often accused by Side #1 of being in league with Side #2, and vice versa, when, in point of fact, those outside belong to neither.

Just the other day a cousin of mine in Massachusetts, brilliant researcher she is, posted something on Bacefook causing me to jot down a quick reply. Before the hour was up,

---

[57] The author freely admits she makes fun of and does not apologize for it.

[58] This explains why music is everywhere but the satisfaction level of listening to it has gone down and listeners cannot figure out why. Echo overuse.

[59] It is amazing how many "tin ears" are out there that can quickly identify crap, and all of them have money to spend on that crap.

[60] The author hopes you are of the first variety of person, namely, one who can extrapolate from incomplete information.

several in her echo chamber jumped all over me with the same types of replies like this:

"You are wrong."

"Yeah, what she said."

"Yeah, what they said."

One then proceeded to say I was "Trump 'splaining" when I had not mentioned the man at all. Another said if I knew history then I would know Russians were never Communists.[61]

When I asked what Russians were, my entire body of comments was deleted, and this self-congratulatory digital back-slapping ensued:

"We are so right."

"Yeah, what she said."

"Yeah, what they said."

When visiting echo chambers, I listen with a discerning ear to what is being said. Those who live in echo chambers do not as they are in love with the echo itself.

---

[61] This is but one example of an echo chamber run amuck.

Explaining a Theme Park to Future Archeologists and Anthropologists.

When you, the future archeologist reading this, carefully remove dirt from an area upon which you will inevitably find a set of machinery, winding paths, and small huts, your findings will make no sense to you. Therefore, it is a sure bet an anthropologist or two will be called. These learned academics will be ready and willing to swoop in and make educated guesses as to what you have found. With all due seriousness and a cute naiveté, anthropologists will come up with some silly notional ideas involving religious rituals, ancestor worship, high holy day feasts, and child sacrifice. They will be so very wrong, though not so very far from the truth.

Therefore, incumbent upon me, a person living during the Rise of the Machines, is the duty to leave behind a written record of what we in these times call *theme parks*.[62]

The title *theme park* is by its very nature a descriptive. A theme is a subject or premise around which a park is built.

A park is a defined and often enclosed community area set aside for affordable leisure pursuits such as eating while sitting on a blanket spread across the ground or at a concrete table, battling stinging insects, swimming in a natural or concrete pond/lake, walking or running along a path designed to destroy knee joints while expecting good health and long life will accrue[63], and for the children: Structures

---

[62] It is the author's hope these words have been preserved, found, and are being read in the future. She hopes this paper will be a benefit to the archeologist and anthropologist of the future in their endeavors to understand their ancestors and maybe shed a bit more light on why their social construct now exists as it does. She has done all she can. Let us begin.

made of metal or plastic for swinging, sliding, and twirling, and for adults: The walking of a domesticated animal while carrying a bag in which one houses the animal's dung after it has been publicly deposited on the ground. Therefore, a theme park is a place people go to spend time away from work-related activities and usually has nothing to do with activities involved in a community park. In other words, credit cards were maxed out[64] in order to bring the family. One wasn't allowed to bring one's dog.

Plus, all theme park guests were encouraged not to bring food that originated from outside the park. Penny-pinching parents were punished if they brought outside food as picnic tables were far from the rides and walking that far made everybody upset because they were "There to have fun dammit!" So small huts, specializing in one or two food or drink types per hut, were strategically placed throughout the park. For instance, Hut 1 refueled children with sugar in the form of Frozen Lemonade and Cotton Candy, while Hut 2 placated daddies with Massive Mugs O' Beer and Ginormous All-Beef Burgers with a side of Crinkle Fries, and so on per hut, all for the low, low price of forty-five dollars per person per order.

However, to maintain these theme parks and their massive and complicated areas of extreme leisure pursuit in a safe, clean, and entertaining fashion, behind the scenes in

---

[63] Many people die while jogging and running or directly after that. You in the future will have the statistics on total body count at your fingertips. It is the author's belief that in the year of you reading this, these pursuits are no longer indulged in by any except the professional athlete for the purposes of winning medals, fame, and fortune or in some weird game show called *The Running Man*.

[64] A credit card was a convenient way of paying later for something one wanted now. Many people used several credit cards as their own personal rotating lines of credit. Balances were transferred from one to another to another in a financial death spiral leading to a rise in Chapter 7 and Chapter 11 bankruptcy filings.

non-guest areas whole teams of people did nothing but work to maintain the machinery and other infrastructure necessary to service park guests. Some front-of-house workers[65] were seen cleaning toilets, hauling trash, making sure toilet paper was available, manning checkout areas in kiosks, delivering food to huts, and serving food, but on the whole most workers were never seen lest the guests' leisure sensibilities and equilibrium be spoiled. First and foremost in managements' minds was the race for stockholder share price to remain healthy, which meant the guest must be made happy so they would return again and again.

This produced one of the biggest conundrums during the 20th and 21st centuries, namely: Where do those leisure-industry workers go to themselves get leisurely? They did not go to theme parks because other than male heads of households with nice cushy jobs, who goes to work to relax? Where these leisure workers went for their recreation was a big secret for quite some time, but since I'm living in this time period I can tell you what I found out after much reading and confabulating of facts and figures: These people hated the idea of leisure in lush environments and went to terrorist training camps in deserts.[66]

This neatly explains the rise of terrorism around the globe because the terrorists' main focus at the time was to destroy those countries who invented and/or housed theme parks.[67] But that is another topic for another time and is one opinion

---

[65] Invariably these people never smiled nor looked directly at a guest.

[66] Little-known fact: Much like universities were after the end of World War II, theme parks were an ideal recruiting ground for anarchists and ideologue traitors.

[67] Notice the author said it was their "main" focus, but obviously some terrorists did occasionally attack less lush areas but these were usually the really stupid terrorists or those who could not get visas to the lush areas.

about which, I am certain, many will argue. I, your guide from the past, have chosen not to address the subject in this paper for good reason. You will find this addressed in my archives that, hopefully, survived intact. Many of those articles will mention Pussy-Hat Wearing Politically Correct Liberal Democratic RINO Socialist Fascist Commies, or P-HWPCLDRSFCs, as this title neatly covers all groups from which terrorists were recruited. First, though, a little history.

Theme parks were traveling in nature when they first began. They were called circuses and traveled from town to town. When animal upkeep got too expensive, someone said, "To hell with lions and tigers and elephants" and portable machines, needing only electricity as feed and a lubricant for gears, were invented to hurl people confined in cages and other receptacles through a defined rotational or other gyratory path guaranteed to make these riders involuntarily hurl from their stomachs in reverse fashion their expensive hot dogs, nachos, beers, and frozen drinks back through esophagi, into mouths, over tongues, and through lips onto those nearby or under them in the crowd. Recipients of the "throw-up", as guests' issuances were called at the time, would scream and holler "Imma gonna kill that bastard" and/or threaten a class-action lawsuit against the company who invented the machine and/or who hauled it around selling tickets to ride and otherwise setting up other inducements to enter the theme park — inducements such as bands playing, jugglers and magicians roaming through the crowds, and other types of entertainment indulged in by those promised the ever-elusive leisureness when they saw slick advertisements full of smiling actors/models pretending to be a family "having fun together".

I say *pretending to be a family having fun together* because families were not meant to have fun together. The concept itself was a false narrative, a phony construct, a sham pushed for the sole purpose of destroying civilization as we know it. You, future anthropologist and archeologist, have seen the outworking of this campaign so you know I am a prophet in this matter. But enough about me and my prescience.

Let us continue.

This involuntary hurling of stomach contents happened so much on these rides, many theme park rider guests chose it as a point of pride to hold inside the stomach said issuance upon riding even the most egregious of gyratory and rotational machines. Whole leisure cultures evolved wherein bets would be taken and food eaten, rides entered, and bets settled after debarking. Those who arrived throw-up free at the end of the ride were the winners of the bets.

Some of the thematic premises of these theme parks were built around popular movies, cartoon characters, dinosaurs, space travel, and countries other than the one it was located in. During national or religious holidays of whatever country the theme park found itself in, decorative hangings, flashing objects, and fireworks and other shows would be placed and planned and everybody going would feel the insidious push to feel the "spirit of the season".[68]

These were huge money-makers as the pursuit of these holiday leisure activities was timed to coincide with breaks from public and private schools and thus the whole family was encouraged to spend "quality time" together.

The implied condition of this "quality time" was that it would be of high quality, though usually it wasn't so high. Fathers always complained about the amount of money it cost to take the family and anxiously spent their time attempting to get out of this leisure pursuit in time to get back to work to earn enough money to pay the high-interest, short-term loan taken through a credit card cash advance to fund the leisure. Fathers could be heard mumbling nearly inaudible swear words and walking around with worried frowns below their ain't-we-having-fun sunglasses.

Mothers hovered over children, slathering them with a foul concoction designed to keep the sun from delivering

---

[68] Suicides increased around these times.

healthy doses of Vitamin D while telling them they were helping the child avoid cancer sure to kill them when they got to be fifty years of age. Mothers were often heard humming, "Let it go! Let it go!"[69]

Children wriggled during those sun-repelling application sessions and cried, often throwing themselves to the floor of the hotel room or lobby and/or the ground while screaming, "I want Mickey!" or "When is Elsa coming?" [Mickey and Elsa were the most favorite characters at the time of this writing[70]. Both were cartoons. The former was drawn as a mouse and his full name was Mickey Mouse who had a girlfriend, Minnie Mouse, who made her name in the shadow of her famous boyfriend. Elsa was drawn as a female human whose last name is never known even though she becomes the queen or something royal like that and things get super cold and freeze over, thus the name of the movie, *Frozen*.]

Eventually fathers, mothers, and children exited hotels *en masse* as early in the morning as possible to ride enclosed elevated rail cars over full parking lots stuffed with the cars of unlucky guests who could not afford hotel fees, and into the theme park to be dumped at the first kiosk built to attract sales revenue above and beyond ticket prices. Both mothers and fathers worked in concert to divert children's attentions away from those. Some mothers and fathers, being Type A personalities and having studied maps of the leisure pursuit

---

[69] This was the theme song of *Frozen*, a full-length animated feature with a particularly homogenous storyline designed to have something that would appeal to everybody but that once exiting the theater one wondered what was so special about it yet found they could not stop humming the theme song sung by Queen Elsa whose main refrain went "Let it go. Let it **go!**"

[70] Some will disagree with the author and point out the rise of the Harry Potter franchise. The author absolutely hates Harry Potter stuff and believes anybody who is enamored of it is an idiot though, and in this she admits she is a hypocrite, the author only hopes she will have a character in a book that will cause people to make her a billionaire.

theme park ahead of time, knew exactly where to go and hurriedly dragged their children away from the debarking station toward the first ride in hopes of beating all the other people and thus having a shorter wait in line in order to "get to the fun faster than anyone else".[71]

Most families, though, determined to be leisurely about their leisure, usually stood exactly where they debarked, effectively blocking the Type A's progress, and reveled in the coming excitement. These people usually lived by the phrase "it will be what it will be" or, later, "it is what it is", of which both sayings caused Type A's to go insane even in their pursuit of insanity-blocking leisure pursuits. When two families of differing personality types but whose children were besties in their neighborhood decided to travel together to the place of leisure, not always, but most often, after returning home the Type A family would move because they could not stand the sight of the "it is what it is" family and for years after would talk about how the "it is what it is" family ruined the leisure trip and from then on closely vetted any other traveling companion families.

In any case, any advantage the Map Study method of making the rounds of the theme park was short-lived because, upon seeing a long line to get onto a ride, most people would pass it and go to the next. The Map Study method was only good first thing in the morning and only for about thirty seconds. With a little bit of forethought, the lesson could have been gleaned, but the Type A's seemed never to learn it before arrival and thought they were the only ones with the idea.

To get into the mood of the leisure pursuit, fathers wore shorts or pants most often used for exercise, which meant

---

[71] These families were usually headed by two Type A personalities. The author is positive they exist to this day, that is, the day that you, future archeologist and anthropologist, are reading this, and therefore it needs no further explanation.

they had to carry their wallets and car and/or room keys around in their hands during the day and often could be seen searching for a place to put those whilst they engaged in bathroom breaks, eating, or holding on for dear life as they were flung, hung, and slung on a variety of machines. Across the globe, Departments of Lost and Found Items were filled with wallets and keys never to be claimed though sorely missed.

Mothers, sometimes known as the father's wife, significant other, or as became commonly used, the father's "baby mama", spent their days offering to hold the wallet and keys for the adult male member of the family unit. The mother could easily do this as she always carried a smaller container slung over her shoulder called a purse, or a tote bag when it was larger. But fathers did not trust mothers with the one credit card they brought and refused to allow their women to "tote their stuff", instead enjoying the knowledge the adult female of the family could not sneak off and spend more money. The men felt good about this and it was the only pleasure[72] they had during leisure pursuits at theme parks.

Of course, this was a false principle upon which to base his actions because the mothers would allow, and sometimes prompt, the children to pitch a fit at strategic moments so that to shut them all up the father would yell "Get whatever in the hell you want, like I have any say-so anyway in the financial future of this family!" while forking over to the front-of-house theme park worker a rectangle of plastic[73] which would then be swiped through a machine capable of reading information from a digitally encoded magnetic stripe on the back of it, thus ensuring the purchase price would be transferred to the business entity handling the commercial transaction on behalf of the theme park minus a service fee of between 3% and 8% of the total transactional charge, and guaranteeing the proper

---

[72] Except for the Massive Mastodon Burgers and Mugs O' Beer.

[73] The aforementioned credit card.

charge equal to the money received by the business would be documented and placed onto the correct person's billing statement which was then hand-delivered to the person's home by a worker for a government agency assigned delivery tasks for publicly traded and privately owned corporations and businesses, a few private individuals, and other government agencies willing to pay an artificially low fee per unit of delivery.[74]

After the purchase, the children of the family would immediately bond to the stuffed representation of Mickey or Elsa whilst the wife would be hollering at the husband "What is the matter with you? Geez. We came to enjoy leisure, so [whispered or mouthed seven-letter curse word beginning in *f* and ending in *ing*,[75]] enjoy your leisure, will ya?"

All this leisure merriment, sometimes mistaken for misery, is only peripheral to the rides themselves. One favorite type of ride was called a roller coaster. These machines could range in height from a portable unit in a traveling theme park of approximately 15 feet to a height of 456 feet for a unit encased within a larger, stationary theme park. Because of their portable nature, the traveling machines had limited thrill factor compared to those installed in a permanent fashion, so we will not discuss the portable versions here because once the permanent fixtures came to be, the portable units fell out of favor with, if not became scorned by, adults and were reserved only for children between the ages of two and five.[76]

---

[74] Please see the paper in the author's archives entitled "The Post Office: A Socialist Dream Come True".

[75] This particular gerund expanded the meaning of the base word it was added to and exponentially increased the ferocity with which it was said.

[76] The little kiddies loved these and lots of parents stood around taking lots of pictures of their offspring enjoying their first "ride". It was a sickening

We will now turn our attention to those "roller coasters" installed in a permanent fashion within a theme park setting. The "train of cars" on these could reach speeds of between 125 and 150 miles per hour. The classic design of the roller coaster was simple. An open-air compartment, or "car", was attached to elevated rails which formed a track along which the cars would travel, seating four human beings per car, each of whom were held in with a simple adjustable strap across their laps.[77] These units were strung together until 8-12 of these "cars" formed a "train". The "train" was then winched to a pinnacle higher than all other rises on the track and released to roll down a steep slope with an angle of between 45° and 121°.

Drop angles and lengths of this first hill were crucial, calculated to assure enough kinetic energy was released so that even a partially loaded complement would make the rise of each subsequent hill, making certain a full circuit back into the "station" was made where, laughing and screaming, rider guests would disembark to the right of the car and new rider guests would enter from the left to take their places. Thus, the roller (wheels) coaster (kinetic energy as opposed to an engine-based machine) nom de guerre.

Some roller coasters were fashioned in such a manner rider guests would be hauled along a track that spiraled, twisted, and/or went into 360° turns, rendering the rider guest upside down then right side up in quick succession. These more vigorous rides often caused fainting spells, heart attacks, "throw-up" spewing, and broken necks.

Because the education system in the overdeveloped, or First World, countries began to mimic those in Third World, or underdeveloped, countries, it soon became clear the

---

display of family happiness and was only ruined when the kiddies threw up or cried from fear and begged to be let off.

[77] Depending on the rotational force of a ride, additional straps went across shoulders, and some featured metal locking bars encased in a soft foam to hold in a body.

general populace was no longer aware of even the basic knowledge of the cause-and-effect of the Law of Gravity and its sister Physics which, according to a highly popular source of quickly attainable publicly curated information at the time called Wikipedia.com, is the "natural science that studies matter and its motion and behavior through space and time and that studies the related entities of energy and force."

Therefore, due to this lack of basic information on how a body in motion will react, rider guests were dying or suffering grievous injury because their bodies were not strong enough to withstand those forces. Lawsuits ensued. Prodded by the insurance industry, governments stepped in and signage began to be mandated to warn of the physical dangers and physiological affect upon the rider guest and asking each rider guest to assume full responsibility for their demise should they have a condition precluding them from arriving alive at the end of the course. This necessitated the clueless get a clue, and that still didn't work.

For instance, pregnant women were not allowed to ride, obviously. There was no choice for them in this matter as nobody wanted a baby pulled from a woman's body by an application of artificial gravity while being slung around in an open car going 150 miles per hour. Only occasionally would a pregnant woman complain and threaten a lawsuit for discrimination, but these lawsuits usually went nowhere as everybody on the jury was usually in agreement the woman was a nut.[78]

However, front-of-house workers were then put in an awkward position. For instance, there are some women who look pregnant but are not. The mandate from management was not to make rider guests angry, but one had to protect the baby. So, what was the front-of-house worker to do? Angry

---

[78] Court records from the time will bear this out.

fat women are just as likely to sue. It was a conundrum causing massive employee turnover.

Also, front-of-house workers could not tell if someone's ticker (a colloquial term for the heart) was frail, or a neck was feeble, or they were just a wussy who got scared easily and could die from fright. Therefore, to limit lawsuit damages, each rider guest, or their parent if underage, assumed full responsibility for life and limb and death at each ride featuring a vigorous shake, drop, fling, toss, or launch.

The future archeologist and anthropologist might be wondering how mothers who were so worried about their children getting cancer forty years hence would be so willing to allow their children to ride such contraptions. This has confounded other anthropologists including those alive at the time of this writing. But I, your pleasant and helpful guide in these matters, shall simply say what I believe is still a universally held truth even in your century:

There ain't no accounting for stupid.

Which brings us to the next thing that happened often at theme parks. Invariably a person — obviously not an obedient Socialist Citizen, but one uneducated in Physics and unaware of the Law of Gravity — ignored signage and front-of-house-worker reminders to secure personal items before riding a roller coaster and would not secure the hat or sunglasses or purse. Then during the more vigorous of the twists and turns, these personal items were sent flying out of the clutches of and off the heads and faces of the rider guests, landing under the ride.

Without fail these items were the rider guest's most favorite and once the rider guest had disembarked he would say to his friends:

"Damn! I lost my sunglasses! They were my most favorite pair. They cost me $875!"

The rider guest's friends would then respond, "Yagottagitdemtingsback!"

The group would then begin a quest for a vantage point to see the ground under the ride to locate the prized possession he simply could not live without. Often this "seeing" was successful. Every single time, again without fail, the item was directly under the lowest point of the track on which "trains" were still running — and sometimes legs hanging. The group would begin an exceedingly excited exchange about the best way to get the item.

The item rescue was always accompanied by the climbing of a high, stout fence designed to restrict access to losers of those items and which fence was full of signs with graphics showing death could occur if one went into the restricted area while the ride was in progress. In the group was always someone who would see the signs and point out the danger, but he would be ignored by the rest of the group with shouted phrases such as —

"Shut up, David. Yer al'ays such a damn pussy."

"Hey, David. Hold my beer."

With one last double-dog-dare-ya hurled at the would-be rescuer, the fence would be climbed and when he landed on the ground on the other side, his buddies would shout the ever popular "Semper fi, brudder. OOO-rah!" and he would make a fist, arch his back, and scream "Gitterdun!", after which he would squat-run to the item to be retrieved.

In all instances what followed was a decapitation of the uneducated "real man" who lost his $875 sunglasses he simply couldn't live without and a hollering by David going like this: "I told you fucking so. But does anybody listen to me? No. They. Do. Not. And now look at what just happened." Additional reaction from his friends included crying, screaming, and throwing up as they watched his head go flying and his body drop next to his favorite sunglasses.

For those who can extrapolate from incomplete data it goes without saying. For everybody else: Stupid is bone deep.

It is the hope of this historian — ergo ipso de fracto moi — that the future archeologist and anthropologist now has enough information to make sense of their findings and that they are grateful for the many hours it took to put this complicated socio-economi-creed information into an easily digestible format. I only ask that you spell my name correctly and have great things to say about me as this is as close to immortality as I will ever get.[79] You are welcome — and thank you.

---

[79] The author is aware she had her little fun with language in this paragraph by making up terms and mangling Latin, so she begs you to have a "wittle fun" with her, too.

THREE STAGES OF
MEDICINAL MARGARITA
RESEARCH

The Medicinal Margarita

When I was just turning twenty, and after much drama surrounding Mother and Honey, her husband, and their damn love life[80], I lived with my grandfather for a few months. When my sister and I moved into his house, my first thought was, "Oh, this just will **not** do!" By **this** I meant his decorating style, which was non-existent. Sister did not understand what was the problem with his placement of the furniture and as was typical of her response to anything doing with me, she called me names such as *stuck up* and *snob* because I had the gall to stop dead in my tracks, look around the living room, and demand, "Hershey Bar![81] This looks terrible. I am going to fix it." And he said, "NOOOOO! I like it like this." And I said, "You only THINK you do. Trust me. You'll thank me later."[82]

And so before the weekend was over drapes were purchased at a yard sale and installed, furniture moved, and the entire house organized except for his bedroom that he absolutely refused to allow me to touch.[83] But one day, as I

---

[80] If you can call it a *love life*. The author says for those details you can purchase **Twinkle, a memoir**.

[81] This was the author's nickname for Granddaddy since his first and middle names were Hershel Briggs thus the Hershey Bar. Look, do not laugh at her. Okay, you can laugh because this is a book of humor, but she was a mere tyke when she came up with that and Granddaddy liked it, alright?

[82] Hershey Bar did thank the author later. In fact, his words were, "Angie...aaaahhhh. It looks better." To which she then said, "Dinner will be on the table shortly. You like salad and spaghetti, right?" To that he looked excited and he ate with gusto.
    According to Dave Barry, Hershey Bar was a "guy".

[83] You will note the author did not touch his bedroom because that was his sanctum sanctorum and the author can respect boundaries, but the other areas of the house were not ignored by her.

walked by his bedroom after returning home from a second-shift job, his door was open.

Hershey Bar sat on the edge of his bed. Holding a bottle in his hand, he was sipping. He had not heard me come in. He looked at me and without one whit of guilt, raised the bottle and said, "It's medicinal."

At this point the reader should understand that while I was raised around the drugs and the alcohol and the other crap people use to get "high", I lived in a world of my own making that allowed me to not only take in all details but ignore them at the same time.

My brain works like this: In my family I saw drugs being bought, sold,[84] and used. I knew what they were. But they did not exist as a part of any life I would ever have once I made my own life, therefore the knowledge of these was carefully stored in an airtight box in my mind and put on a shelf. So, it wasn't until years later that I unpacked that box in my mind and realized my grandfather was drinking alcohol.

I remember the bottle.[85] At the time, though, he said it was medicinal, which meant Granddaddy was sick. So I said, "Oh, no! You're sick? What's wrong? Should you go to a doctor?"

His stare is hard to explain, even today after having unpacked all the memories, but it was a lot like the same expression he used when I, at four years old, asked him why watches had to be licked.[86] In any case, he had to explain that by "medicinal" he was warding off *future* illness, not treating any particular ailment existing at that time.

---

[84] Stepfather had to make his extra money somewhere since Mother couldn't earn enough to keep his lifestyle fully funded.

[85] Jim Beam.

[86] Based on a famous ad campaign Hershey Bar quoted several times to help the author understand a gift he had given her: "'Timex. It takes a lickin' and keeps on tickin'. Angie...aaaaahhh."

He went on to explain how it was that a swig applied every night before going to bed helped him to live so long and so well.[87] Interesting.

Which brings me to Linda Sands[88], my really good friend and fellow crime novelist and researcher into all things medicinal. You see, we are both health nuts. We've been through the wars of pregnancy and childbirth and not being able to jog anymore.[89] Yes, the pain is terrible. So, together yet not always at the same time or in the same U.S. state, Linda and I took notes and compiled them about the medicinal use of alcohol.[90]

---

[87] Granddaddy Hershey Bar was about 67 at the time. He died dramatically a few years later in a grocery store aisle in front of the eggs and orange juice. Yes, he was DRT (Dead Right There). The author's mother complained about having to pay the EMTs for trying to revive him. Her exact words were, "He was dead. They couldn't tell? And now they want me to pay them for trying to make him not dead? Sheesh. I'm not paying 'em for them doing something they didn't need to do and shoulda known they didn't need to do."
Mother said this about somebody she would miss every day for the rest of her life, so the author is not under any illusions that her death will be mourned in the least.

[88] You remember Linda, right?

[89] The author was never able to jog because her knees swelled up bigger than basketballs. Let it not be assumed this swelling began when she was — ahem — older. No, no, no. This happened from all the way back when she was a kid and her friends said she should run with them, but she couldn't without being in pain for at least a week.
She didn't understand the medicinal uses of Jim Beam at that time. Though it is doubtful Jim could've cured her bad knees, he might've made it easier to forget about them.

[90] Those notes go back years and years. Much of this research has been put to good use in advising other novelists on how to write on the medicinal use of alcohol by any type of character. They have conducted entire day-long seminars on this subject at international writing conventions as they are considered the foremost authorities on Medicinal Margaritas and Other Alternative Alcohol-Based Health Solutions. Their hands-on approach to learning (that is, they bring the shakers and salt and other

We have both come to the same conclusion, that is we agree about which works best in most situations. To give an equivalent *for instance*: For instance, aspirin works very well in most situations, though naproxen sodium may have a more specific and beneficial result in limited applications. In the same way, Medicinal Margaritas work very well in most conditions while straight Medicinal Tequila works best on a narrower spectrum of health conditions.

There was this one time when I acted as documentarian while Linda acted as the Identified Patient. We met at our local doc's office[91] and proceeded with the study. I have to say that Linda was a trouper in this research experiment. After three hours we came to the following conclusions:[92]

Medicinal Tequila administered alone via a series of shots in quick succession, say thirty seconds apart, is good for what ails you and is fast to treat the condition.

---

ingredients) leads to the seminars always being well-attended, if not packed out, by other health nuts.

[91] Dr. David M. "I've Got The Shaker" Hooberry was in, but he was merely the supervisor of the study. All he did was dispense the Medicinal Margarita and standalone shots of Medicinal Tequila per the author and Linda's precise instructions.

[92] The author and Linda have four times replicated the study to confirm initial hypotheses. Their findings have remained consistent therefore you, dear reader, can trust the study.

The after-effect of the above treatment, or the Residual Result as is the scientific name for it, should be noted: Short-term[93] loss of memory. Clothes fall off.[94] Headaches. Sunlight hurts the eyes. Whispers are as loud as roars.

Medicinal Margaritas, which have Medicinal Tequila as only one ingredient in the mix, can be sipped for hours on end delivering smaller doses of the stronger core pain-killing component, and usually cause limited memory loss for a much shorter period while delivering enough pain-killing benefit that the Identified Patient was able to function well[95] during the test, she did not lose her boots,[96] and the following morning sunlight was only mildly irritating.

---

[93] By *short-term* the author means "lasting eight to 12 hours" by which time boots have been misplaced but one still remembers what a boot is after memory returns. This memory loss is in stark contrast to the family of dementias which neither Medicinal Tequila nor Medicinal Margaritas can relieve.

[94] The author notes that both she and Linda are not the only researchers in this health matter. A song was written about the use of Medicinal Tequila by one Joe Nichols, a singer/songwriter and lay researcher from a small town in Tennessee called Nashville, who wrote "[Medicinal] Tequila Makes Her Clothes Fall Off".

[95] By *function well* the author means sentences were finished in an appropriate fashion and did not end with the typical Medicinal Tequila "WHOO-HOO! GIRL-HOWDY-DO-EWE-DOOOO ewe know whutI'm sayin'?"

[96] Linda's husband, we'll call him...ummmm...Mike, is happy when she returns from our research outings and she has both her boots on. He said, and I quote verbatim, "Linda, what are you going to do with all these half-pairs of cowboy boots?" Linda's response is always, "Whaddayamean whadamIgonnado? Make art, you wittle silwee wilwee."

The author has documented this husband/wife exchange for future studiers of Medicinal Tequila and Medicinal Margaritas. Therefore, if you experience these when you apply Medicinal Tequila, please note this is normal and not out of the ordinary.

Linda and I are two of the healthiest people you will ever meet. And by healthiest, I mean *most* healthiest.[97] We are happy to provide you with a copy of our study's results — for a price, of course.[98] Hey, we have more studies to conduct and somebody has to pay the bills.

We aren't a charity, you know.

---

[97] The author is certain her editor will insist upon taking out what he says is redundant phrasing at which time the author will reply "But, I'm having fun, so...your point is...*what?*" and the editor will sigh and shake his head and say "Whatever. *Youuuu* know best, as *always*" and he will not be sarcastic in the least.

[98] Only serious researchers will want to pay the asking price of $575,000, though researchers Linda and Angela have said that they will give the results to any non-researcher who can pony up $1,000,000.

Conversations in Hyperreality and Other Thoughts
Umberto Eco and Dave Barry Never Had

A Hardee's Halloween

Recently, due to circumstances beyond my control, I found myself in the little town of Courtland, Virginia, staying at a cheap motel that, for that town, was pretty good. It was clean (though I did have to change rooms because the carpet still had major cleaning chemicals on it from not being rinsed well). But it was definitely a clean room. I do not mean to disrespect the town or its people, nor the owner of the hotel as the old man has provided employment for many through the years as well as a service to those in need of rooming for the short haul, of which I was one as I went about helping a friend in need. We arrived late October 30, a Tuesday evening, making the next morning I woke up Halloween.

I don't celebrate Halloween and neither does my cousin who was born on October 31. In fact, she hates that's the day she was born. Oh, the many times I've heard her complain. But what can she do about it? Nothing. I always think of her on that day. And since I refuse to celebrate any birthday either, including my own, I never call to wish her happy anything on that day. Yes, I call her other times.

There I was on a Wednesday morning, my cousin's birthday, in Courtland, waking in a cheap but clean motel on the morning of All Hallows Eve, when I realized I was hungry. Somebody on a review site said the motel provides breakfast. Maybe they did at one time, but they do not anymore, which forced me to head down the street to a Hardee's, next to the Food Lion.

I like Hardee's.

They make a damn good hamburger and, for the most part, their employees are usually kind country folk who know what is on the menu and can answer any questions about it that a sometime-diner would have and are willing to accommodate a request should a person ask. A person such as myself who ordered for my breakfast a biscuit with sausage gravy[99], browned hash rounds, and coffee. In other words, the Number Five breakfast. The girl behind the counter, though, got all flustered when I said to make the coffee large.

"So, let me understand you," she said, not kindly. "You want the Number Five, which is a biscuit with sausage gravy and a coffee?"

"Yes."

She continued. "But *you* said to make it *large!* So, what do you want?"

"I want the Number Five with a large coffee."

She started searching all over her little keypad ordering system and could not find what I ordered. "Well, you either have to have the whole thing large or the whole thing small. You cannot have a small breakfast and a large coffee."

"What's the difference between them?"

Her eyes got all wide and frantic and she said, "ONE IS SMALL AND ONE IS LARGE. DUH!"

By this time a supervisor came over just as I said, "Then make the whole thing small."

I finally got my breakfast and found a table. That's when I looked around at the other people there. The place was packed with old people. I mean *old people.* Walkers and canes and hearing aids out the wazoo. I was the youngest customer in the place. In the middle of the room at a round table was one woman dressed up in a costume, fake diamonds glued to her face, a wig on crooked, face painted, wearing tennis shoes.

In front of her sat a wire roller cage with numbered balls in it. She was rolling out all the balls and matching them to numbered perfectly round divots in a wooden board. The divots were arranged in five rows. Above each row was one

---

[99] OH MY GOSH! THE BEST EVER. YOU GOT TO GET YOU SOME.

letter that when all the letters were taken together spelled BINGO. That's when I looked around at the rest of the room and saw every old person in there with a bingo card in front of them and holding a red place marker in their hand.

These old people were not messing around. They were ready for action. I looked at their faces and saw major intense concentration. Most were staring at the woman with the wire cage as she slowly put all the balls back in the cage and mixed them well. She rolled the cage until eight balls slide down into a feeder groove. One man held his marker up, ready to claim his first number. I could see the child in him, so eager and excited he was. Another man had two bingo boards in front of him. He stared intently my way, but it wasn't me he was seeing. He was seeing victory snatched out of the jaws of defeat. He was a soldier in a foxhole waiting for the enemy to show his ugly face. His eyes were cold, unflinching. He. Would. Win. Then the woman with the wire cage spoke.

"Listen up, everybody. Who in here likes to play bingo?"

Of course, I looked around fully expecting each person to raise at least one hand. But I was surprised. Only three people raised their hand. Everyone else just stayed as they were, frowns in place. Now, I say these were frowns, but technically I think that's just how their faces fell naturally. What with sagging bags and such, and having such intense concentration, smiles were the furthest thing from their minds. The woman continued.

"Okay. Then let me tell you this. Management!" she looked around the room with her hand on the first numbered ball. "You hear me? *MANAGEMENT* has said if there is any more complaining about bingo, then there will be *no more bingo*. You hear me? Do ya? Huh? No. More. Bingo."

Oh, they heard and how. In fact, I could tell who were the guilty parties right away because these squirmed in their seats and dipped their heads and eyes in a classic guilty fashion while the others gave them hard looks. I felt like I was back in elementary school.

"Okay, O-61!"

And they were off and running. The story does not end there. Management made herself known a few minutes later. She walked through like she meant business, too. Putting a hand on the shoulder of Guilty Complaining Party Number One, she said loudly, "We good? No complaining this morning?" GCPNO shook her head that she wasn't complaining just as O-67 was called out. Management repeated that questioning two more times with other players. Oh, she was good. I bet she used to be a teacher. The kind that didn't mind publicly humiliating a student when that student made it clear they had to learn the hard way. In other words, a great teacher.

You will never find Wednesday Morning Old Folks Bingo anywhere in Decatur, Georgia, except maybe at an assisted living home on the memory care ward, but never in public at a fast-food place. That's the difference between small towns and big city university towns.

Still, what was it those three old people had to complain about that they did it so loud and long that *MANAGEMENT* had to step in and threaten them with eviction should they ever again complain about bingo in her store? I cannot even imagine it unless…

Nope. I've got nothing.

Then again, maybe when I get that age and I'm sitting in a Hardee's on a Wednesday morning waiting for bingo numbers to be called, I'll understand what there is to complain about. What if the only prize is the honor of winning? What if the complaint I'd utter is that Hardee's is mean because it doesn't want to reward my win by giving me a free breakfast? It's possible. And shouldn't they at least favor me with a free coffee just for showing up? You know how much effort that takes from an old folk? It's a lot. Not that I know from experience, but I've heard tales, and I am a close observer of humankind.

Which brings me to another topic I find interesting: 55+ Active Living Communities. Let's explore that, shall we?

Active Living

"Independent **living communities** are designed for the **active** and **healthy** senior who is able to live independently on their own. You can live in a home, condo, townhouse, apartment complex, motor home or mobile home."

By that explanation, I will never live in such a community because what the definition does not tell you is that it costs a lot of moolah to live in one of those, which is why active and healthy are requirements: You'll still have to work because they want your money for "programming", not meds.

Obviously many people have that kind of money, but not me. Besides, even if I did have that kind of money, I wouldn't do it. I'm too damn cheap. Do not doubt me on this. I've been that way since I was a child. My husband, now The Ex, was happy to have such a wife as myself, though he honestly didn't know what to do with me. On the one hand, he kept telling me to spend. On the other, when I did spend (on necessary items like food and shoes for the kids) he would pitch a fit and call me a spendthrift. He was a confused man in this matter, among other matters. He had all sorts of replies ready for when a woman would go out and blow a paycheck on a new pair of shoes, but I never did it; he couldn't use his really good insults and so he was always having to revise them on the fly. He wasn't good at that.

But would The Ex like to live in an Active Living Community? I think he would but only with a woman he could complain about because something else interesting happens in these 55+ Active Living Communities.

Previously, these folks have lived quiet, upstanding lives. Gone to church. Paid their taxes. Didn't party. Babysat the grands and gave them lots of sugary items so they would stay awake all night crying and keep their parents awake as they came down from their sugar highs. SuhWEET revenge these

55+'ers had. But now they move to another state far, far away and what do they do with their time?

They boink.

Yes, they are all going around boinking each other's brains out. It is easy to do in these communities because there are no grandchildren to worry about influencing. There is a huge increase in sexually transmitted diseases because none of these 55+'ers are using protection. And why should they, they think? They've been faithful all these years and they don't have any diseases and they believe everybody else has been faithful, too, and everybody is healthy, like the ads say they should be. But it doesn't work that way and now doctors report rises in STDs because the men and women aren't managing the "risings" like they should.

Of course, once dementias and other health problems set in and folks are no longer active and healthy, you would expect them to move. But guess what? They don't because — damn it! — they bought this place and used up all their money to make sure this was the last place they would ever live. This tells us something about these 55+'ers: They are determined to screw over their families and their neighbors yet again. They are probably every last one of them a damn...you know what? I am not going to bring politics into this essay in the least bit.

Suffice it to say, you will never find me in one of those communities. Number one, I'm cheap — which I've already told you I am and if you were to meet me and say "Angela, you are cheap," I would hug you and say thank you so much because that is high praise indeed. Number two, these people are boring. I've never wanted to "party" at any time in my life and that's all these people want to do. Number three, I would not fit in in any social activity they find attractive. For instance, they watch plays, cook out in the backyard, and go to concerts, whereas I write, don't like mosquitos, and put on concerts. They boink willy-nilly while I do not believe boinking is sport-related.

I've always been odd man out. To live in a 55+ community one cannot be such an odd man out because one must contribute to the homogenous nature of the fun-loving group by "participating". Though — and you now know this to be true — "pasteurizing" doesn't seem to be so high on their list of priorities[100]. While I fight against my germ-hating nature[101] — I want to make it through alive when the Big Bug tries to wipe out the world — I'm not so eager to be boinked willy-nilly to put myself around more germs that mutate. So, you see, I just will not get any participation award in a 55+ Active Living Community.

Plus, I'm cheap.

Look, I'm so cheap that my drug of choice is putting a pack of Planter's peanuts inside a bottle of Coke, shaking it, then slugging it down — swig after swig of salt, fuzzy bubbles, and nuts. You haven't tried that? You are in for a treat. However, do not use Dr Pepper. You must use the Coca-Cola brand of Coke but not Coke Zero.

Another way to use your Coke well is to mix it the Jack Daniels, in just the right ratio of course. Too much Jack or too much Coke and it won't work. You'll have to work out the percentages for your use. Best to use a glass glass and not a plastic glass for this. Then pop that in the freezer and go check on it a few hours later. Stir with a spoon to slush it up. Oh, yeah. Homemade Coke-and-Jack slushy is delisioso.

This recommendation is not meant to take the place of the Medicinal Margarita. After all, the latter is research while the former is just all for fun and would be the only way I would fit into a 55+ Active Living Community and, since that is such

---

[100] See information about boinking and spreading STDs.

[101] The author often does not wash her hands before she eats. When she drops a piece of food on the floor, she counts to five (exactly) so that she hits the Five-Second Rule smack dab in the center no matter which way the rule bends, then eats the food. See? She is allowing her body to build up a natural immunization against those germs that mutate.

a narrow skill set and does not contribute to the betterment of mankind, it is obvious this is yet another reason I would never be able to visit such for over two days[102] much less live there.

---

[102] The author follows the old Friends and Fish rule.

There's a bit of a disconnect here.

I've got a quick question for you.

So, there I am Tuesday night and I go to Venkman's for the Joe Gransden Jazz Jam. For those who do not know, Venkman's is a club in Atlanta run by men who claim to be music guys. True, they are the Yacht Rock guys who play lots of covers and they do an okay job of it for those who are drunk on yachts. But as restaurant guys, they have the gig down to an art form, which is to say, they are damn cheapskates when it comes to making the sound better for other artists in that room. But I'm not here to talk about them right now. Maybe later. Then again, maybe not.

So, I go to Venkman's on Tuesday night for the Joe Gransden Jazz Jam and on this particular night Matt Miller, a killer sax guy, is doing hosting duties. His Supremeness Gary Motley is on keys. And Craig "Shawboxx" Shaw is tickling Dora Darkness. No, not his girlfriend. It is the name of his instrument[103]. Dave Potter is pounding on the skins.[104]

Joe was late to arrive on this night because it seems Joe was at the Fox hanging with some ninety-something-year-old dude by the name of Tony Bennett who was doing a secret show, or so my friends told me the next day. Everybody was very unhappy that Joe was late. How dare he blow off the Venkman's crowd for Tony Bennett, right? Anyway, I'm not here to talk about Joe and his fan-disrespecting ways either.

I'm here to talk about me. That's right. Me.

I was feeling quite fine on this particular Tuesday evening and because my duo partner Alan Dynin was out of town, I was able to sing earlier in the evening than is normal. Usually

---

[103] Not that instrument! Shawboxx's instrument is an upright bass, gitchermindouttadaguttah!

[104] Drums! Sheesh, gitchermindouttadaguttah!

Alan and I don't get to go on before 10:30 (and the show ends at 11:00) because Alan has lessons and rehearsals and such which run late so I'm always giving Joe the heads-up.

"Hey, Joe. Alan just texted. ETA 15," I say when Joe passes by the table with a worried look and asking about when in the hell are we, Alan and I, going to be able to go on because don't we know he, Joe, can't have a show without us, right? Of course, right. But, I'm not talking here about Alan's schedule either or Joe's OCD ways.

So, Matt is being accosted by three women singers (of which I are one[105]), fighting to be first to tell him what they are going to sing and the key in which they will sing it. Madeline and Tina and me[106] are all elbows and insults as we push and shove our way toward the man of the hour screaming, "Me! Me! Me! Me wanna sing!"

Matt, saxophone slung to the side, is furiously working his thumbs over his smartphone making the list of who will play or sing as he looks from one to the other and he's saying, "I gotcha! I gotcha! Uh-huh. Uh-huh. Say, what was that song title again? And the key?" But I'm not here to talk about diva drama in the Jazz Club scene.

I finally get up to sing ("Hey, Gary. Summertime in C. Swing it after my comedy routine." "Hey, baby, I'll follow you!" he says.) I open with, "Helloooooo, Venkman's. What time is it?"

Some smartass friend of mine, who knows what I was gonna sing, hollers, "It's Summertime" which, of course, totally steals my whole routine's thunder, but I didn't care because the audience laughed, and I had their attention and I do know how to recover from interruptions by smartasses. So, I'm killing it. Now, in the music world "killing it" is a

---

[105] Please take off your editor hat and join in the fun of language's many facets.

[106] See above footnote.

good thing. That means the audience is having a good time because you are there. Well, at least they are laughing.

Granted, they could be laughing because I was horrible, but I don't think that is the case because after being laughed at my whole life I know the difference between haters and likers and they liked me.

But they liked me better because the band was effin'[107] killin' it and in the music world "effin' killin' it" is better than "killin' it". But even that is not what I'm writing about here. No, I'm writing about the next day, Wednesday.

So, there I am, riding high on the memories of the previous evening and thinking I'd go to the Gordon Vernick Jazz Jam at the Red Light Café on Wednesday evening. But I wake up early Wednesday and I feel like I've been drugged. I know it isn't because I got drunk the night before because, though I have lots of stories of watching others do so, I myself do not get drunk.

I walk down the street to meet friends for coffee and a bagel at our local independently owned coffee shop called The Corner Cup. I'm thinking I'll feel better after I walk a half mile to and fro and put something on my tummy. But no. By the time I get home, I'm feeling worse and I fall into the bed and promptly sleep for about an hour and wake up feeling even more drugged.

This situation goes on all day. Get up. Feel drugged. Work on the computer a bit to try to make some damn money. Go to sleep. Until around 4:00 when I text my friend Amy and say let's go to Red Light Café for the Jazz Jam. I said I would pick her up at 9:00 and we would arrive properly as divas should — with a splash and a little late — and then sing and such. Amy thought that was a grand idea. I told her all about

---

[107] For those in your century, "effin'" is a polite way of say "fuckin'".

how I was feeling drugged and she said, "Well, you didn't drink a lot last night, so I just do not understand that."[108]

"I don't either, Amy. I think I must have something wrong with me genetically because Awesome Cousin Number One says she often feels drugged when she wakes up, so I think I must have inherited something from the Kell side of the family, which is Daddy's side, you know. I think I might be dying."

Amy says, "Oh, nooooooo! I'll see you at nine."[109]

We hang up and I fall asleep and wake up again feeling drugged about twice more and then I decide I must need some food and proceed to eat. It makes me feel worse, but I ignore it because I must get stuff done for a client before I die from this horrible affliction visited upon me by my father's DNA. I'm on the phone with the client when I almost throw up on the phone.

"Hey, gotta go. Call you later." Barf!

I fall onto the bed and look at the clock. Damn! Two hours before I have to pick up Amy. Okay. I shall will myself to overcome my DNA's assault and I proceeded to take ninety minutes to lose the fight. At 8:30 I'm calling Amy with the sad news: I do not want to spread germs and what I thought was my father's DNA attacking me, must be —

"Gotta go!" Barf.

Then I did the really smart thing. I cranked up the TV, got Hulu going (Netflix is verboten in my home) and found a comedy special because, after all, laughter is the best medicine. Only the comedian was Ron White, a foul-mouthed

---

[108] Amy is such a nice and caring person and if you could've heard how she said that it would make you feel just damn swell.

[109] Amy said that so encouragingly.

Southern boy who said some hilarious things if I was into foul-mouthed stuff, which I am not.[110]

But I did not have the strength to turn Ron off or turn him down and so, there I am, on the bed, fighting the barf reflex only to have Ron make me want to barf more. But this is not what this story is about either.

The real story here is I am so disconnected from my own body I cannot tell the difference between a life-threatening condition caused by inherited DNA and a damn stomach bug. It is my understanding some folks might call me a hypochondriac, but they would be wrong because you ain't one if you really are dying of something, therefore you could, at worst, say I am vigilant with my health.

But look, let's get back to the question I wanted to ask you: Is anybody else disconnected from their body like that?

Anybody?

---

[110] Granted, the author agrees that occasionally she does use the F-word, but that is only occasionally and when directly called for. Not like Ron White, who never frickin' stops saying it.

 **WHAT IS IT?**

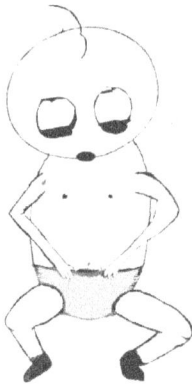 **DON'T KNOW. BUT...**

 **I LIKE IT!**

The difference between boys and girls, from someone who knows.

Invited to dinner by a childless couple, my husband[111] and I were not about to turn down an opportunity for a free dinner somewhere else and proceeded to pack up everything parents of two small children, four and one, needed for an excursion outside the house, even if the excursion was next door, literally.[112]

The reason I am making such a big deal about adding the word *literally* here is this: In the South we tend not to measure space and time by the same things Big City Yankees do. For instance, a Big City Yankee would say, "I'm going down the block." Everybody up there knows how long a block is and that down the block means *one* exactly defined *block*.

Therefore, the Big City Yankee has let everybody know the extremely limited general area in which he will be and they can extrapolate an approximate segment of time before he is determined to "be missing". This is why Big City Yankees are always getting caught with their hands in the ol' proverbial "illicit nookie jar" iffenyaknow whuttamean because they also don't look at clocks thereby misjudging the passage of time and then somebody comes looking for them because they are "missing" and then they are found because they are only one block away and if they aren't one block away and they cannot be found, then she always knows

---

[111] Now called The Ex. At the time of this incident, the man was married to the author and was the father of her two children, both of whom were spawned after the marriage was officially registered and signed off on by all legal government entities and the preacher.

[112] Literally next door. The author, husband, and children *walked* from their yard to the next yard and into the neighbor's front door.

where the old girlfriend lives and steps onto the next block and proceeds to make a scene.

But not in the South. If we have blocks at all, then they are limited to very small areas of each town[113] and none of them are the same length, breadth, or depth. Some towns only have one block, yet it could stretch alongways[114] and be different town to town.[115] Southerners don't say block much and we do not say alongways out loud. Instead we say "apiece" used like this: "I'm going down the road apiece."

Based on how and where it is said, *apiece* could indicate going to town to the grocery store[116], or visiting Mama[117], or going to the deep woods to sit in a deer stand for three days[118]. Therefore, when I say next door, it could mean all sorts of distances here in the South, which is why I clarified for you that when I said *next door* I *literally* meant *next door*.

For our sojourn *literally next door,* it took one hour to pack up all we would need and check the list twice lest a child not have what it needed and therefore would make our lives miserable. These needful items[119] included:

---

[113] This does not include Atlanta, which has tried its best to make "blocks" but failed dismally because — as anybody knows and that includes visiting Big City Yankees, those from The Left Coast, and those born and raised in Georgia — there is not a single well-defined block in Atlanta around which you can make four consecutive right turns without ending up at Stone Mountain, or as natives call it, That Big Rock Over There.

[114] Alongways, not a long way, is proper Southern for alongways.

[115] The author may or may not delve into this further, but then again maybe she will and maybe she won't.

[116] If female.

[117] For both male and female.

[118] Which could *literally* mean the woods, if male.

[119] The modern reader will note a severe lack of "digital mobile devices". There was such a time.

- One diaper bag (contents listed later)
- Two sweaters
- Three favorite blankees
- Two sippy cups
- Juice, Welch's grape, one bottle of
- Dollies, two favorites, three changes of clothes each
- One shaker toy, or rattle, with flashy visuals
- A homemade chocolate dessert as a contribution to the meal

We were ready! The husband led his little band of merry visitors across the yard. I say he led, because that's all he did. He did not carry the baby. He did not hold the hand of the four-year-old. He did not carry the diaper bag. He did not carry the necessary bag. And he certainly didn't balance the cake plate. I did all that. If I had worn a burqa, from the back you would not have been able to tell the difference in the scene from my neighborhood and one in Iraq or Iran or any country that makes their women wear long black full-body veils in the dead of summer.

That's right. Men are men and when spittle-filled preachers get involved I don't care what language they speak or what sort of headwear they don, men feel invincible and start saying things like "Woman! Get me mah cawghfee."[120] Or "Woman! Get your sangak in the oven and your lavash[121] in the bed." But that's another essay for another day. Let's get back to the trek next door. We arrive and are, as expected, invited in. Interesting side point: Our male host.... Never

---

[120] Southern for a hot beverage brewed from the caffeine-loaded bean of a plant grown on mountains that when said beans are roasted and ground produces a delicious aroma making it a desired beverage around the world.

[121] Two favorite bread types in Iran. In the South we would say, "Get your biscuits in the oven and yer buns in the bed."

mind. That would just take us around the world, so I'm not gonna say anything about the time when I was thirteen and had a crush[122] on him or when I was seventeen and experimented with manipulating his little mind[123] and found him wanting even if he did have a Trans Am or when I was fifteen and our hostess asked me not to tell her mama she was smoking.[124] I will not mention these things because to do so would be to diss a generous host and hostess and, at the time, they were generous in their hosting.

Dinner was eaten. We slogged through conversation that kept getting interrupted by children screaming "See me, Mommy! SEEEEE MEEEEE!"[125] and snotty-nose wiping and sippy-cup refilling and so forth. We retired to the living room where — and this is where we get to what this essay is all about — the difference between boys and girls became apparent.

What happened was that The Boy[126], who was still in diapers, laid on the floor kicking his little legs and then got quiet and still. Then he got all red in the face because he was holding his breath and experiencing a "brownout"[127] and within seconds produced a room-filling stench.

---

[122] With attendant fantasies of getting locked in a church overnight. Do not ask for details.

[123] The author dressed up and flirted outrageously and said to herself, "If he reacts like I expect him to, then he is not a man for me!" He was not the man for her.

[124] The author did not tell on her but she got found out anyway and assumed the author told and got mad at her.

[125] That was The Girl. The Boy did not yet speak and wouldn't for six more years.

[126] Hereinafter to be understood to mean "The Boy Child of My Ten-Month Pregnancy and I Ain't Lying!"

[127] This one has nothing to do with brownouts associated with electric grid fluctuations. See essay "Brownouts vs. Blackouts".

Now, as a mother of two, this was normal. Our hostess and cooker of our free dinner was annoyed because the stench overpowered her home's flowering bouquet smell; I still don't know where it came from. But she kept her say to herself. Totally not caring and simply wanting to remove the offending smelly deposit from the room, I sat on the floor next to The Boy who, by now, knew the routine and laid himself flat with legs spread, and I removed from the diaper bag the following items:

- Five wet washcloths
- Two empty bread bags, one lining the other
- One clean cloth diaper
- One liquid- and brownout-proof rubberized changing mat
- One bottle of baby powder, half empty
- One tube of zinc oxide cream, almost full

Holding his ankles and thus pulling his legs up, The Boy rolled to his right. I laid the mat next to his back. He rolled back on the mat, assuming the spread-eagle position once again. Our hostess whispered, "Wh-wh-what are you doing?" I replied slowly while staring ironically, "Changing? His? *DiaPERRRR?*"[128] Our hostess reached out a hand to her husband for support and stared in fascinated horror.[129]

---

[128] The author admits that the Ironic Spoken Question Mark was invented by her. She apologizes to humankind.

[129] **Hang on, now. Don't be getting all in a hurry for the author to get to the point because you think she's digressing because, she will have you know, she is not only not digressing, she is getting mighty close to the point of this essay. That's the problem with all you Google-iPhone-MeFirst-Generation types. Always in a hurry. Gotta have it now. All about the destination, not the journey. Sheesh.**

The bread bags, washcloths, cream, powder, and diaper were staged for use in that order. Off came his little plastic diaper cover[130], laid to the side after confirming brownout did not spread to it. Out came the safety diaper pins. Down came the diaper. Down went the hostess' face buried into her husband's shoulder as she gasped for a breath of flowery bouquet air.

And that is when it happened. I said, "Huh. What is this?"

Laying right there, embedded in the brownout, was a large black rubber tire from a toy truck, clearly of the yellow iron[131] variety. The Girl[132] had never eaten anything that wasn't food. I had never found a toy part in her brownout. Not even if it was part of a doll. Her brownout was always pure brownout. And that is when I knew the difference between boys and girls.

So, as I'm sitting on the floor looking, our childless host sat up straight and leaned forward. "What did you find?"

I said, "Look!" And I held it up with a washcloth for all to see. Our hostess fainted onto the sofa after screaming *ewwwwwww!* Our daughter was screaming and fainting with her.[133]

But you see? Our host and the father of the child were not surprised at all this was there. Instead they made comments

---

[130] The reader may believe at this point that the author had her children in the 1950s or 1960s because she's talking washcloths, cloth diapers, and such. That would be incorrect. Both her children had super-sensitive skin and were highly allergic to everything modern that would've made their mother's life easier, thus forcing her to go "old school".

[131] That is, from the Caterpillar company who produces that yellow construction equipment and of which miniatures have been fashioned and sold successfully.

[132] Hereinafter to mean "The Girl Who Was Born Mad and Stayed That Way For Two Solid Years".

[133] They were such *girly girls!*

like, "Wow! That's a big one!" and "How did such a little boy swallow that biggathang?" If high-fiving with children was popular back then, I swear they would have high-fived The Boy. But it wasn't, so they just kept up with the attaboys which, of all things, The Boy totally understood, and his little legs wiggled in the air and a big old smile spread and he made little fists of approval[134] causing male-bonding moments aplenty.

But the story takes an even weirder turn because, you see, there were no toys in our house featuring large black rubber tires. We had none. We didn't know anybody who had any and if they did, as the hovering mother ever worried about choking hazards, I always thoroughly vetted any home we went into for small choking hazards and made sure those were put under lock and key so my precious children would not die.[135]

So the big question was, and one we discussed at length between us[136] while The Boy's poopy bottom was still awaiting service, was how did a child barely walking, whose mother hovers to keep him safe, who doesn't drive, and cannot yet crawl out a window to get in the back of his redneck friend's pickup truck to go searching for the same, manage to lay hands on such an object?

It is a mystery and one that can only be explained by saying God has a sense of humor.

It is sufficient to say we were never again invited, and in fact the woman began lobbying for her husband to "get me the hell out of this crazy place *right now!*" Within two

---

[134] Fist-bumping would become a highly popular thing, indicating extreme approval of the person receiving the fist-bump or of the event, saying, comeback, movie, or performance being attended.

[135] The author was a **very good mother**. Her children said so.

[136] Excluding The Girl and Hostess.

months they had hitched up their trailer and they were gone. Within a year they were divorced.

I believe their marriage would have lasted except for one thing. And this thing was the Great "Large Black Rubber Tire in the Brownout" Event because, you see, when this couple had married they had both agreed they did not want children. They were both the babies of their families and were self-absorbed. But when our host saw how much fun it was to discover buried toys in a heavy diaper he started yammering for a baby boy and our hostess really did not want kids. So, they divorced, and he found a woman who did want toys in diapers — I mean, children — and they've had several and been happy. Our hostess moved to Florida and became the childless skin-sunburnt-to-leather party girl she longed to be. Yes, God has a sense of humor alright.

The more things change, the more they stay the same.

On October 12, 2018, at 8:20 AM, a news item that got not one glance from the mainstream media showed up on my desk. Entitled "Personality differences between the sexes are largest in the most gender equal countries", it went on to say, in part:

"The study was conducted by University of Gothenburg, University West and the University of Skövde. Over 130,000 people from 22 countries [took the self-rated] personality test [that] measured openness, conscientiousness, extraversion, agreeableness, and neuroticism.

"Average differences between men and women's scores were computed for each country, then compared against that country's gender equality level as measured by the World Economic Forum. The study showed higher levels of gender equality were associated with larger differences in personality between the sexes.

"Sweden and Norway showed differences in personality between the sexes…twice as large as countries with substantially lower levels of gender equality, such as China and Malaysia.

"Furthermore, women generally rated themselves as more worried (neuroticism), social (extraversion), inquisitive (openness), caring (agreeableness), and responsible (conscientiousness) than men. These relative differences were larger in gender equal countries.

"'Insofar as these traits can be classified as stereotypically feminine, our interpretation of the data is that as countries become more progressive men and women gravitate towards their traditional gender norms. But, we really don't know why it is like this, and sadly our data does not let us tease out the causal explanations,' says Erik Mac Giolla, Ph.D. in

Psychology. 'A combination of social role theory and evolutionary perspectives may ultimately be needed to explain these findings.'"

A combo of social role theory and evolutionary perspectives may be needed to 'splain? Holy cow. Let me, your Autodidact Polymath and Magnificently Methodical Southern Woman, make it simple for you: The more a country pushes stupid theory as fact, the more people push back even if they don't consciously recognize they are doing it. But the study is clear. They only needed someone else to give meaning to the results.

Look, I've made plenty of fun at the expense of RadFems, those who wear pussy hats (male and female), and women having meltdowns for other reasons, but every one of them only wants to get laid. They just don't recognize the symptoms. Let me explain using myself as the example.[137]

You've heard me mention The Ex. Everything I'm saying about him now does not in any way negate the truth that he needed divorcing. Nevertheless, when I got all cranked up and on a tear about something or another, it never failed he would eventually sáy after about a week of that, "You just need a good f***ing."

Well, I would proceed to tell him how he was a no-good so-and-so who didn't care but for himself and his needs, but he'd just keep on hounding me with how he was willing to sacrifice himself for the cause until finally, to prove him wrong, I'd agree and in we'd go, lock the bedroom door, and proceed to getting busy in a robust and angry fashion.

After which, damn him, he would be right. Wow, how my attitude got so much calmer and happier. Though smiling while I said it, I'd remind him that just because he was right about this didn't mean I was wrong about that thing which

---

[137] You see how humble the author is?

bothered me so a few minutes ago. And thus, the divorce was needed.

However, my point is clear: Everybody just needs a good servicing every now and then, even in anger and frustration, and perhaps maybe we wouldn't have so many frowns on baristas' faces or be invited to attend so many women's conferences and other seriously serious crap like that.

It's confusing to know me both personally and in business.

If I had a hundred-dollar bill for each time somebody looked at me sideways in a confused manner and said, "I had no idea you could do all that," then I would have enough money to keep me comfortable as long as I didn't get too crazy with the spending thing.

In this response from other people I'm just like Umberto Eco. Even when told that Eco was a polymath and a semiotician, American interviewers did not understand how it was Eco could be so…so…widespread in his interests and knowledge base. It's as if they did not do their homework or touch a dictionary to find out what a polymath or semiotician was.[138]

I can sympathize with Umberto because American interviewers, customers, audiences, and men have the same problem with me. No matter what I tell them, or how I tell them. No matter the patience I use as I walk them through whatever subject about which they are interviewing me.

They. Get. It. Wrong.

Which is why I prefer to write the interview and give it to them or have them "feel good" about writing it and send it to me for "a few tweaks".

Not too long ago, a female reporter was assigned the job of interviewing me. I asked her which part of my life or businesses her paper wanted to focus on. I got a blank stare. Ah, so no prep was done by her. Eventually she asked what I did. I do a lot of things, so that meant she needed a synopsis

---

[138] But that's the horrible state of journalism in the last 40 years, a devolvement brought about by the consolidating of news sources, journalism classes that stressed politically correct terminology over well-researched facts, and the overall smackdown in the newsroom when you mention a viewpoint in opposition to Socialism.

of the various businesses I'm involved in as well as the thought-leader and Citizen Journalist stuff I manage to do in my spare time.[139]

She wrote the piece and, as all serious journalists do, she did not ask me to fact-check her understanding or representation of the subject in her article before she turned it in to her editor. After all, she is a serious journalist, don't you know. Her editor rejected the piece and it did not run. The serious journalist was furious at me. Somehow it was all my fault the editor refused her words. How do I know this?

Because the editor told the writer, "This is the most confused and boring woman. Furthermore, she is making all this up because no one person does all this."

By now, I was curious about the piece. What in the hell did the journalist write that would make an assigned interview go this horribly wrong? Through hook and not-a-lotta crook (I knew somebody who knew somebody), I managed to lay hands on what she had turned over to her editor. My first response was "Oh. My. Goodness. They *pay* her to work there?"[140]

My second response was, "I do not blame the editor for turning this down. I would hate me, and I would think me a bore and a liar, too."

My interviewer could not wrap her head around anything I do, therefore, in trying to explain how and why and where and so forth, she had screwed it up royally. You see, Umberto

---

[139] The author is not bragging, but it is a fact that when no children or men are in the house with you, a girl can get a whole hell of a lot done in her spare time.

[140] The author's actual response and one that she did not want to include in this book was, "Goddamn it. How stupid can that woman be? F*&king *itch wasted my time. See if I ever talk to her again." Now you can see why the author did not include it in the book, though she does want you to note the correct use of the effing word in all its glory.

Eco explained to American interviewers that how he operated — that is, writing on and opining about a broad array of subjects in the popular press, books, articles, and so on — was common to all European intellectuals in Germany, France, Spain, and Italy.

Which means I would fit right in over there, but am considered abnormal in the U.S. That explains a lot of man interactions I have. Except for one particular rich German man who manages (in a business situation) to make me the bad guy as a way to get his even-richer German dominatrix wife to be mean to him like he likes it. Of course, well-traveled American men and visiting European males with any intelligence say I am The Most Brilliant Woman In The World. These men are correct.

Other American men for the most part think I'm a liar, a poser, an ugly man in drag, and/or a dominatrix.[141] They are wrong, but they will never understand Angela.

Oh, well.

Whatever.

---

[141] The author is not kidding and looks at these comments as opportunities to hold her ego in check and remain accessible so that the roar of the greasepaint and the smell of the crowd does not distract her.

How to train the public to hold a P-HWPCLDRSFC[142] opinion.

First, buy up as many independent radio and television stations and newspapers and magazines as you can legally lay your hands on in as many countries as possible. Then form a conglomerate of those business entities. Next, hire people who are good at signaling[143] and put them in charge. Of course, confirm they can be trusted to pass along messaging intended to divide and control. Messaging that says:

- Families made of a male and female married to each other are bad.
- All men are evil.
- All women are victims even when they aren't.
- Laws are made for picking and choosing.
- Faithfulness is to be shunned.
- All police are malicious.
- Proudly Brown and Black peoples[144] are slaves-in-training and must be protected against all Whites who are nothing but plantation owner wannabes.

Then no matter what happens in the real world, have your pretty talking heads repeat ad infinitum, "What you just

---

[142] Pussy-Hat Wearing Politically Correct Liberal Democrat RINO Socialist Fascist Commie

[143] See the essay entitled "The Most Brilliant Woman In The World nailed it a long time ago".

[144] All peoples of color do not include White.

saw is not what really happened. What you just heard is not what was really said. You are too stupid to realize that, so listen to us. And remember" — long pause delivered with unflinching stare at The Big Red Eye That Never Blinks — "if anybody tries to tell you differently, they are trying to enslave you. If anybody disagrees with us, we know who you are and will make your life a living hell if you speak up. You are getting slEEEEEpee."

Final step: Continue to push the DILDOS[145] narrative ad infinitum and ad nauseum until, just like water torture in all its forms will do, citizens have been driven insane.

Heck, these DILDOS even think wearing a condom will keep them safe during sex. They must have missed the news story about this pussy-hat wearing guy who was wearing a condom, but he got shot anyway by his girlfriend's wife.

Does that make him the murdered master[146]?

---

[145] DILDOS: Desperate Intolerant Liberals Destroying Our Society. The author saw this on the World Wide Web where one can find both indexed and non-indexed Internets and other stuff like men setting their balls on fire. The acronym was not attributed but widely spread, so she figured finders-keepers.

[146] The author simply despises those who cannot read in context. Even though no color has been mentioned, some pussy-hat wearing reader will accuse the author of supporting White Colonial Male Privilege because she used the word "master".

It is a surprise The Master Lock company has not yet been sued, especially as their HR department makes them a prime target because the company used White Colonial Male Privilege language, boasting that "We believe fostering an *inclusive* and positive environment where *all* individual differences are recognized as a competitive advantage is a business imperative. Accordingly, we leverage the strength of our *diverse* workforce to consistently exceed the expectations of our customers and shareholders, simply by treating *all* employees with the dignity, respect, and trust they inherently deserve."

When filtered through the P-HWPCLDRSFC mind, that statement shows the company is trying too hard to prove they are not a White Colonial Male-based employer which, of course, means they totally are. And, just like the ex-president they follow who has been called "The absolute worst and a criminal racist failure dementia patient", The

A Gender Scholar goes to Hooter's to find out why it is so popular.

Okay.

So.

I must confess I did not come up with this title but heard it on Ben Shapiro's radio show. Seems there are these three academics[147] who are completely sick of Gender Studies hijacking universities through political corruption. They decided to prank[148] and wrote several articles based around fake, non-existent scientific studies. One had the title above. They then submitted these to — let my fingers stop laughing so they can type the words — *HIGHLY RESPECTED* gender studies journals around the world.

One paper they submitted used incidents of dogs humping as evidence of a rape culture in humans. It was accepted and officially honored as excellent scholarship, even though one reviewer said she was worried the writers of the paper did not respect the dogs' privacy while inspecting their genitals.

Master Lock company cannot win for losing so they may as well give all their profits to Planned Parenthood and PETA and ANTIFA because those organizations surely know how to spend money more responsibly than anybody else, right?

[147] If you are asking what gender these academics are, then you are normal. Two men, one woman. And we're not talking here "self-identified as", but rather "actually born as and did not feel the need to change".

The author realizes this is a "water statement" she has flung in the hopes gender studies people read this footnote and melt like a certain evil — and maybe misunderstood — character in *The Wizard of Oz*.

[148] "To prank" is an action clause made up of a functional word — "to" — and a verbed noun — "prank" — that when completed goes like this: To prank or not to prank: That is the question.

As we have seen, the three academics decided to prank.

Another paper the three wrote and submitted to a *HIGHLY RESPECTED* queer studies journal proves that a man who privately diddles himself while thinking about a woman without her consent, or her ever knowing or even finding out he was thinking about her during said diddle, has in fact committed sexual violence against her.

This fake paper, pranked out the wazoo, was *published* and lauded as gospel.

I — your own personal Autodidact Polymath Magnificently Methodical Southern Woman and The Most Brilliant Woman In The World — have been warning for years about this type of university hijacking sh-…errr…crap. When both my children definitively stated they did not want to go to college, I thoroughly respected their decision because it proved they had listened to their mother. All mothers want their children to listen to them and often wonder if they do. I have proof mine did which, of course, makes me the Mother of the Century. Thank you. No really, thank *you* for the applause. Give yourselves a big hand for recognizing my awesome mothering abilities.

Thank you.

Thank you!

Oh, hush now, y'all. You're making me blush…

…except I never have and never will.

That is not a lie.

I have never once in my whole life blushed. I think it is a genetic condition, but since I was unsure of whether it was passed on by DNA, I did some research. While the World Wide Web was loaded with information about why one does blush, there was not one bit of indexed information on the WWW about why one never does.

But reading deeply into the first paragraph of a paper by The Karen Smith[149], these gems came out about why people do blush. This is quoted bervatim:[150]

> "When I was really young I was really shy, and sometimes someone only had to speak to me and I would blush. As I got older and more confident this decreased. Except if I was in a large group of people I didn't know, then I would feel very uncomfortable and blush I don't know if it is genetic I doubt it. There is usually an underlying reason for these things. Such as lack of confidence or even a trauma. Don't worry as you get more self-assured your confidence will grow. I traced the reason I had this problem back to a childhood experience, when I was in school, which I hated! And hardly ever went. But now I know the reason why."[151]

Lest you are wondering if The Karen Smith hated her school or her childhood experience, let me say right now: It doesn't matter. What does matter is The Karen Smith has brilliantly identified why I do not blush. She said blushing is caused by a lack of confidence and/or trauma. Even though the sad recounting of my life in *Twinkle, a memoir* indicates the contrary, according to The Karen Smith, the reason I have never blushed is because I have always been so very confident and what traumas I went through were not sufficiently bad enough.

---

[149] "The" Karen Smith as opposed to "a" Karen Smith since this Karen has her own section on Quora.com that answers such questions as "Do you think a person who cannot keep secrets can turn over a new leaf completely?" Her extremely detailed and helpful answer was: "I don't know." I ask, though, "Where is the leaf and can the person bend over?"

[150] Or verbatim if one has no sense of humor and fun.

[151] In this passage, did the use of commas make your eyes cross?

Well, that explains it.

Not.

I went looking further and found another scientific-ish answer. Fear of blushing made for more blushing. I've never been afraid of it, so there's my answer. But wait! There's more.

Another study said sudden and strong emotions — such as stress or embarrassment — cause the sympathetic nervous system to widen blood vessels in the face, increasing blood flow to skin producing redness associated with blushing. In addition to emotional triggers, other causes of blushing can include: **Alcohol**.

So, I don't blush because I don't drink enough?

According to the book *The Expression of the Emotions in Man and Animals*, only higher-order animals (humans) blush. So Charles Darwin classifies me as a lower-order animal?

Another study on the subject said not blushing proves one is a liar at worst, or insincere at best. That totally explains what one man said to me when I told him something about myself. He said, "Oh, now you're just being disingenuous." I snapped back, "You callin' me a liar?"[152]

Another study was done on the Dearth of Studies on Blushing, so I didn't find out anything there other than there aren't enough studies, God help us.

Then there is this: The Impact of Avatar Blushing on the Duration of Interaction between a Real and Virtual Person by Xueni Pan, Marco Gillies, and Mel Slater of University

---

[152] He was not calling the author a liar. But like many men do when they first meet her, this man became disconfabulated with what he thought was dichotomous information. He could not reconcile all the disparate data he was intaking as existing in one woman and therefore his lack of understanding simply meant she had to be tricking him because obviously the lack could not be in him.

College London, UK and ICREA-Universitat Politècnica de Catalunya, Spain, which said:

> "This paper describes an experimental study on human participants' reactions towards a blushing avatar. As one of the 'most human of all expressions', blushing serves an important role in interpersonal communication. In this paper we describe an experiment in which there is an interaction between a person and an avatar who 'blushes' in an embarrassing situation. Our major question of interest was whether participants would be influenced by the blushing, and whether they would tolerate the avatar longer than in the situation where there was no blushing. Moreover, two different type of blushing were considered: whole-face blushing and cheek blushing. This work uses behavioural and questionnaire responses. The results show first, participants tended to withdraw early when the avatar was blushing only on the cheek; second, the whole-face blushing improved participants' degree of 'co-presence'."

Well, well, well, cleared that all up. What the hell[153]?

And this is what passes for *HIGHLY RESPECTED* research? Maybe I should submit some of the essays in this book to these institutions and let them throw some money at me. I mean, I've got lots and lots of footnotes and quote plenty of people; if I cannot find anybody to actually quote, I am not above making it up. Wouldn't you agree I fit right in? As I state this, I am not blushing.

Another study, however, proves I am not alone in not blushing as all Pussy-Hat Wearing Politically Correct Liberal Democrat RINO Socialist Fascist Commies also never blush

---

[153] For readers in Southern parts of the United States, the author is here saying *"Whut da hay-ell?"*

because, as the report entitled <u>Intrapersonal and Interpersonal Concomitants of Facial Blushing during Everyday Social Encounters</u> pointed out, "Frequent blushers generally reported lower levels of dominant behavior, higher levels of submissive behavior, and perceived their social interaction partners as more powerful and less affiliative."

Bullies never blush. According to all the research, my not blushing means I am a disingenuous, lying, bullying, non-alcoholic cold bitch of an inhuman animal.[154] I might as well just commit suicide except, as another study pointed out, people who do not blush never kill themselves because as confident as they are why should they?

---

[154] The author's ex would agree, and he claimed he made a study of her.

Justified Smackdowns

Denese A. Rodgers, a friend of mine in real life, posted a question on Bacefook[155] the other day. It went like this: If a gnat is hovering your wine, is it a justified smackdown?

Denese is a Southern Woman, so of course she knew the answer to that question, and only asked to make a funny so her friends would laugh. And laugh they did, including those who replied with humorous remarks of their own. Remarks such as "Yes! Smack that biotch!" and "Not if you smack it down into the wine".

When I first read the *Smack that biotch!* comment, my inner RadFem was mighty angry. Here was one female attacking another female as if male gnats do not bite. Then I remembered: Male gnats don't bite. And so another justified smackdown came to be and my inner RadFem was told to lighten up and have a good laugh.

Back to Denese. For her comment, she used one of those fancy backgrounds Marky Z has put in place to help us build our individual echo chambers in order to attract more eyeballs he can then deliver to his corporate clients who purchase his mailing lists. One of his new ways of attracting eyeballs is something called Bacefook Watch. Its effectiveness is being tested. I know this because I thought it might be an interesting way for me to do some of my marketing and so research commenced on how to use it, but the company is not taking any new "shows" at this point and asked for my name, email address, *and show idea*. They would get back to me.

Right.

"Tell us your show idea."

---

[155] Bacefook is the name the author has given to a certain Social Media Platform that if you are the type that can extrapolate from incomplete information you should already have understood.

Hahahahaha. I am not LALOTIing but full-out ROTFL.[156]

So, of course, I had to ask a la my friend Denese: If Bacefook asks to hover over your show idea, is it a justified smackdown not to tell them?

The answer is yes.

Another justified smackdown is to remove the Bacefook app from your mobile devices. First, you cannot tell me watching shows or reading friends' witty posts is anywhere near an engaging or relaxing experience on such small screens.[157] That's why we have big-screen TVs taking up entire walls in our homes, and giant computer screens on our desks. Second, are we so desperate to "stay in touch" with other people[158] we carry around a machine housing an application allowing a highly manipulative algorithm to do it for us?[159]

I could come up with more reasons as to why we should do a justified smackdown of social media apps from our mobile devices, but you get the point, so why beat a dead gnat horde, right?

---

[156] LALOTI: Laughing a little on the inside. ROTFL: Rolling on the floor laughing.

[157] Yes, we all know people are so broke these days they save money by only having a portable device with a Wi-Fi connection. Which is why these people spend so much time in coffee shops staring at their phones with wires attached to their ears and not interacting with anybody. I say to them, "Yer sucking up all the oxygen. Get a room!" You know, like a living room or something, where traditionally TVs and other "entertainment centers" are located.

[158] These people would be those who are not physically near us at the moment, but which usage requires us to ignore those who are physically near.

[159] In this I speak of Bacefook Messenger. User agreements started getting creepy and ever-changing, so the author said "To hell wit dat" on her phone and deleted it and the parent application.

But back to Denese. Denese is a good example of a Southern Woman. She loves her mama. She loves her husband. She is helpful to her community. And she does not get sentimental about pesky gnats. Speaking of gnats. For those of you not from Georgia, or who have not traveled throughout our great state, Georgia has The Famous Gnat Line.[160] It begins not too many miles south of Macon, though the line has been known to occasionally meander into the city limits, and if you get out of your car anywhere below that line on any day with a temp above fifty degrees, you will immediately be surrounded by millions of teeming gnats, each one heaving with passion to either bite your skin or suck the moisture out of your eyes, mouth, and nose cavities — and not a one of them blushes.

Besides waving your arms like windmills to set up a turbulence throwing them little suckers out of orbit from around the body proper, one will also find oneself immediately ventilating the lungs by keeping the teeth as tightly together as is possible while thrusting out the lower lip in various configurations and aiming short bursts of air toward one's nose and eyes.

These are autonomic responses no one need be told to do. That's right, these smackdowns just come naturally.

Folks below The Famous Gnat Line might look like they are laid-back, easygoing types. After all, this is the genteel South. Where slow is the name of the game and Southern witticisms fairly drip with charm like Spanish Moss off oaks of stately stature.

In this you would be wrong.

---

[160] There is also another line in the northern part of the state. It has nothing to do with gnats but once you cross this line you wonder where these people buy their clothes. Even when the author lived above that line and shopped in the same town in which she lived, she never could find those styles in any store she went to. It is a mystery that, to this day, haunts the author and if she could find a *HIGHLY RESPECTED* institute of higher learning to finance the study, she would commence with it.

There is a lot of drama the likes of which are too dark[161] for a book of humor and so will not be included here.[162] Above The Clothes Line in the north is a special kind of crazy. Again, the stories are cheerless and not for inclusion in this most wonderful book of humor. Why bring you down, right?

But gnat fighting, echoes of banjos, and pig-snorting at the point of a gun aside, both above and below the two invisible lines are some mighty fine folk. Farmers and hunters, makers of carpets and ceramics, renters of tubes for splashing in The 'Hooch, sellers of fudge and windchimes, real flea market booth operators, cookers of funnel cakes in any size you want, suited money lenders in swanky banks, earthy bootleggers[163] with babes and broods.

All of whom used to be willing to put the smackdown on anybody who "crossed the line" of what would be considered good manners in their neck of the woods. Unfortunately, and here is where I get completely and mighty sad, many in these areas are becoming wussified. I kid you not.

Which is why I was so pleased to see my friend Denese step up and bring back even the idea of a justified smackdown.

You go, Girl!

---

[161] Think "brothers and sisters and drinking and guns and Granddiddy's Last Will and Testament" and other such and you should have a colossal hint as to what types of "dark" stories I mean. The author's ex was related to some of these, as she learned too late.

[162] The author says, "You'll thank me later."

[163] Who have doors at banks opened for them by suited money lenders.

An axiom for Young People: You can't row a boat with one foot on the shore.

Let me start out by saying it is technically possible to row a boat with one foot on the shore, but it's a sure bet nobody will be going very far in any sort of a successful fashion.

Furthermore, it is also a sure bet somebody will have a camera trained in that direction so within a few months all of the Internet and viewers of *America's Funniest Home Videos*[164] will have seen the clip several million times.

And thus begins the lesson for people who grew up in the age when everything could be ordered with a swipe of a finger[165] and delivered with hardly a wait. In other words, those who were born well after 1990.[166]

Returning to our axiom and the lesson it teaches, we find an interesting thing happening. After years of pushing for technology to turn everything digital so that we have phones with cameras and electrified frames sitting on mantles and shelves showing those pictures in a randomized rotation, we now have an advertisement showing a gaggle of five teenage girls taking pictures with their smartphones, then placing them on top of a little machine that will then print a copy of the picture it "sees" and then the girls pass around printed

---

[164] Future anthropologists will have a hard time explaining the popularity of this show that is so popular it has been running weekly since 1990. The author will give you a hint: People have been tired of "fake" for a long time and like to see people be "real".

[165] Including sex with strangers at no charge through an app called Tinder that, according to the company, is a "location-based social search mobile app that allows users to like or dislike other users and allows users to chat if both parties swiped to the right. The app is often used as a hookup app."

[166] The author hopes you have learned your lesson well.

photos and all of them are giggling and getting totally, like, psyched into major delirious happiness as they admire the printed pictures then hang them around their rooms and on their headboards and on their school lockers with fancy tape in totally groovy colors.

Before you know it we will again have phones hanging on walls in the kitchen with handsets attached by curly cords and only the rich will be able to afford the super-long cord in matching colors with padded shoulder rests and avocado green matching appliances throughout the house.

You mark the words of this Autodidact Polymath Magnificently Methodical Southern Woman and The Most Brilliant Woman In The World.

Passport Reading Material

Have you ever looked at your passport? I mean, really looked at all the elements of it? From the color of the cover to how the words are placed on it or the interior pages and the organization and flow of the information in it? I had not looked at it when I got mine. In fact, I simply signed where I was supposed to, put it in a fireproof box, and waited for an opportunity to use it.

That opportunity came five years later when I went with seven other people to the British Virgin Islands for eight days of sailing from island to island on a catamaran. Leaving the U.S. and landing in the U.S. Virgin Islands did not require using a passport, but to get to the British side meant I would finally get my very first stamp in the book. I was so excited I could hardly contain myself. Even the lady who did the stamping was smiling, and other folks in line with me enjoyed my childlike enthusiasm. Yes, as frequent international travelers often are, they were jaded.

I held the passport up for all to see. Opened to the page with the stamp. Held it in the air. Woo-hooed my way through the other checkpoints while saying "First stamp!"

But never once looking at the page contents.

Time passed. Renewal was needed. I hated turning in the old one with the application. My very first stamp was gone. Sadness followed. Thankfully, the U.S. State Department returned the old passport with a hole drilled through it. Happy surprise that was. With both passports in hand, and having lived through one of the most, if not ***the*** most, important and meaningful presidential elections in modern history[167], I was now more conscious than ever before of the

---

[167] This would be 2016 election between Hillary Rodham Clinton, who thought being the official president was her long overdue due, and Donald John Trump, who finally decided to run for real and — as reported by all FLOTSAM — was surprised he actually won. The

role the U.S. and its foundational documents — the Constitution, Bill of Rights, and Amendments — played in the stabilization of economies and governments around the world and in the quashing of the rise of terror.

For many years I had been aware the Constitution was under attack, but until 2016 I had not realized how broad were the powers of what we are now rightly calling the Deep State from whence the attack came, how systemic was the internal rot, nor what the aftereffects of the attack would look like. Even President Trump did not know how bad it was and he was pretty well "plugged in" — or so he thought. Say what you will about Trump, this is a guy who likes to make deals that will benefit as many people as possible. Trump has said if America wins, the world wins. He is right — and countries like China and North Korea, among others, are agreeing with him.[168]

All this caused me to take a very close look at the document I had to jump through hoops to get, but that would validate me to other countries when I visited. Here are only a few of the quotes from the current version and others from the past:

...And that government of the people, by the people, for the people, shall not perish from the Earth.
— *Abraham Lincoln*

The principle of free governments adheres to the American soil. It is bedded in it, immovable as its mountains.
— *Daniel Webster*

---

difference between the two candidates was huge and will not be delineated here.

[168] As of this writing, France is burning, Yellow Vests are everywhere, and President Emmanuel Macron is under a lot of pressure to stop being a whiny butt and grow a pair.

We hold these truths to be self-evident: that all men are created equal, that they are endowed by their Creator with certain inalienable rights, that among these are life, liberty, and the pursuit of happiness.

— Declaration of Independence

We have a great dream. It started way back in 1776, and God grant that America will be true to her dream.
— *Martin Luther King, Jr.*

Whatever America hopes to bring to pass in the world must first come to pass in the heart of America.
— *Dwight D. Eisenhower*

The cause of freedom is not the case of a race or a sect or a party or a class — it is the cause of humankind, the very birthright of humanity. — *Anna Julia Cooper*

Let every nation know, whether it wishes us well or ill, that we shall pay any price, bear any burden, meet any hardship, support any friend, oppose any foe to assure the survival and the success of liberty.
— *John F. Kennedy*

Liberty is never out of bounds or off limits; it spreads wherever it can capture the imagination of men.
— *E.B. White*

Democracy is based upon the conviction that there are extraordinary possibilities in ordinary people.
— *Harry Emerson Fosdick*

The God who gave us life, gave us liberty at the same time. — *Thomas Jefferson*

What wonderfully inspiring thoughts. Frankly, I was proud of the sentiments expressed within. What a great way to let the world know where the country stands with regard to how important freedom is to all citizens and what we are willing to do to keep and defend it.

Except…

Except all citizens aren't willing to keep freedom, much less defend it. For instance, we have one Mr. Thomas Geoghegan of Slate.com in a 2014 article called "American Passport Exceptionalism: Why does our passport boast so much about how wonderful America is?" who decried the design, saying:[169]

> "Isn't it kind of an embarrassment?...What unfolds now inside is a whole tie-dyed history of the United States...There are quotes from great Americans, usually presidents, or at least their speechwriters, pumping up America...aren't 26 pages of quotes overdoing it?...Something about this passport doth seem to protest too much. Page after page, it starts to seem neurotic... Without us...there would [have been no] democracy. But in the 21st century, we're just one of 150 or so. Now, like it or not, [government of the people, by the people, for the people] wouldn't perish at all...I'll say this about Germany and countries like it: Even if their democracies are less than perfect, at least they don't endlessly gloat...What's in the Australian passport? ...Wombats, dingoes, koalas, emus, and kangaroos, but they don't say a word."

What an absolute ass is our Mr. Geoghegan. He ignored Abraham Lincoln who said "…And that government of the

---

[169] The rest of his article was so insulting the author did not want to include it here. But she is sure the readers of Slate.com, P-HWPCLDRSFCs that they are, loved it.

people, by the people, for the people, *shall not perish* from the Earth." It was Lincoln's wish that diligence be paid to the forces trying to destroy it because the United States of America was a great and first experiment never before done in the history of mankind. The natural order of things until then had been fighting between kings and despots and uncles and nephews to get power and keep it in their line. The commoner be damned. Little duchies broken apart by murder and war and joined back together through marriage, and trade came and went and went and came. Damn the commoner who complained.

Execution: Summarily performed.

Therefore, isn't it an embarrassment what Mr. Geoghegan wrote? His entire column was nothing but a kumbaya Pussy-Hat weenie roast where none of the women or men, straight or gay, would share their buns with him no matter how much he said he respected their self-identified gender role. As he dissed the country that suckled his freedom of speech, it became painfully obvious the man does not understand: Reciting facts of history is not gloating. Maybe Mr. Geoghegan should understand the nature of what a reminder is and why this miniature history lesson is needed so very much both abroad and at home.

When certain presidents of the near past, and their dictator wannabe Deep State cabinet appointees including a former president's wife, began to disrespect freedom and forget the price a lack of it would cost, then freedom around the world began to disappear. Christians and anyone else with a different ideology came under attack in multiple countries as mass killings by terrorists seemingly could not be stopped. Male and female. Old and young. All countries saw victim counts grow.

A well-funded terror network around the world gloried in triumph after triumph[170] as U.S. presidents spoke big words but privately wrung their hands and offered up a nonstop string of pussy-whipped conciliations and mollifications while lamenting the super-duper power that was these terrorists.

Then along came Donald "The Hammer" Trump, who found out how terrorists were funded — through the United Nations — and said, "Not gonna contribute to that anymore." And because the United States was the only country paying their full dues, it was U.S. funds paying for terrorism. The Hammer shut off the tap and, oh gee, what happened?

The PLO started whining their gubment checks were late, Hamas stomped their pretty little feet and cried in their hummus, and ISIS attempted to open negotiations with al-Qaeda saying, "Hey, dudes, why don't we work together and, uh, you know, go kick some pussy-hat wearing ass?" Al-Qaeda did not put out a press release stating their position on the ISIS proposal, but they didn't have to because ISIS went broke and got disbanded. Still, al-Qaeda's leaders are rumored to be thinking of how to get out of the terror business though they might have to go enroll in college for retraining. I suggest Nursing as a new career.

Heck, they're already halfway there: They don't have to get over the blood phobia.

---

[170] YouTube.com, a Google Inc. company, was forced to decide whether to allow on their site video of speechifying terrorists beheading and immolating journalists, soldiers, and regular folks. Night after night, CNN and other network news outlets enjoyed scaring the bejeezus out of viewers with the icky parts of photos and videos carefully blurred so as not to offend the delicate sensibilities of viewers who, immediately following blurred scary parts of beheadings with swords, would hear all about "Guns are bad. Guns should be outlawed."

Hunter: Not a computer in sight.

The Decades Channel is great. It runs whole weekends full of back-to-back episodes of various series from the mid-20th century to the 21st century. On a weekend in July 2018, this channel was running the late-1980s hit network show *Hunter* starring the sure-enough hunk Fred Dryer, #89 Defensive End for the New York Giants (1969-1971) and Los Angeles Rams (1972-1981) who eventually became an actor with his own series. Yeah, he was a police detective, last name Hunter. His co-star and fellow detective was hottie Stepfanie Kramer whose character name was Dee Dee McCall.

The team of talent was very good and even today the show holds up well. It was smart. It was politically incorrect. (Oh, for the good ol' days when men were men and women were happy about that. If you want to really see some politically incorrect police action, watch Angie Dickinson's *Police Woman* series back when bras first weren't worn so much and clingy polyester was introduced. In both shows, you can see where a lot of now-famous folks got their starts.)

As I watched *Hunter* I kept saying to myself, "What is missing from this squad room?" Didn't take me but two seconds to realize there was not a computer screen on a desk anywhere in sight. Nobody had a computer. Nobody had a cellphone. There was only one fax machine in the whole office and it was shared, which is why Cover Sheets were invented. There were no digital display screens taking up an entire wall for the whole room to see.

There were desk lamps, pen/pencil holders, phones, and stacks of bad-guy jackets, or folders, stuffed with paper on top of metal desks. Room lighting was harsh fluorescent and the colors of the room were grayish blue and it wasn't pretty. No directional lighting, strategic shadows, or designer paint anywhere. In other words, these cramped rooms were for working; they were not designed by decorators for sitting around and looking pretty.

To see any computer, the characters had to go to a different floor of the building to make an appointment to get something "run through the computer". It was fabulous.

And when the results came in, if these detectives were out in the field, they didn't receive text messages or emails with last-minute butt-saving messages. They were alone and all they had was their wits as they existed where their boots hit the ground.

If they could make it back to their car, then they could call the police station with their radio, but otherwise, they had to wait to read messages left for them when they got back to the office and saw the stack of pink *Please Call* slips on their desks, one of which would have scrawled in ink, "Computer Room. Results in."

Not "not The Most Brilliant Woman In The World."

As you know, Mark Twain and Will Rogers have both independently and post-life proclaimed me, Angela K. Durden, to be their successor in all things brilliant and humorous. It is a mantle of praise I wear with great humility. These are facts you know because you are constantly reminded of them by the person who knows it best: Me.

Yes, Twain and Rogers have called me The Most Brilliant Woman In The World. However, some readers have misconstrued my title and have ascribed to me all knowledge of all things. Oh, the times I am in public and total strangers stop me and ask questions because I look like I know everything. It gets so tiresome. However, to help you understand where I am going with this, let me make a list of only a few of the things of which I know nothing and, furthermore, have no hope in Holy Hell of ever knowing about, much less mastering.

These are, to wit:

- Navigating a submarine, even in the wide-open ocean.[171]
- Flying a plane without crashing on either takeoff or landing.[172]
- Writing computer code that will make something function properly.[173]
- Operating on any part of the human body and not killing the person.[174]

---

[171] The author would have been of no use in hunting for the Red October.
[172] The author would have been no use to Captain Sully.
[173] The author would have been no use to Gates or Jobs.
[174] The author would have been no use to Dr. Ben Carson.

- "Signaling" to those with useless and expensive "higher educations".[175]
- And changing the oil in a car.[176]

I can hear some of you now. Cackling away with your sniggering snide comments saying such things as, "Hahahahaha! See? By her own admission she isn't even the sharpest knife in the drawer nor the brightest bulb in the pack nor the most reliable condom in the box. I told you she was not The Most Brilliant Woman In The World. Did I tell ya? Did I, huh, did I?"

Well, you can stop with the sniggering snidely cackling comment-making right now because you would be wrong to make that conclusion. In fact, I am not "not The Most Brilliant Woman In The World" and since a double negative cancels itself out, that means I am. For those of you who are overwhelmed by my prowess in the language department, please read the following paragraph. Those who already understood what I said (extra points for extrapolating from incomplete data), you may skip this next section.

- - - BEGIN PARAGRAPH OF EXPLANATION - - -
I shall explain the concept of "double negative". Not is a negative and it means something isn't. But not not — See the double negative? — means it isn't isn't, which means it is. I hope I've made it clear. I am only one woman and I cannot work miracles.
- - - END PARAGRAPH OF EXPLANATION - - -

---

[175] See the essay in this book entitled "The Most Brilliant Woman In The World nailed it a long time ago".

[176] The author was of no use to her husband when he did this and he just couldn't understand why and got mad, though he often said she was the best gofer ever.

So how is it I can *not* know things and still be more brilliant than those who had to read the paragraph of explanation? It is because brilliant has several meanings, one of which is clear. Another is strong. I know the following fact because I asked other truly brilliant people when we held our annual convention at The Corner Cup Coffee Shop in Decatur[177] in this year of our Lord. (Our exclusive inclusive crowd loves the toasted Jalapeño bagels with buttah. To die for!) There is one thing truly brilliant people know for a certainty and are very clear in and feel strongly about and that is that they don't know everything.

Unlike stupid people who do know everything but who still manage to end up dying or maiming themselves in ill-conceived break-ins, silly rescue missions[178], or the taking up of double-dog-dare-yas that should never have been uttered[179] much less taken up, truly brilliant people know their limitations and it never hurts their feelings nor puts their ego in any sort of disrepair to ask for more information, even if the asking is done in front of a stupid person who will judge harshly.

Therefore, since I am willing — Nay! Able! — to thoroughly make an ass of myself in front of strangers and friends alike by saying "Why, I do not know", then it is a sure bet I am the only Autodidact Polymath and The Most Brilliant Woman In The World you know and I have made my case for being not not.[180]

---

[177] It is on Lawrenceville Highway just ITP, or Inside The Perimeter. You can tell the owner Angela says hi.

[178] Read essay in this book entitled "Explaining a Theme Park to Future Archeologists and Anthropologists".

[179] See footnote directly above and do what it says.

[180] See paragraph explaining the power of the double negative.

"I do not apologize for my insensitive tweet."

I get nauseous and weary when I see yet another headline-making tweet by an actor, politician, sports figure, or other high-profile type who says, "I apologize for my insensitive tweet."

I apologize for my insensitive tweet is usually said by White Males[181] (though not always[182]) when they have had the gall to say something like *Serena's style of playing has a guerilla effect*. Of course, the excrement hit the fan. But why?

Guerilla Tennis was a successful Nike ad campaign tagline in the 1990s. Nobody had a problem with it. Doug Adler, a longtime authority and commentator on the game, remembers that ad campaign and how much respect it got the players involved. He described one of Ms. Williams' moves as having a guerilla effect.

Those in the armed forces, mercs, and guerilla soldiers themselves completely understood Serena was complimented by Mr. Adler. But the rest of the world has gotten much too sensitive — and stupider — since the 1990s and took Mr. Adler to say Serena, a black woman, had moves with a *gorilla* effect.

---

[181] As we all know, White Males are the worst offenders in the world when it comes to insensitivity on all mediums, all subjects, everywhere, across the board, bar none, on all planets, for all time, and throughout the universe.

[182] The next-largest offender group, though running a far second to White Males, is White Females Who Take Yoga Classes. This group even includes those super-caring White Females who wear pussy-hats but who can afford to go to the best yoga huts...errr...salons...the author means studios, and who look very nice in yoga pants no matter the pose they assume but are still accused of being insensitive to other cultures simply because they do yoga, which is Culture Co-opting.

That's right! Stupid people who did not know their history but wanted to prove just how caring they are called for Adler's firing and ESPN[183] kowtowed to those rousers of rabble. Mr. Adler cannot get a job and is suing for wrongful termination. After all, it isn't his fault people are stupid and don't know about homophones[184]. Yet, he is the one being punished.

It seems the only ones who do not apologize for their insensitive remarks and do not get in trouble for it are members of ISIS, the NFL, the DNC/Democratic Party, RINOs[185], and tree huggers.

Research into this showed a disturbing trend: It is called *digging*. In 2018, several trolls went digging way back in time into several Major League baseball players' accounts and that which was dug up — tweets made when Twitter was barely a newborn company — had to be apologized for.

Do you know how hard it is and how much time it takes and what databases you have to access in order to go digging through the Internet? That's right. Mere mortals such as I do not have access to these databases no matter what.[186]

---

[183] ESPN began losing viewers when they started wearing pussy hats, and their management has not seen the correlation between loss of viewers and being "too stupidly caring".

[184] No. We are not here talking about a method of communication meant only for homosexuals but not for any other LGBTQ+ group, therefore we are not advocating for exclusivity nor making a judgment statement. According to Webster's Dictionary a *homophone* is each of two or more words having the same pronunciation but different meanings, origins, or spellings. Examples are: *new* and *knew* and *gnu*, and *guerilla and gorilla.*

[185] Republican in Name Only.

[186] The author readily admits that Google has deeper pockets than she for fighting court cases, and that all the power to grant access is on their side. But she reminds them they only have power if people depend upon

In any case, I am looking for a stouthearted man. One who makes a comment and then does not come back and apologize for it with "I promise to never ever never say that most insensitive thing again and I'm so sorry I hurt the feelings of [insert title of group representing the professionally offended] ever never again. I am such a bad boy. Spank me. Spank me hard."[187]

Just one stouthearted man will do and before you know it, there will be thousands of such brave and courageous men willing to stand for the rights[188] they adore.[189] Men who will make a strong woman's heart go pitty-pat-pitty-pat-ker-thunka-fer-her-hunka-hunka-burnin'-lurrrrvvv.

Oh, where are these men? Hello? Helloooooooo?!?

---

them and, as more of the world does not, the user base will decline and then who's gonna have the last laugh?

[187] The last three short sentences in this quote are not real. Well, they are real, but they are never released to the public, though I have good reason to believe that within the groups of the professionally offended are, hidden deep within their own closets, not less than a few doms. How did doms get their name? DOMS stands for Delayed Onset Muscle Soreness. It is the pain and stiffness felt in muscles several hours to days after strenuous exercise which, as we all know, defines a really good spanking with a whip, wooden spoon, purse, hairbrush, etc., and so those who are "spanked", upon finding themselves in need of more pain or Delayed Onset Muscle Soreness, would say, "You know, I think it is time to have more DOMS" and then they would call their pain practitioner and next thing you know, presto-change-o, an industry acronym takes on a new life.

[188] Free speech.

[189] Please go to YouTube and search for "Stouthearted Men Barbra Streisand". The author assures most people will like it. [Ignore this recommendation if you wear a pussy hat.]

Stupid is Bone Deep

"No Selfie Zone"

BBC.com reported a 2018 global study revealed the quest for extreme selfies led to 259 people offing themselves between 2011 and 2017.

As has been mentioned by me at least nine thousand and forty five times in this book alone, Stupid is bone deep and there ain't no accounting for what Stupid will do. We all know Stupid is as Stupid does and Stupid never listens to anybody and will not read signs.

I know a woman who was married to Stupid. She was three months pregnant and went on a hike with Stupid, the father of her child, whereupon they made it to the bottom of a beautiful waterfall and he said, "Hey, watch this!" Five minutes later Stupid was dead, she was crying, and the child got a new daddy[190] when she was three.

Immediately after Stupid fell, a government agency put up a sign that said "Do not climb up the waterfalls. People have DIED from climbing."

Well, I disagreed with the sign from the get-go. People did not die from the climbing. They died from the falling. You know I am not wrong in this and that is why I completely disagree with the researchers at the U.S. National Library of Medicine's recommendation that "no selfie zones" should be introduced at dangerous spots like tops of mountains, tall buildings, lakes, where motorized vehicles can be used, anywhere a fall might occur, where the wild things are, next to anything electrical, around fires, and when holding devices that propel projectiles designed to explode upon impact. Why will this solution not work? Here I go saying it for the nine

---

[190] This woman has been known by the author since the author was thirteen, which means she is not lying about this when she further reports that Daddy #2 was also named Stupid and which thoroughly explains why this woman and the author's mother got along so well.

thousand and forty sixth time in this book. Y'all say it with me now:

> Stupid is bone deep.
>
> There ain't no accounting for what Stupid will do.
>
> Stupid is as Stupid does.
>
> Stupid never listens to anybody.
>
> Stupid will not read signs.

Stupid's own mother, wife, sister, brother, uncle, good friend, or boss can say, "Please do not do that. You will get hurt." But does Stupid listen? No. Stupid does not. Here is another example:

There is a tiny faux-German town in North Georgia (U.S.) called Helen wherein Octoberfest is a big deal. There is also water in the form of lakes and rivers. Two tourist couples partied hearty and went for a responsible walk as opposed to driving drunk. Nobody is sure how they managed to walk this far out of town, but they did and eventually made it to a big bridge and stared over into what looked like a really great place to dive as the water appeared still and deep. According to reports, here is how the conversation went:

Stupid #1: Hey, look at that water way down there. I bet I could dive in and not do a belly-flop.

Stupid #1's Wife: I don't think so. You always manage to land on your belly, then you whine and complain for days and use up all my Aloe gel with Lidocaine.

Stupid #2: Do it! I double-dog-dare-ya. OOO-rah!

Stupid #2's Wife: Wait! Let's get a selfie first.

[Group selfie is taken, and it is awesome because that woman knows how to compose a great shot!]

Stupid #1: [Climbing up on railing and posing.] [To wife:] Get a good picture of me!

Stupid #1's Wife: Hold it right there. **[Framing the pic.]** Okay. Got it.

Stupid #2: You gonna dive or whut?

Stupid #2's Wife: Stop rushing him. He'll go when he's good and ready.

Stupid #1: Here I go!

Stupid #1's Wife: [Showing pictures she took of dive.] Wow. Look at this one.

Stupid #2: [Looking at pictures. Then looking over railing.] Man, he musta gone deep. He ain't come up yet. I didn't see him do no belly-flop neither.

[Everybody looking over the edge. Waiting.]

Stupid #2's Wife: Oh. My. Gawd. He can't hold his breath that long. Can he?

Stupid #1's Wife: Baby! Baby! Don't you be hiding on us. Where are you? BAAAAAYBEEEEEE???

Stupid #2: He's in trouble. Imma gonna go git 'im.

Stupid #2's Wife: Wait. Whut?

Stupid #2: [Dives in without taking a selfie.]

Stupid #2's Wife: Baby! Baby!

[Wives staring over edge waiting for either Stupid to surface. Waiting. Waiting. Stupid sighting does not happen. Slow dawning begins.]

Stupid #1's Wife: Oh, Jeezus, God.

Stupid #2's Wife: WhattaweDOOOO?

[Concerned citizen pulls over when he sees two women crying and screaming and pointing over the rail. 911 is fetched.]

This is a true story. The two Stupids did come out of the water eventually. Like, two days later. In bits and pieces. With the help of a team of divers from the company that built and maintained turbines under the bridge. Turbines which helped with keeping water in the lake upstream at tourist-pleasing levels, making sure water release downstream didn't flood anybody out. Turbines which have a massive sucking action when working. Turbines which don't care who Stupid is or what Stupid does. Turbines which chop up Stupid when Stupid clogs it and does not hear wifey screaming.

Yes. There were signs like: Do not jump off this bridge. Do not fish from this bridge. But did Stupid read them? Stupid did not.

Stupid also needs signs to keep them from drinking bleach, using a stepladder on a roof while installing a metal antenna in a thunderstorm, and drinking hot coffee before it has cooled enough, among other activities. This book is not long enough to list all the ways Stupid manages to die around the world. No amount of signage in any language will stop Stupid from offing himself unintentionally.

Now, I would never say this myself, but it has been said by others and I merely quote them here as I am not so uncaring as to have originally had this thought, but I promise it has been said by others and I merely quote them. *Others* say the reason mankind has managed to stay a viable entity is because Stupid manages to take himself (and yes, herself) out of the gene pool with awe-inspiring promptness. In other words, Charles Darwin was right and Stupid proves Darwin to be so:

Survival truly does happen to the fittest.

I hear you. You're saying, "But, Angela. If survival of the fittest means survival of the smartest, then why with each generation do we continue to have so much Stupid still show up?"

The answer is easy and clear: DNA. Yes, there is a stupid gene. Sure, nobody has found it yet, but it isn't for lack of trying. As recently as 2014, both SmithsonianMag.com and Cardiff University weighed in on this. The former said, "Rather than looking for the **genetic** regions responsible for a person's high IQ, maybe we should be looking for the opposite: the root of **stupidity**." The latter said…well, that link was dead. Therefore, let me tell you what was said by one Sally Hingston, a wise, deep-thinking, and fair-and-balanced reporter for Phillymag.com:

> "For an article I wrote about Penn professor Adrian Raine's studies of psychopathology and children, Duke University ethicist Walter Sinnott-Armstrong told me that 'eugenics — the policy of weeding out bad genes — should not be government policy. It's a family matter.'
>
> "I agree it's not my place to decide what other parents should choose. But I do think there should be more public discussion about the choices involved — and, for that matter, about what makes for 'a good life.' Of course, if anti-choice activists have their increasingly restrictive way, none of the discussion will matter in the end."

As you can see, super-smart and very wise Duke University ethicist Walter Sinnott-Armstrong agrees with me, The Most Brilliant Woman In The World:

Dealing with Stupid should be a family matter.

As an example of this, for instance, my earlier story about the woman who was widowed by her man who fell from the waterfall. She went on, with her family's blessing, to marry another Stupid. Finally realizing his severe limitations[191], the family built a psychological and monetary fence around their daughter and two granddaughters[192] so the second stupid husband could continue with his Stupid ways while not having their precious blood relatives inconvenienced.

---

[191] The family was big into "signaling" and signaled that he shouldn't be punching holes in the walls and that he should not be getting drunk all the time. But the man missed all those signals because he was…*what???* That's right. Stupid.

[192] Yes, stupid husband #2 added to the gene pool.

See? Family took care of it, as family should. They had freedom of choice. They used it. They didn't have to ask a government agency about how to handle Stupid.

In the second paragraph quoted above wherein our precious writer from PhillyMag.com decided to dump her wise thoughts on the reading public, she let it be known she is a Pussy-Hat Wearing Politically Correct Liberal Democrat RINO Socialist Fascist Commie who believes — she said this in her own words, mind you — *it's not her place to decide what other parents should choose. But*…Ah-ha! Here comes the big Socialist buttinsky: *She thinks there should be more public discussion about the choices involved.* What does that mean? It means she believes she has the **right** to tell other parents what **they** should choose but she has not been given enough time to **legislate her belief into law**.

So, here is a woman proclaiming she is all about freedom of choice but who wants the only choice to be one she agrees with because obviously anyone who disagrees with her must be stupid. But this woman is clearly about not having freedom and she doesn't see it because she is what…??? That's right. I'll let you say it. Go on, now. You know you wanna. Say it. Okay, I'll start you off —

Stooooooo…

There you go! Well done.

In any case, it is people like her and P-HWPCLDRSFCs who think putting up signs will cure Stupid. What a waste of taxpayer money.

One cannot wave a weenie.
One can only waggle it.

John and Lorena Bobbitt would say this is a misleading headline. I prefer to say it does not address all instances of penile usage, abuse, or assault.

If you do not know who these people are, let me say they made worldwide headlines after John woke screaming to find Lorena waving his disattached weenie as she held it aloft in one hand with a sharp knife in the other. One can infer she gloated. As John was not in a position to give chase[193], Lorena ran out the door, jumped in her car, threw it in gear, and hauled ass…I mean, hauled genitalia…down the highway in a fit of jubilant exultation that she would not have to touch *that man's dick* ever again. When she realized she was still holding it, she threw it out the window.

At some point she called 911 and that's when the story went viral before the Internet was as big a deal as it is now and before viral stories were a thing which could be planned using Google AdWords.[194] I won't even go into how his severed man part was found much less reattached in a nine-plus-hour surgery. Nor shall I mention his reattached part never regained full sensation or that to pay his medical bills John started and failed with a band called The Severed Parts or that he was a featured actor in a few adult films or that he ended up beating up a girlfriend or that he appeared on World Wrestling Entertainment's *Monday Night Raw* television program or that he worked as a bartender, limo driver, mover, pizza delivery driver, tow-truck operator, thief, and wife beater, or that he served at a wedding chapel

---

[193] It is doubtful he even spoke, but if he did he would've said, "Woman! Give it back!"

[194] Which does not work when blacklisted by Google.

as a minister of a Universal Life Church or that in 2014 he was severely injured when he broke his neck. I will not mention any of this because none of that matters.

What matters is that this essay title is accurate as written because I am discussing another instance altogether. Here's what happened. There was this man, Justice Brett Kavanaugh, who was accused by a professor, Christine Blasey Ford, of trying to rape her. The falseness of her accusation aside, "We Believe Her" became the slogan of the #MeToo day. What was interesting is that in one news report a screaming pussy-hat wearing person[195] was holding a sign which said —

IT IS ILLEGAL TO WAVE A WEENIE IN THE FACE

At this point, in public, flew out of my mouth the words, "One cannot wave a weenie! One can only waggle it!"

All the men around me blushed. According to the aforementioned research — "A Gender Scholar goes to Hooters to find out why it is so popular" — these men blushing meant they were not disingenuous, lying, bullying, non-alcoholic cold bitches of inhuman animals, and might kill themselves because they were not confident.

All the women nodded at my sage wisdom.

We women know weenies cannot wave.

They can say "Heybebbiewhuzzzyername?"

---

[195] Future archeologists and anthropologists will tell you the author is not lying. While the pussy-hat wearing person looked female, what with the fuzzy lines at the time around gender and some folks passing as everything but what they were born as, the author cannot say for certain this person was female though she dang sure looked like it in the face. The sign covered the chest area and even if it hadn't and bumps could be seen, who was to say those bumps were natural-made, surgical enhancement, rubber appendage, or were natural-grown on a guy who liked to smoke his wacky weed.

They can take — and sometimes pass — the Dance Floor Dick Test[196]. But they cannot wave when they are attached. It just cannot happen. Look, if a weenie is waving, it is of no use to a woman. Obviously, it is only Real Women who know this.

But you see how these pussy-hat wearing people just cannot deal with real facts. They wouldn't know a real fact if it waved in their faces. Speaking of real facts…you must read the essay in this book entitled "Lily-livered actresses".

That's next.

---

[196] When a man is dancing with a woman and she is shining his belt buckle — that is, they are dancing to a slow song and snuggled up nice and familiar — and his male member gives its opinion about the nearness of the woman. Now, if they are married, then *no problemo*. But if they are not married, often the man is embarrassed. But women know how to handle such things: They ignore it. They pretend they feel nothing. However, the Dance Floor Dick Test gives a woman empirical evidence of a man's ability and interest.

In other words, if a man does not take the test, then she can be assured his sexual interest in her is nil and will not waste time with him. However, let's say that the woman likes a man who isn't sexual, and his male member is opining, she can walk away from that too with a "thank you so very much" handshake and he is none the wiser.

Furthermore, you got your size preference. Some women prefer tiny, others ginormous, though most fall somewhere in between and are happy with normal-sized man parts. So, you see, the Dance Floor Dick Test allows for further sorting into and out of preferred and non-preferred columns without any words being spoken or feelings hurt. See how it works?

Lily-livered actresses.

The Hollywood Reporter headline read: 'Lost' Producers Apologize After Evangeline Lilly Says She Was 'Cornered' Into Nude Scene.

I then went on to read the article and was disheartened. Before I was a mere twinkle in the eye of my mother, measures began in earnest to empower women. It was called The Feminist Movement and it focused on two things. The second was finances. The first, and main one, was sex.

The second one is boring, but I shall recap here. Women wanted to be able to get a loan or credit card without having their fathers or husbands go surety for them. This was successful and now just as many women seek protection in the bankruptcy courts as males.[197]

The first, sex, is a more powerful and fiery subject, so this is where we shall focus our concentration.[198] The fight for equality in this arena began with the dual rollout of bra burning and invention of The Pill. The Pill promised — with 99.99% accuracy — the female user would not get pregnant. Thus The Pill allowed for spontaneous sexual activity in myriad locations and reduced males' responsibility to "come prepared" for the event. No more tell-tale large rings on wallets anymore.[199]

The Pill also reduced opportunities for begging. Males were over the moon with this turn of events. Well, all males

---

[197] See? Equality.

[198] Also, since everybody knows that sex sells, maybe this book will become a best seller.

[199] These rings or circles on wallets indicated the long-term presence of a wearable prophylactic designed to reduce the risk of pregnancy with its use to a mere 5%. These prophylactics were also called a rubber, condom, raincoat, top hat, cock sock, and insurance policy.

except certain fathers whose daughters were burning their bras and getting their prescriptions filled for The Pill because somehow or another those daughters fell into the 00.01% The Pill did not work for.

My mother was a forerunner in this area and thus I came to be. At least, that was her oft-repeated claim that she was so easy and free with "gittin' and givin' some". But after carefully ascertaining the dates of marriage to my father and my subsequent birth, unless I was a freak of nature (which some claim I am and have made a compelling case for) there was no way I was conceived out of wedlock.[200]

Back to the sex without the mother overtones. Though that is going to be hard to do because around the same time as The Pill and bra burning and spontaneous sex came into being, men started calling their female sex partners "Mama" and women called their male sex partners "Papa". This was so common that a popular singing group known for their strong yet delicate harmonies was called The Mamas and the Papas. So maybe there is something of the Oedipus going on here and I just missed it.

This so-called freedom went on for about twenty years, then men were forced to again begin "coming prepared" to the event because lo and behold sexually transmitted diseases (STDs), the names of which had only been mentioned in dark back alleys where disgraced doctors plied "cures", came roaring back into the vernacular and were proving to be resistant to old cures.[201]

Popular songs were written about this. The most famous was called "You Ain't Seen Nothin' Yet". Written by Randy

---

[200] Yes, the author knows her conception date does not prove her mother was not a forerunner in The Feminist Movement. Geez, can you just drop the subject of her mother? What? Are you an Oedipus type?

[201] The prevalence of these STDs became so prevailingly prevalent that magazines and newspapers and TV shows were written and filmed to show how to inform your next lover that you were "in remission".

Bachman for his group Bachman-Turner Overdrive, or BTO to hep cats, the song featured a driving 4/4 beat the drummer kept up like a train rolling down the tracks with a head full of steam, wailing electric guitars, and funky thumb action on the bass. Some of the lyrics are included here, and I have appropriately noted copyright ownership to Sony/ATV Music Publishing. Not that they could sue me for use of these lyrics since they are used in an essay purely for educational purposes, but one does practice CYA[202] when one must.[203] Here are parts of the lyrics with inserted commentary (IC):

I met a devil woman

She took my heart away

IC: According to all fundamentalist religions — and I don't care which one you name be it Judaism, Islam, Buddhism, Christian, and some atheist cults — all women are from the Devil and thus are devil women. So, in this Randy Bachman spoke for these men.

She said, I've had it comin' to me

But I wanted it that way

IC: Randy Bachman stated the obvious here and, as lyric writing goes, this was not inspired, but it got the point across well when he sang it and it did rhyme.

---

[202] Acronym used in polite company for the more vulgar term of Cover Your Ass. As a side point, the CIA, or Central Intelligence Agency, often deploys CYA methods in their work.

[203] Sort of like a legal prophylactic, if you will.

I think that any love is good lovin'

So I took what I could get, mmh

IC: Randy Bachman was a Mormon and they are fundamental so this song was not about him as he was married and had six children and did not like the wild ways of his industry, but he did see what happened to others and, like all good writers, he could write about it.

In this spot here are a bunch of lyrics about eyes and promises to keep, and they get repeated below, so let's get on with it.

IC: Here comes the part that references the disease process:

She took me to her doctor

And he told me I was cured.

He said that any love is good love

IC: Obviously, the doctor meant that any love is good love *as long as there is a cure.*

So I took what I could get

Yes, I took what I could get

And then she looked at me

with them big brown eyes

And said,

You ain't seen nothin' yet

B-b-b-baby, you just ain't seen n-n-nothin' yet

Here's something, here's something

you're never gonna forget, baby

And those men Randy wrote about never did forget, and neither did we because I bet you were singing along with the song and knew exactly where the hard instrument hits were and did those in your head.

I'm telling you all this because from the 1960s when Free Love began its reign, females have been told in school (sex education classes mostly run by agents of government schools), through movies (*Pretty Woman*), in announcements made to service the public (No Means NO *unless I change my mind*), and in song ("I am woman, hear me roar") that all the power over their bodies belongs to them.

Therefore, having been thoroughly indoctrinated in this, why is it so many actresses, like Evangeline Lilly did, complain they were forced or cornered into taking their clothes off for a scene in a project they have already been hired for?[204]

According to <u>The Hollywood Reporter</u> story, Lilly saw the script ahead of time. She rehearsed it privately and with her fellow thespians yet missed all the written clues as to what the scene called for and — **this is important** — did not speak up to the producers ahead of time.

But, for grins and giggles, let's just say Lilly missed the clues in the script, or when she got on-set the director got a bright idea and said, "Hey, Evangeline. We're gonna go off-script here. You see, I think your character should be somewhat naked in this scene. It fits the interplay between your character and the others and will add an added dimension to the depth in the role by showing her to be bold yet somewhat timid, strong yet emotionally fragile. Whattaya think? You up for the stretching of your acting chops?"

So, explain to me how a woman — in our day and age and after almost seven decades of systemic training in how to

---

[204] The author is not talking about the famous Casting Couch audition style, which is a whole 'nother topic.

say no including updates to politically correct thinking —
who would not want to take off any or all of her clothes,
would do it anyway because she felt...

Hang on one sec; let me check <u>The Hollywood Reporter</u>
for the correct quote. Ah, here we go. Lilly was...

..."mortified" even after she "fought very hard to have a
scene" under her control but the big bad boys just wouldn't
let her do nothing but take her clothes off, boo-hoo-whah-
whah-sob-and-such.

Now, an even more interesting question that I, The Most
Brilliant Woman In The World and Autodidact, Polymath,
and Magnificently Methodical Southern Woman to boot, need
to ask is this:

Mizz Evangeline, why did you stay on the show for seven
years and not speak up?

Let me put on my Jim Acosta CNN Reporter hat here and
ask follow-up questions:

Mizz Evangeline, why did it take you a further five years
to say something about it? Come, come. I think you owe it to
us, your fellow Sisters (and that includes those who self-
identify as females though OEM parts are still attached), to
tell us, Mizz Evangeline. Are you playing false to the
Sisterhood in this matter?

Or were you perfectly happy to trade for fame and
fortune what you did on-set but, now that we are in the
#MeToo era wherein no woman will ever be accused of
making up a false claim — and all wussy men cave to it,
issuing public apologies with no blowback on the poor
powerless woman — you've decided to get free column
inches by playing the victim?

Because, Mizz Lilly, as I check my notes, we see it has
been a long while since the media has given you any
meaningful attention or the phone has rung with an agent on
the other end.

Therefore with those thoughts and needs in mind, did you conspire with an easily duped press to get much needed public face time you did not have to pay for?

If the answer is yes, then you are in company with several others (Kathy Griffin, Snoop Dogg, Lido Pimienta, to name a few). You are not the first to generate fake controversy P-HWPCLDRSFC[205] reporters and publications are eager to print if it fits the RadFem narrative.

However, such use of the media is a Pyrrhic victory, Evangeline.[206] Last words to ya, dear: *Baby, it's cold outside.*

---

[205] Pussy-Hat Wearing Politically Correct Liberal Democratic RINO Socialist Fascist Commies.

[206] You'll have to look that up yourself, Lilly.

Angela listens to braggings[207] and questions the recollections.

Angela has been the recipient of many a man's brags.[208] They mostly occur in two different situations: When he's making his case for Angela to allow him access to her goodies; and when he has been turned down by her. The brags do not change in content, but the tone of voice in which they are delivered does.

In the first instance of brag, wherein he is making his case to Angela, the tone can vary from a shy admission to confident aggrandizement.[209] In any case, it is simply self-reporting as the man does not actually bring around the other women he claims to be quoting nor does he bring third-party certified letters of endorsement as to his prowess, range of talents, and size of his package.[210]

The second instance of brag occurs after the turndown. Each man sounds the same in all instances: Brags repeated in a whining voice as if they cannot believe they have been rejected.[211]

---

[207] Used as a plural noun, not a verb.

[208] This is a fact, and everybody knows a fact is not a brag in and of itself.

[209] Men will change their presentation style according to what they believe the woman wants, so that the same man can be by turns both shy and confident, confessional and boastful.

[210] The author fully understands that it would be even creepier should a man actually produce the women and/or letters attesting to his prowess, talents, and size. Therefore, his not producing them is not a negative against him and any man reading this is not being encouraged to put together his *curriculum vitae of love*.

[211] There are two types of men. Those who know they will be turned down and therefore they approach a woman with the well-practiced whine in

I feel for these men because it is obvious they have given much thought to their presentation and put in hours of practice in front of a mirror. But like a resumé sent out to blanket the corporate world, most of those presentations will never see the light of day. Would these men go whining to the corporations that do not respond or who send letters of rejection? No, they would not. But they have no problem whining to Angela when she turns them down for what they have admittedly said is only "a bit of fun".[212]

Even all that, though, is not the most interesting part of these human interactions. The most interesting part is, contrary to what most females do, Angela genuinely listens to what men say.[213] Do not mistake what she is telling you. She is not telling you she has never ignored a man as he bumped his gums, because she has. Most notably The Ex to whom for years she gave massive opportunity to make his argument for why she was not a good wife but which ex, after failing in those attempts, was subsequently ignored.[214]

In all the *bragging with intent to snare* these men indulge in, one thing quite a few do is reminisce about parties they went to and how drunk they got. It never fails they say something along the lines of "it was such a good party and I was so drunk, I don't remember it!", after which they then say what they did and to whom they did it and how grateful the gal was. After a while, Angela made it an operational standard to

---

place like a self-fulfilling prophecy; and those who cannot believe they are being turned down and are not used to whining.

[212] Thank you, but no thank you. And what does she look like to you anyway, man? A woman of easy virtue? Get lost.

[213] And the author takes them at their word.

[214] As proof that he failed in his attempts to prove the author was not a good wife, she asked one simple question: Who's missing who after the divorce, huh? That's right. Case made. Deep breath. *Ooooohhhhhhmmmmmm*. Moving on past the digressive tangent and back to the topic: Listening to what men really say.

clarify. So, she asked, "How can you be drunk and not remember the evening yet can still remember enough about how grateful she was?"

Angela can hear some of you now. You're saying, "Angela, ain't no man gonna forget it when he gets the good stuff. Nor will he forget it when the woman is grateful."

Granted, you make a good point to a certain degree, but it is her opinion, and she believes it is a sound one, men do not have sex when they are drunk[215] and that what tales they tell are simply their drunken fantasy they have convinced themselves is true in order to keep their ego undamaged. Further, if they do remember, then they weren't drunk.

There are men who will not dance until they are drunk. They tell Angela this. Then when they are drunk, they still don't dance. True, they may get out on the floor under the sparkly lights to twirl and hurl, but that's not dancing. And they won't remember it either, but the ladies on the floor will remember dodging the spew, that's for sure.

Oh, Angela has had her share of men who got close to her after having over-indulged with the drink then proceeded to do something stupid, like picking her up as if she needed the Hindlick Manipulation[216] and then twirling her so fast her legs stuck out straight, hitting other dancers. That turned into the best bragging memory ever...if he could have remembered it. But these men do not remember what they do because if they did they would not have come back the next week and asked to dance again.[217]

---

[215] Something about not being able to "git it up"?

[216] Yes, the author is aware this is not the correct spelling. But this is a book of humor and she is a Southern Woman who wants to have her fun, so take off yer editor hat and continue on with the story and laugh a bit, okay?

[217] Yes, the author said no because she remembers.

Hollywood Walk of Fame, Tax Assessments, and Vandals

The Hollywood Walk of Fame is famous. It was thought up in 1958 and originally built using a tax assessment that was ruled legal after several questioned the funding source. But in the 1960s and 1970s, times got hard and nobody would show up in the bad part of town to receive their star and the Walk of Fame lost its luster.

But all was not lost. The area began rebounding and in 1980 a $2500 fee was assessed, payable by the person or group or business nominating the recipient. The fee was for upkeep. It didn't hurt that taxpayers didn't have to foot the whole bill, either. The fee rose gradually until by 2017 it was $40,000.

If you've got five or more years in radio, TV, live performance, film, or recording; have been nominated for or won an award; do philanthropic work; and have somebody to pony up the $40K fee, then the committee will happily peruse your application.

There are now more than 2600 stars on Hollywood Blvd. and Vine St. You don't have to be an actor to get on it. Directors and producers, fictional characters, bands, acting duos, and more bring in the tourists. Which is what this whole thing is about anyway: Economic Development.

But some of those stars represent folks who are lightning rods for controversy, and vandalism has occurred. Bob Marley had a sledgehammer taken to his star. Hugh Hefner had a crown drawn on his in blue crayon. Bill Cosby, Sofia Vergara, John Lennon, Harry Houdini, Ed McMahon, the Olsen twins, Mariah Carey, and Donald Trump's stars have also been vandalized. That's not the complete list, either.

The thing is that nobody knows who committed most of the vandalisms in this list, or if they do know, they are keeping it to themselves. In any case, except for one fellow, nobody has ever been charged with anything, much less the felony that it is.

But Donald Trump's star. Oh, folks seem to be proud and not shy about admitting to defacing and vandalizing his plaque. From a toilet placed on top inviting people to "Take a Trump!" to colorful stickers with Pussy-Hat Wearing Politically Correct Liberal Democratic RINO Socialist Fascist Commie phrases on them to comedian George Lopez taking a fake pee on it to several other attempts to vandalize it to it finally being destroyed by a pickaxe wielded by one Austin Clay, 24, who was finally brought to justice.

He paid a $400 fine and spent one day in jail.

He was assessed 20 days of community labor and three years of probation. He also had to repay the Hollywood Chamber of Commerce a restitution of almost ten thousand dollars and attend psychological counseling where almost certainly his group will love it that he hates Donald Trump and think the government is a big bad meanie for compelling him to make restitution.

However, keeping Trump's star clean and bright and beautiful is more than anybody wants to deal with and the committee who decides these things decided to not only stop repairing but remove his star.

I don't agree with that removal. That's caving to bullies.

Now, while Trump gets accused of an ever-rotating list of crimes for which there is absolutely no evidence, amongst the 2600 and growing list of stars are some not-so-nice people who did some bad, bad things.

Let's talk about one of those on the list, the convicted serial rapist Bill Cosby. His star is still on the street, yet you would think the people who care so much about women victims would band together, go there on a bus, and make a day of destroying Cosby's star while turning it into a media event with the theme No Means No. They should invite Evangeline Lilly in her #MeToo T-shirt. But have they done it? They have not — and they won't.

In fact, quite a few of those who say they care about women's rights have defended Mr. Cosby, calling his many women accusers liars. Does that make sense to you?

It doesn't to me.

The committee vets the "street star potential" by looking at philanthropic works. Instead, they should be doing exhaustive background checks to see if these people are criminals so the community isn't building a walk of shame.

Youngest Jaded Retro Hipster Millennial[218] Retires at 12

According to BabylonBee.com, Millennials have been struck with a disease rampant among them. It is called "I Can't Even". The fake news outlet[219] reported on this disease and did a fine job of explaining it in three short paragraphs.[220] One story BabylonBee.com did not write about is the one this essay is on: The retirement of the youngest retro hipster Millennial and his descent into a jadoistic weariness. Here's how it went:

Suze Orman[221], a self-proclaimed financial guru, wrote a book just for this young group. It was entitled *The Money Book*

---

[218] JRHM throughout the rest of this essay.

[219] The term "fake news outlet" as used here is not hurled as an insult. BabylonBee.com's specialty is writing news stories that are tongue-in-cheek blatantly false, such as:

"As part of his new trade deal, Trump just strong-armed Canada into taking Jim Carrey back."

"Mike Pence admits to heavy root beer drinking while in high school."

"10 out of 10 Nazis recommend not opening the Ark of the Covenant."

[220] BabylonBee.com never goes over four short, simple paragraphs because they know their audience well. The reader of this footnote is invited to decide if by that the author means that online portal's audience is stupid, shallow, humorless, and riddled with "I Can't Even" disease.

[221] One bookstore owner near Conyers, Georgia, is still mad at Orman after she had a book signing event that attracted not one person and sold not one book but which managed to cause an unnatural flow of other customers around her table as they attempted to avoid the new author and the book she was vigorously and unsuccessfully flogging called *You've Earned It, Don't Lose It: Mistakes You Can't Afford to Make When You Retire.*

of the Young, Fabulous and Broke. Orman's financial advice has never been good and I am not the only one to say it. Look, just because she's an "expert"[222] doesn't make her right, a concept I'm sure my astute readers understand; yet blatantly wrong advice has never stopped someone being exalted to guru status. Astute readers would never have bought that book because, after all, if the woman can so thoroughly miss one little yet highly important comma in the short title, then just how much attention has she really given to the many all-important decimal points in the spreadsheet?

My. Point. Is. Made. ***Boom Shakalaka!***

Nevertheless, JRHMs bought her book because the words *young and fabulous* were on the cover and they were *broke*.[223]

Future readers[224], you need to understand that at the time I write this there is a peculiarly interesting demographic: Young people who virtually live at Starbucks, hunched over the newest and most expensive smartphones with unlimited

---

The bookstore owner is mad is because Orman promised to come back and draw a huge crowd when she "got big" and he hasn't seen hide nor hair of her since except on television. And she won't return his calls either.

[222] Ironic quotation marks are used here on purpose.

[223] "Broke" is a relativistic term as you will obviously infer upon further reading. The author knows what "broke" really means and has nightmares of coming home to an empty house as a child after a visit by the repo man and of having to answer the phone and pretend the bill collectors reached a wrong number.
"Broke" as used by JRHMs means they cannot call a ride-share service but twice per day.

[224] And by "future readers" the author is implying all those readers in the future who discover her brilliance after she dies thereby making her the "Van Gogh of Authors" and her heirs rich if they have properly handled copyright registration updating and protecting and defending the huge body of intellectual property their ancestor produced for them.
But knowing her children's aversion to paperwork, she despairs that the money stream her works generate will only serve as dividends to stockholders of the Big Five publishers or a copyright troll on the ball.

data plans including video chat while updating their social media du jour's feed with genuine fake news stories and boring memes, that have never known a day of hunger except that which is self-imposed after they embark on a cleanse designed to move the sludge out of their intestinal tracts. While Starbucks denies their culpability in being the producer of this sludge to be moved, it is nevertheless a fact that cannot be denied that these JRHMs seek the cleanse because they feel stove up.[225]

One reason the JRHMs' intestines don't move is because these young'uns never see one whit of fiber[226] in their politically correct diet which, of course, logically gave rise to the sub-disease of *"I can't even* take a poo without an artificial cleanse".

It is this group that purchased Orman's book of financial advice that allowed them to retire early. Astute readers are now asking the question: Angela, if Orman's advice is so bad, how is it these young people are able to retire young while I — slaving away for fifty five or more years and living responsibly and cutting my own grass and eating fiber and never once having to take a cleanse and avoiding the sub-diseases of *"I can't even* take a poo without an artificial cleanse" and *"I can't even* pay my taxes even when that idiot[227]

---

[225] This condition named "stove up" means that the body is not moving properly. Parts of the body that cannot move properly, or that get "stove up", at various times within a person's lifecycle are: Joints (including the nose joint), intestines (lower and upper and small and large), the brain (all quadrants), and male genitalia (even if one has those hangy-down parts and self-identifies as having female genitalia and is riddled with the "I Can't Even" disease).

[226] *Fibre* if you are reading this in Great Britain.

[227] The author is, **on purpose**, not naming which idiot or which local, regional, or national political office as that will totally change the nature of this essay into a slingfest of insult and innuendo and the author does not want to call her dear readers any names nor start any public fights at this time.

was in office" — can't? I thank you for your questioning interruption and answer you thusly: Let me get on with my story and I shall tie it all together and tell you. *Sheesh!*

These people bought Orman's book by the tens of...I can't even! In any case, they soon found themselves with no challenges to look forward to other than should their half-caff with added triple espresso shots, rice-milk-infused, low-foam, fat-free latté be large or small today?

What kind of challenge is that?

Some say that challenges are just problems in disguise and that we could all do without problems. Logically it follows: Why complain when there are no challenges? It is simple, really. Think about your muscles. If those muscles do not regularly meet challenges that stretch their limits, those muscles wither, weaken, and waste away. This current crop of young'uns can be likened to unused muscles.

Orman's advice, therefore, is contraindicated and thus wrong as is evidenced by the jade factor so early in the JRHM lifecycle. What usually takes people fifty or more years to achieve is now theirs in only six or seven? I mean, what is the fun of going on a trip around the world when you're in your twenties, huh? One should do it when one needs to carry along a box of meds, two styles of canes, and a convertible walker/mini-wheelchair and can afford to hire a foreign local young'un who is not riddled with "I Can't Even" and is grateful to get the five American dollars to push that old ass up the hill and which traveler is willing to be told about the view if they cannot see it through their glaucoma and cataracts.

These JRHM young people have absolutely nothing to look forward to.

No wonder their suicide rates are higher than any previous generation including The Greatest Generation, who saw major challenges in overcoming the Nazi and Japanese problems (1933-1945); and those who went through the Great Potato Famine of Ireland (1845-1852); the rise of the Radical

Feminist (1965-1975) — or what came to be called the Great Balls On Fire Movement[228] (1989-2016); and the Great Meltdown of the United States House and Senate[229] (2009 to present), among others.

This youngest JRHM who, at twelve tender years of age, said when interviewed that his "greatest desire is to live where I can make my own soap out of lye, that is, in the mountains where I can be what I truly am without having to apologize for it." He lived with his two daddies[230] in a Midtown Atlanta loft with a Starbucks in the building.

---

[228] Wherein to prove they were not anti-woman and were supportive of all feelings, opinions, and other thoughts of all women, men set their balls on fire, and there are videos online showing them doing that.

This movement ended when a subset of the Millennial Generation said "Ta hell wit dat!" and began regularly to make offensive jokes about women after seeing previous generations self-immolate and yet still not get laid: A condition that was so brilliantly written about by one Jim Butorac who, to great applause (the bastard), fictionalized his life story of missed opportunities with the women in his famous series of books.

In response to many men finally "growing a pair", Georgetown professor Carol Christine Fair tweeted that "entitled white men" should have their corpses castrated and then be fed to pigs, causing Twitter's coveted Blue Check Mark to be removed from her account. [Please see the essay "'Verify' your Twitter account, or *More* busy work designed to keep you a slave to Tech Giant Algorithmic Bull Crap".]

[229] Some contend this is just the continuation of the Great Potato Famine of 1845 wherein the blight that struck the taters of Ireland traveled across The Pond and hibernated itself in DNA only to come alive in the brains of certain politicians, causing massive cognitive dissonance between reality and fantasy in both parties.

[230] The two "daddies" are actually two man-hating "politically correct" heterosexual women who have chosen to live as lesbians and who self-identify as daddies though they insist that anyone who uses the term daddy and infers the male gender is homophobic, misogynistic, misandristic, and/or a hater of gender fluidity.

Their closets were filled with identical pairs of faded blue jeans, black faux leather belts, and shirts with stripes in varying hues of brown, and brown shoes and boots with thick rubber bottoms. Not one other color or pattern was found in their closets.

While this essay has focused on the negatives, I must point out that this young man[231] gives me hope that males will survive as long as they heed the inner yearnings of maleness and don't get petrified and terrified by crazy women and pussy-hat wearing men who desperately want to be pussy-whipped. And even with hard pressures at home, if a young fellow like this can #standfirm in ways his two daddies never thought he would, then there is hope for the human race — yes, yes, *man*kind! — because, after all, if a man can't make nice with a woman on a regular basis and upload new generations that will be downloaded eight to ten months later and who in turn will grow up to repeat the cycle, then it doesn't matter what is in that fancy retirement account nor when you fund it, and all Suze Orman wannabes can just go to hell because they won't have anybody to flog their financial advice and services to until they go to the Seventh Circle of Hell[232] which is what they inflict while on Earth.

However, they had two hidden drawers filled with girly-girl stuff of lace in colors men like to see "bad girls" wear. When their human unit was at gender fluid summer camp, these two "daddies" would close the drapes, lock all doors and windows, and dress up in those pink and red diaphanous lacy bits and watch *An Officer and a Gentlemen* while they drank wine spritzers and dreamed of getting The Big D from Richard Gere in such a fine fashion that it would make them want to slap somebody.

Publicly they have been quoted in the press when they were interviewed for the Atlanta Journal-Constitution article about the youngest JRHM ever to retire. "We are so proud of our human unit. Our human unit even paid off the mortgage."

[231] The young man's two "daddies" tried everything they could think of to get him to self-identify as anything but male, but the young man showed a gritty spine and refused, causing no end of nights of worrisome debate after the young'un had gone to bed to get his sleep. The two "daddies" had to refer to a specialist to advise on how to talk to their human unit about nocturnal emissions.

[232] Which is the "Punishment" level.

"Verify" your Twitter account, or *More* busy work designed to keep you a slave to Tech Giant Algorithmic Bull Crap.

Never mind that Twitter.com has been a force for good in some countries dealing with civil unrest [read *civilians standing up against tyranny*]. Never mind that Twitter billed itself as a way to save time in communicating with customers and/or fans attracted to "follow" users, thus growing the user base for the company at no charge to themselves. And never mind that Twitter Inc. has well over 50 impenetrable subsidiaries around the world: MoPub, WiredSet, Ubalo, Fluther, and Magic Pony Technologies, to name only five.

Never mind any of that because, you see, it seems their flagship product Twitter.com was in bad need of their user base being homogenized and pasteurized. To that end, I received a message from Twitter [@Lovedoggey][233] inviting me to become a Verified Twitter User Worthy of a Blue Check Mark. Intrigued, I clicked the link.

After some ego-fluffing language about the benefits of becoming a verified user came the process itself.

Step 1: Fill out Twitter's Verification Request Form

Using Twitter's verification request form, start the process of getting verified on Twitter. Login to your Twitter account to complete the form. However, before your account can be considered for verification, confirm you have these eight elements your user profile:

1. A verified phone number.

---

[233] Contrary to what everyone believes when they hear her handle, this is the long story short: In the early days of Twitter.com, all user names the author wanted were taken and in frustration she turned to her Jack Russell Terrier and said, "Lovedoggey! What am I going to choose as my handle?" Ding! Ding! Ding! She became the first Lovedoggey on Twitter.

2. A confirmed email address.

3. A bio.

4. A profile photo that *matches all your other social network* profile photos.

5. A header photo that accurately represents your "brand".

6. Your birthday, unless you are the brand.

7. **Your website.** If you do not have a website, you are not considered legitimate.

8. Tweets must be set to "Public".

In the eight steps above is where multi-organization homogenization and pasteurization begins. Notice 4: A profile photo that matches all your other social networks[234]. Whoa. That flies in the face of why different social networks exist in the first place: Attracting different audiences by using different approaches. But no. Twitter wants you to match everywhere.

Now, notice 7: If you do not have a website, Twitter says you are not legitimate. What does "not legitimate" even mean? A fake? A sham? Unlawful? Forbidden? Criminal? Dishonest? Now Twitter is telling me on what I need to spend my money and time without asking if it works for me?

Hello, McFly? Is anybody home?

Okay. Moving on. Let's say having that Blue Check Mark is important to me and I jump through all their hoops and submit myself for verification. Does this mean I will get the

---

[234] This only works if you are highly focused on bad financial advice [such as Suze Orman] or are a plastic surgeon with your own television show [such as Dr. Andrew Ordon], but *not* if you are an Autodidact Polymath and Magnificently Methodical Southern Woman who is The Most Brilliant Woman In The World because that just blows Twitter's ever-loving lid and makes their eyes cross and rotate superfast.

coveted Blue Check Mark? It does not. Now, somebody or something inside Twitter will make the determination: Thumb up or down. But do they tell you why?

They do not.

But all is not lost! If Twitter displays "Account Not Eligible for Review", you will "have another chance to fill in the missing information for another chance to submit yourself for verification". Their words.

They even supply hints as to how to have an increased chance of getting your account verification approved. First, your bio should specify an area of expertise and/or a company mission. To do that, you must optimize your Twitter bio to their specs.

What are those specs? They do not say and you cannot find out.

Second, carefully confirm the validity of the information you want to submit — this implies that the first time you confirmed the validity you were just playing, you know, messing with their minds — and now they want you to *actually, really, truly* confirm it.

Now you wait. How long? Nobody knows. But Twitter will email you as soon as a decision has been made and you will know you've been verified once @verified follows you.

According to an expert in this process: "If your request is rejected the first time around, know that you can apply again after 30 days. And if you do get verified, note that verified Twitter accounts that do not follow Twitter terms and conditions (or use the account for another purpose) can have their verified badges revoked."

This same expert listed the benefits of having your Twitter account get a highly-sought-after Blue Check Mark. These include:

1. Signals high authority and authenticity.
2. Builds thought leadership.
3. Special account management advantages.

4. What was once reserved for celebrities and key personalities that Twitter verified through their own methods, now has been made available for all of us peons to apply.

Let's look at benefit 1: The Blue Check Mark signals high authority and authenticity. I beg to differ. Kathy Griffin, the comedienne who thought it would be a great idea to pose with a representation of President Donald J. Trump's bloody head and tweet it out all over the place, as of this writing still has the verified Blue Check Mark.

Now, she may have high authority (expert joke teller) and be deemed authentic (true and reliable) within certain circles, but just because she "signals" it does not make it so. Don't get me started on 2 because leading in thought is not what Griffin has ever done. Number 3 is never explained. And number 4 is feel-good Socialism at its best.

Twitter has let their users down in other ways, too. Please notice what I call "weasel words" in their application for verification process: Twitter "will remove verification from accounts whose **behavior does not fall within these new guidelines**. We will continue to review and take action as we work towards a new program we are proud of."

You read correctly, you wonderful reader you. Twitter will not provide a list of verboten topics or behaviours[235], but will make you read their ever-loving politically correct corporate mind[236], and if you read that PCCM wrongly, you will **not** get the coveted Blue Check Mark and it could be removed if you do have it. Effectively, Twitter is bullying. Again, though, all is not lost because —

---

[235] Behavior in the U.S., but behaviour everywhere else including Great Britain.

[236] PCCM.

Twitter has suspended their Blue Check Mark Verification Program indefinitely because…***actually, really, truly*** they don't say, but my guess is because it sucks and because when employees quit they are not hiring anyone else to take their place and the algorithm they thought was going to handle the process didn't work as planned sooooo…

Now that you have been thoroughly slammed with an impossible to-do list from the Tech Giant's First Circle of Hell[237], you will now need…

---

[237] Limbo.

Your Moment of Zen

Become one with the blankness.

Say oooohhhmmmm.

Close your eyes.

Turn the pages slowly.

oooohhhmmmm

oooohhhmmmm

oooohhhmmmm

oooohhhmmmm

oooohhhmmmm

oooohhhmmmm

oooohhhmmmm

oooohhhmmmm

Open your eyes.

Continue reading.

If This, Then That: Or How to Spin facts in an Alternative Universe.

On September 29, 2016, in the Great State of Virginia in the United States, as reported by The Washington Post's Laura Vozzella, The FBI and police from Richmond, Virginia, began investigating how 19 dead Virginians from the Shenandoah Valley city of Harrisonburg re-registered to vote.

Long story short, a private group was on the James Madison University campus registering voters. Granted, the folks in this publicly unnamed private group thought it quite possible that since the laws as written do not specify a voter is required to be alive when they register and vote, that registering dead people was not breaking the law.

Yes, I agree. This group might live in an alternative universe where such makes sense. But more than likely the group — no charges were ever filed against them — was just hoping to get away with registering dead people to vote in this critical swing state. How can we tell who might have been behind the scheme and thus infer from an incomplete story who would have been benefited by the votes from the dead? Easy-peezee: We look at the rest of the article.

First, it was State House Republican delegates who held a conference call with reporters to call attention to the investigation. So, even if some mainstream reporters — or as other might call them: serious journalists — knew about the investigation and, being Liberal themselves, chose not to report it, the nature of the conference call (where everyone identifies themselves as being on it) would make it nigh on impossible not to report on the unlawful events.

So report they did and this is how the time-honored and proven equation of *If This, Then That* was completely ignored and the alternate universe was again visited. Let's allow House Minority Leader David J. Toscano (D-Charlottesville) to tell us in his own words:

"First of all, there was no voter fraud — they caught him," Toscano said. "Nobody cast a vote. . . .There's still no evidence of [voter fraud] going on in the state."

Do you see how *If This, Then That* was completely ignored by Toscano? That's right. Toscano wants us to believe that the person[238] registering dead voters would not lead to votes being cast. Stopping a crime during the commission of it does not mean a crime was not intended to be completed. Let's look at this logically with an illustration.

Three men go into a bank. One sits in the lobby as if waiting on a loan officer. One goes to a teller window. Another goes to a desk and pretends to fill out a deposit form. A fourth sits in a vehicle outside, waiting. Each, though, is tasked with "casing" the joint. That is, locating cameras, guards, possible escape routes, crowd load, and other areas of danger in need of control so they can successfully get away with the money. They do as they wanted to and leave for home where they will solidify their plans. They will use the equation *If This, Then That* to come up with alternate methods to handle other scenarios. If they are smart, they even acknowledge a Black Swan's effect on their plans.

In any case, they have taken steps to commit a crime, which shows intent, and will continue with the crime if they are not caught. But one of them has a girlfriend who, unbeknownst to the group, has just found Jesus and accepted Him as her Lord and Savior. She knows of the plan and, not wanting to tick off Jesus, she goes to the police and tells them all about the plan. She even knows when the crime is to happen. She spills her guts and drops to the floor of the detective's office and prays for the soul of her boyfriend and also begs them to go easy on him because, God HELP HER!,

---

[238] Obviously Toscano knew the "group" was one person which, of course, brings up a whole other topic for discussion that the author will allow you to have with your fellow.

she still loves him and thinks his heart is good and can be saved.

Detectives assure her they will not hurt the love of her life and ask that she keep quiet about having told them. She isn't stupid and, not trusting her boyfriend's gang members, agrees to be prudent.

Then detectives do what detectives do in upholding the law, catching the men before they go inside the bank. The gang is hauled away in the bus and promptly upon arriving say one word each, "Lawyer." They clam up.

Lawyers come and a few hours later they call the press to meet them at the front of the cop shop where they issue a joint press release that goes like this:

"First of all, there was no bank robbery because they caught them," said the lead attorney. "Nobody robbed a bank. There's no evidence of bank robbery going on. Further, we will be suing the police department, the individual officers involved, and the FBI because every time you turn around, Law Enforcement is trying to make it more difficult for men such as these to actually get their job done."

I can hear you laughing right along with me, yet that is just about what state Delegate David J. Toscano (D-Charlottesville) said about the person who got caught forging 19 voter registrations for dead people. Here's his own words: "There's still no evidence of [voter fraud] going on in the state. But there is evidence every time you turn around that the Republicans are trying to make it more difficult for citizens to vote in elections."

O. Emmmm. GEEEEE.[239] I can't make this stuff up. Not even in the land of Conversations in Hyperreality that I made up from scratch for comedic effect, I can't even make that up

---

[239] Readers of the Future, note: O.M.G. stands for "Oh, my God", or if one is Jewish "Oh, my G*d", or if a good Christian "Oh, my gosh".

because I cannot think up such nonsensical, self-serving, felonious thoughts.

But…

I know that type of thinking exists and that is why I can identify it when I see it. Yes, these eagle eyes cannot be fooled. Though she may not know when they will show up, this writer knows Black Swans exist. Thank goodness there are others who can do the same. Unfortunately, too many others can be fooled. That is why I use humorous stories to write on these subjects. Humor often gets points across that a serious discussion cannot.

And because humor can get the point across, that is why Evil tells jokes. But Evil's jokes are always vicious with the only nugget of truth you'll ever find in them twisted beyond all recognition. But hey, they make the blind laugh even as that laugh does not make anyone feel better, learn a beneficial lesson, or be able to understand a complicated concept.

Evil always simplifies everything. There is no gray with Evil. Evil always paints itself as an angel of light on the side of God, children, and puppies while describing enemies as overlords of dark dungeons who feed children and puppies to pet dragons.

Oh, dear. I can hear some of the simple-minded folks saying, "But Angela, I remember that time ol' So-and-So did this-and-that bad thing, and they belong to Party X. Whaddaya say about that, Angela, huh?"

To that I say — listen really close because I'm only going to say it once — Evil can be found anywhere.

Down here in the South of the United States we've simplified one way of recognizing Evil. When somebody comes to you and says "Do business with me. I'm a Christian," we all know to grab our wallets and run like hell.

Caution: Prone to break out in song.

Somehow, I got hold of a black T-shirt that said in bright yellow letters: *CAUTION Prone to break out in song*. I don't remember if I bought it or Awesome Cousin Number One did. In any case, every time I wear it, something interesting happens. The first time I wore it was in Atlanta, the downtown area. I'm walking down the street and every man walking toward me looks at my shirt, their bodies getting all tense and tight and their eyes wide and fearful. Each looked away quickly, then looked back, and relaxed.

What in the heck was going on? After about an hour of that I realized they were all looking at my T-shirt. CAUTION, it said. And sure enough, they took caution. But the next line allowed them to smile and relax.

Not one woman thought anything about it, if they noticed it at all. So, I've been giving a lot of thought to this. You see, young and old and white and black and yellow and red and brown, all men continue to have the exact same reaction every time I wear it. The big question is why?

I will tell you why.

You are asking, "Angela, why do you think you have the ability, knowledge, and other stuff necessary to answer such questions? Just who do you think you are?"

Let me answer, you smart aleck you. First, did you pick this book up from a shelf and flip to this essay so that you missed the introduction explaining exactly who I am? Or are you just trying to pick a fight?

Don't answer that. It doesn't matter.

I am an Autodidact Polymath, Magnificently Methodical Southern Woman, and The Most Brilliant Woman In The World, that's who I am, and don't you forget it because this information will come in handy later.

Getting back to the purpose of this essay, the reason all men, young, old, and every color and nationality (that can read English, of course) had the same reaction is because many women went batshit crazy and emptied out the exact same amount of RadFem whoop-ass on menfolk whether all they did was hold a door for them or ask them out on a date.

The recent manipulation[240] by the Liberal Democrat RINO Socialist Fascist Commie Deep State produced what could only be termed an overreaction in certain women and pussy-hat wearing men. This overreaction involved a schoolteacher asking publicly "Who is going to take one for the team and kill Kavanaugh?" Another overreaction involved women beating on the door of the Supreme Court on a Saturday demanding to be let in so they could complain about Kavanaugh's appointment. The Court is closed on Saturday, but all they did was say the Court was not letting them in on purpose and ignoring them, too, those big bad SCOTUS men with scrotums.

So, the flinch of these men reading my T-shirt was a sad thing to see. I knew men had it rough but did not realize that even the young woke men had it as bad as the old misogynists walking beside them. But they do.

More women are now publicly speaking out against the RadFems' practice of unloading whoop-ass for no good reason. I applaud those strong women.

Finally, I am not alone in this.

---

[240] The author is writing this essay at the end of 2018 when Justice Brett Kavanaugh was being confirmed as an associate justice with SCOTUS.

Speaking of T-shirts that get a reaction.

There are two types of people in this world.

Those who can extrapolate from incomplete data

Yes, these are the words written on a bright yellow T-shirt I remember buying, which means I know how it got in my drawer. The first night I wore it was when I was hosting the Atlanta Songwriters' Club at Red Light Café in Midtown Atlanta. There were two reactions from attendees.

One: Hahahahahaha! Exactly.

Two: [Read it. Read it again with lips moving.] I don't understand.

The second group then had four further reactions:

Two-One: [From the back of the room ten minutes later.] Oh! Hahahahaha! Got it.

Two-Two: [From the back of the room sixty minutes later.] Oh! Hahahahaha! Got it.

Two-Three: [Two weeks later.] Hahahahaha! I got it.

Two-Four: [Two weeks later.] Hahaha! I still don't get it.

These real-life reactions have continued no matter where I wear the T-shirt. But what I'm finding interesting is that the message on the shirt was thought of by so many for such a long period of time. And, they came back and said something. This is amazing to me. The reason is because, other than my own T-shirts, I can't think of another whose message I've ever thought of again once I passed it by.

Truly. As I write this I'm thinking back to all the T-shirts I've ever seen and I cannot remember a one with any clarity. I know some of them have been interesting because I remember laughing at their witty humor; I just do not remember the message or the person who wore the shirt.

So, all these people coming back to me up to two weeks later means…what? Do they have better memories than I? It seems so…at least when it comes to T-shirts. How do they do it? I don't know. I doubt they know either. Yet, they remembered that it was me who wore a particular shirt with a particular message and that the message attracted their attention enough that they thought to orbit back around to me and say something. I love it. But what does that say about me that I cannot remember these types of shirt messages?

I've given it much thought and, frankly, I'm loath to say, the initial messaging was boring. I am a polymath, and as such I tend to take any bit of information for a trip around the world. I always end up tripping out…errrr…I mean going somewhere much more interesting than the point of departure. With me, it's about how the journey gets me to a destination I did not know was connected to the point of departure. That is string theory at its most primal. Bet you never thought about that, did you? But, see, a polymath such as myself does. And that is why I am, humbly speaking of course, a Magnificently Methodical Southern Woman and The Most Brilliant Woman In The World.

Now, take Dave Barry for instance. He would remember the T-shirt messaging. I bet if you were to ask him, he could tell stories about T-shirts with all sorts of implied and overt messaging such as the name of a brand of beer that on a hot Miami summer day is hosting a wet T-shirt contest on a swanky beach. I bet Dave remembers the brand name very clearly. But, could he take that and do what I do? No. He could not because Dave is not a polymath and he definitely isn't a magnificently methodical or brilliant Southern woman.

"Can you wait one week before you kill yourself?"

On an early morning school day in 1997, my daughter said, "Mom, I think he's getting ready to kill himself." I hot-footed it down the hall to my son's room where I saw him holding a noose made from a rope.

In the middle of his room there he stood, straight and still; eyes, dull and dark.

"Son? Are you thinking of killing yourself?"

His eyes registered my presence. "Yes," he said firmly.

"Well, I tell you what. You don't have to go to school today. Is that all right with you?" I asked. My son nodded. "May I have the rope?" He nodded again, but did not hand it to me, so I gently removed it from his hands.

Daughter left for school and I formed a plan.

Let me break here before I continue with the story to tell you this: As far back as I can remember and continuing to this day, I've thought of killing myself. Suicide is an almost daily thought for me. In fact, when I was very young, I made a promise to myself that upon turning eighteen I would kill myself. I chose eighteen because then I would legally be an adult and my life would be mine to do with as I pleased, and nobody could tell me otherwise.

Life was not pleasant, and it wasn't worth living, but I was an obedient child who did as she was told because the adults in my life had the legal rights, not me. Yes, I was a child and did not come to the best conclusion; still, that was my reality.

Obviously, I did not kill myself because here I am writing this. The reason I didn't suicide is because at sixteen God made Himself known, which gave hope that one day I would see justice. That allowed opportunity for other solutions for living that had not been seen, which is not to say the thinking about or planning it stopped; it was merely postponed.

So that my outward calm reaction to my son's intention to self-harm does not seem to be uncaring, it is important for the reader to know this about me. I promise you this: Inwardly I was reeling, heart and soul. I reeled for the next ten years of his life, always on tenterhooks, wondering when my son would make good on his plan. After all, even in the midst of this hadn't I continued to make plans for my death at my hand? Losing a mother is the natural order of things and I believed he would be fine without me. Losing a child, though, is not the natural order. Could I live without my child?

I did not know.

When my children were small I had twice come close to killing myself by what I called a socially acceptable method: I ignored two major health issues, both of which came close to killing me. Medical help came only when my husband forced it. Yes, I am happy he forced the issue. In any case, thoughts of and planning for death were normal for me and so I was able to calmly approach the situation with my son, thus not exacerbating his emotional balance.

"Son, here's what we're going to do. I'll take you to school —" quickly raising a hand to forestall any jumping to conclusions on his part — "and we'll go tell the counselor that you won't be in for a few days. Does that sound okay?"

He thought for a moment and nodded. Once in the car and backing out of the garage, we headed toward the school. "Son, just so I can understand where you are at this moment and can figure out how best to, you know, work through this. Do you think you would be able to hold off killing yourself for… say… one week?"

His eyes widened in panic. "One *whole* week?"

"Yes. One whole week."

"No!"

"Thank you for telling me that. How long do you think you can go without killing yourself?" We continued to the next stop sign, where I engaged the right-turn signal.

"Ummm…uh…*maybe* one day," he answered.

"Excellent. I fully understand."

We arrived at the school, walked directly to the office of the counselor assigned to ninth- and tenth-graders, knocked on her door, and were invited in.

"Good morning. I am Angela Durden and this is my son. I believe you know him?" The counselor nodded and said hello to him and said that though they had never met in person she was certainly aware of all the students in her charge.

Continuing, I said, "Listen, I just want you to know that my son is — Son, may I say exactly? [He nodded] — wanting to kill himself. He had a noose in his hand this morning."

The counselor was fabulous. She did not overreact but had a matter-of-fact calm about her expression as she acknowledged the news. "Oh, I see."

"We just wanted to stop in and tell you that he would be out of school for a few days, not sure how many, and that we are heading over to Brawner — his sister works on the front desk in the evening, so we know them there — to get an assessment and see what would be a good course of action. Would it be possible to let his teachers know he will be out for a few days?"

"Absolutely. Of course. And I agree. Brawner is a great place." She turned to my son and had some kind words to say about how she sure was going to enjoy seeing him back at school. We stood and all three shook hands. We left and drove to the hospital.

Upon arriving at Brawner, I explained the situation again and introduced them to my son. They were kindness itself and asked if he would mind answering a few questions so they could get a point-in-time snapshot of his thought process. He nodded and followed a woman into an anteroom off the lobby. A few minutes later he came out with the woman who explained to us the results:

He was definitely actively suicidal.

But Brawner was not on our insurance plan, so another hospital was called and informed we were on our way. Imagine my surprise to find that the director of the hospital was a neighbor in our subdivision. He met us at the unit servicing teenagers.

With my son standing next to me I told the nurses and the director that he was suicidal and that I did not know why, therefore if to help him they needed to ask him any questions about alcohol or drugs or any abuse he may have suffered, please do so because all I cared about was helping him.

A nurse got snarky and said they would do that whether or not I gave permission. The director stepped in and said to the nurse, "This is not that kind of family. But we will do all of that." The nurse calmed down. Then my son was led to the unit, placed on suicide watch, and I did not see him for another 24 hours. My neighbor, the director, said, "Angela, don't worry. I'll keep my eye on him."

I walked out the door of the hospital where I was met by my husband, who I'd managed to call at some point and leave a message telling him where to meet us. Upon seeing my husband — and knowing my son could not see me — I proceeded to collapse and cry and have a general meltdown.

Twenty four hours later I was back at the hospital. The nurse who had been so snarky the day before had a completely different attitude. Here's what they found out. First: He was not using any drugs or alcohol. Second: No matter how many times or how they asked, he absolutely denied abuse by anyone and credibly affirmed that his parents had never done so. Third: Why would he want to die? Simply because certain chemicals in his brain were way off balance. Keeping him on suicide watch, they plied him with liquid Prozac.

Was I ever happy for that report! They let me in the back where I sat next to him on a sofa watching television and where, like we always did at home, we talked about the TV shows and various thoughts those brought up.

Sitting on another sofa at a right angle to us was a girl about my son's age. She did not watch the television but watched me and my son instead. Her eyes darted between us until finally she blurted to my son, "Who is that woman?"

"My mother," he answered.

"Hello," said I.

"That's not your mother," said the girl. "Mothers don't act like that."

Gently my son said, "Well, my mama does."

The girl stared for a few seconds and said, "I want a mama like that."

Visiting time was over, son was hugged, and I left. The next visit would be twenty four hours later, which would make that a Saturday, mid-morning. Both his father and I arrived to find the place packed with adults and more children than we had originally thought were in the unit. But other than the TV, there was no sound. Nobody was talking. We had brought two decks of cards and when our son saw us, he was relieved. We found a table, cards were shuffled, and a spirited game of Rummy became the focal point of the room as parents and children alike watched us as if we were aliens from another planet.

After about an hour or so of playing, our son leaned toward the center of the table and crooked his finger at us. We leaned in. He whispered, "I don't belong here."

We nodded our heads and said, "We know." Two days later we took him home.

The nursing staff said they had never had a suicidal child who had never been abused and/or was not misusing alcohol or drugs. They said it was such a pleasure to treat an actual medical case for a change and wished us well.

However, by the law at the time my son was required to see a psychiatrist or psychologist once a month for the next several years. I dropped him off and picked him up. When I asked him what he did during the sessions he said, "Well, the first few times the doctor kept bringing up abuse, but I kept telling him that wasn't my problem. So now we just play chess and talk about video games."

I didn't care. He was alive.

That was all that mattered to me.

Recently I was telling this story to a friend of mine who asked, "Why didn't you ask your son why he wanted to die? And try to find out if he was on drugs or abused or whatever?"

Because it just wasn't the right time to have that conversation, that's why. In other words, if those were his issues, then it would be better to get him stable in his thinking before we delved into why it was unstable. Yes, I know the hospital staff had that conversation, but they also did it after blood work and liquid Prozac identified and eased an underlying medical condition, both of which I could not do.

I had blamed my suicide ideations squarely on my terrible home life. A consequence of the abuse. A fallout. But clearly there was another triggering condition in me as five years before this event of my son's, I too had been diagnosed with the same brain chemical imbalance. Obviously, DNA is a powerful thing.

My son and I have had conversations about that time and how my OCD Mother Genes kick in until I finally simply must check in with him and make sure we're all still percolating along. We are blunt in what we say and share, but neither are ever surprised that we agree with each other about death and how we want our lives to end. More specifically, how we do not want our endings to be. Whoever goes first will be missed by the one who remains, but we won't be overly sad since we agree on what death is. It is The Big Sleep.

We both agree: We are more worried about living so long that we can no longer indulge our passion for learning. We are both afraid of being bored to death.

Thus far we have avoided that. I told a friend the other day that when thoughts of death come, somehow I always manage to think "Let me just do this one thing and then I'll die."

Do people fear death itself? Or do they fear more the being left behind to deal with loss? Are they afraid of being alone? Losing something they can control? Have they put all their emotional eggs in one basket and don't know what to do when that basket breaks?

Or is it lack of living they fear, and not death itself?

In the Christian Bible at 1 Corinthians 15:26 the Apostle Paul said: "As the last enemy, death is to be brought to nothing." In verse 31 he said: "Daily I face death."

Paul faced death in many ways.

He did not run from the realities of it.

When you look an enemy squarely in the face, it loses its power over you.

If I write a tell-all about my affair[241] with a married[242], big-time[243], well-known[244], highly lauded[245], and not-too-much-younger-than-me[246] crime writer, will my other books sell faster?

Let me say at the outset I do not want to be famous for:

• Having boinked someone famous.

• Or having someone famous boink me.

The list of women (and these days, men) who are famous for doing that is endless.[247] To even begin listing them would

---

[241] The author is clear: This didn't really happen. The author is purely asking a rhetorical question. Rhetorical. That's it.

[242] The ideal situation would be they are separated, but he would, of course, be lying.

[243] His books will all have BEST SELLER written all over them.

[244] If you were ever to hear his name you would, of course, know him.

[245] He is very good...at finding an agent to pull the wool over eyes of editors and publishers and get them to pay the big bucks in a ten-book deal, though his writing sucks.

[246] Ideally, he would be fifteen years the author's junior, you know, still able to "get it up" without artificial enhancements and having had enough practice to know what do with it once it arose.

[247] In fact, the book publishing business saw fast growth from the early 1950s to the late 1960s as early Hollywood female actresses (now known as actors) began writing their life stories. Once the public no longer thought of these escapades as titillating, sales fell off but the publishing companies did not understand what was happening to their falling sales numbers. This led to a growing decline in profits. The

take longer than I am willing to take. However, we could mention just a couple. I am thinking of Barbi Benton. Wikipedia.com says:

"Barbi Benton is an American model, actress and singer. She is known for appearing in Playboy magazine, as a four-season regular on the comedy series *Hee Haw*[248], and for recording several modestly successful albums in the 1970s."

Her one hit notwithstanding[249], everybody might talk about her song but it never failed they would then leer "You *know* she's Hef's[250] girlfriend, right?" And that will always be what Barbi would be most well-known for. But she did get the roles, and her albums sold more than if she had not been Hef's girlfriend. I'm sure she lived a pretty much stable life, financially and otherwise, as three years after Hef she married a nice man in 1979, and they had three children. As of this writing, they are still married. That is a success I cannot stress any more fervently as being just plain awesome. So, good for you, Barbi.

---

companies employed an accounting method called "robbing Peter to pay Paul" which only worked for a short while. They then began buying each other up until finally they were all gnawing on their own legs. In other words, it ain't pretty out there in book publishing land.

[248] *Hee Haw* was a variety show featuring Country music and cheesy jokes.

[249] The author's younger brother, Michelangelo Darling, was madly in love with her and hated it when their mother said she was sleeping her way to the top. If one wanted to "crank his engine", one need merely mention just that.

[250] Hugh Hefner, famous misogynist who used women to build an empire devoted to boinking and was a beloved target of radical feminists such as Gloria Steinem. Steinem went on to marry a rich man, father of Christian Bale the actor, and was subsequently hated by other radical feminists for not being faithful to the cause.

However, to get back to the most important thing in this story: Me.

I don't want to go through all that. I never wanted to be a Playboy Bunny, even though my stepfather wanted me to be one.[251] I didn't want to be arm candy if to be arm candy meant I had to boink somebody and parade around nekkid[252] in a mansion somewhere to be ogled by other misogynists.[253] I'm particular like that.

I've written about this subject before in a column entitled "If I self-identify as a Female Native-American Caribbean-African Disabled Male Machinist Righty-Tighty-Lefty-Loosey Author, will my books sell faster?" The column struck a nerve with a huge amount of people, most of whom were writers I bet. Yet the question is still the same: How can one get attention for one's creative works? It's the worst bugaboo for any creative. Creating scandal these days doesn't even work anymore. Just ask Snoop Dogg and Eminem. People yawn when they see a ginned-up scandal. Hell, they yawn when they see a real one.[254]

---

[251] Please purchase and read the author's memoir *Twinkle, a memoir* to learn about this story.

[252] This is the way Southerners say "naked", though genteel well-bred Southern aristocracy say "NAAAAYked".

[253] Bill Cosby was a frequent visitor to Hef's mansion and one of Hef's good misogynist buddies. So you can't tell me Bill's wife didn't know of what her husband was made.

[254] We know this because ratings are down, as is ad revenue, and layoffs just keep a-coming.

The main way to tell a scandal is fake is when the story is spread by mainstream media. #CrunkNewsNetwork[255] is the hugest[256] of the lot. You can bet the gullible reporters can be counted on to spread in print or on the telly some gushing and highly favorable version of statements of caring[257] and hatred[258] for hours and days on end at no charge to the writer or artist or rapper or sports figure.[259]

---

[255] By "hugest" the author does not mean to imply they have many viewers or high ratings, because they do not. Look, when a cooking show on PBS gets more viewers late at night than prime-time CNN — the #CrunkNewsNetwork mentioned — then hugest in this case takes on another meaning, namely their ego.

[256] Yes, this is a real word.

[257] The caring spoken of here is for the money they want to make via sales and the money they save by not having to pay for editorial placement.

[258] The hatred mentioned at the time of this writing is for President Donald Trump and all his relatives, friends, business associates, anybody who lives in flyover country, Blacks who are for White Supremacy (that is, they publicly say they like Trump and/or Conservative values), all White Males and White Females unless they are wearing a pussy hat, and all Autodidact Polymaths like the author of this book who is The Most Brilliant Woman In The World.

[259] Ha! Made you look at the bottom of the page. Just the author having a little fun. Say, have you bought any more of her books?

Living life *tempo Snapchato*[260]

Dear Snap Inc.,

I want to thank you for bringing your app to market. It is my wish that your company will remain or, in the case of not yet being such, will become financially stable and solvent and be in business a long time. Here is why.

Your company is saving me a lot of money in doctors' bills and plastic surgery recovery downtime.[261]

As I have so famously written about in the past, my dear friend and fellow crime writer novelist Linda Sands introduced me to your app[262] when she said, "Hey, open up your Snapchat and let's have some fun" and I went "What in the hell is Snapchat?" and she went "Woman! What do you mean 'what in the hell is Snapchat?'" and I went "What I mean is 'What…in… the…*HAYLE*…is…Snapchat?'" and Linda went "You really don't know?" and I went "Linda, will you just [bad word here that ends in *ing*] show me for God's sake" and Linda went "Of course, darling, all yousehaddado wuzzask" and Linda did show Angela and Angela downloaded the app right there and then and then Linda and Angela spent the next four hours in the absolute best therapy

---

[260] This is a bastardized musical term taken from *tempo rubato* meaning "free in the use of stolen time".

[261] For the reader and Snap Inc: The author has never had any surgery involving her face or paid doctors for their opinion on how to employ plastic surgery, nor does she plan to do so. This sentence is merely here to get the point across that should the author have ever even thought of doing something stupid like that, with the Snapchat app from Snap Inc. she would not have had to do so.

[262] The author admits that when it comes to fun tech, Linda casts massive shade.

session ever because we did nothing but laugh and laugh and laugh.[263] Here's why we did such as we did.

First, Linda and I, both being savvy self-promoters[264], are always taking selfies as we go out and about in our mobile lives while promoting our various creative endeavors and events and so forth. Now, Linda and I know how to use an iPhone camera better than just about anybody when it comes to taking pictures of our own faces, and we do a damn good job of it. Though I will say it now *in print* that Linda is like a lot of folks when it comes to taking pictures of others, that is, she is not so good, as opposed to me that takes awesome pictures of everything and everybody because my compositional eye is just that good.[265]

Anyway, there we were at Killer Nashville and staying up until three in the damn morning playing with your awesome app and giggling and laughing at the filters and the voice changer thing which, by the way, is simply fab. Oh, the comedy routines involving the publishing world that Linda

---

[263] Massive worldwide studies have shown beyond a shadow of a doubt that laughter is the best medicine. Which, as a polymath who puts together disparate thoughts and ideas, the author posits the theory that with the rise of seriously caring P-HWPCLDRSFCs who do not understand humor and think all laughter should be derisive in nature and not joyous comes the rise of all disease. So, buying this book is good for your health. Help your friends with their health without the use of nagging by buying them a copy of this book and other humor books by the author.

[264] If we could only find out how to promote our books, we would be over the moon.

[265] The author reminds the reader that stating a fact is not bragging. Further, please be advised that the author also knows when not to use a photo and deletes those that did not turn out well as opposed to others who think every picture they take is just freakin' usable when they are not.

and I came up with on that night[266] were beyond amazing.[267] They were so full of truths and we looked so freakin' good that we have not shared them with the world lest the world get depressed at just how bad the book business is and how awesome we are, and a rash of suicides should break out.

Do you see how caring we are, Snap Inc.?

You agree? That is awesome.

However, to get back to this letter to your company. We both thank you for first focusing your attention on the Youth Market. The person who said "Hey, let's put some filters on an app that will even out skin tone, get rid of bags under the eyes, add perfect coloring to the cheeks, make the lighting flattering to the *nth* degree, and add fake eyelashes and make the pupils dark and sparkly and large for all the young female people out there who do not need these types of helpers but to whom we can serve ads and upsell to at the same time" was a total genius.

I say this with all seriousness because for some time I had been seeing these pictures on my social media feed that showed all these parents sharing pictures of their daughters with captions like *My beautiful and caring daughter at the soup kitchen* and *My beautiful and highly intelligent daughter on a STEM track on her first day at high school* and I thought, "Crap fire. These girls are absolutely drop-dead gorgeous and stunning. Look at that skin! Look at those heart-shaped faces! Look at that: NO BAGS under the eyes." I was fairly blown away at the sophistication of these young beauties and wondered why it had taken me all of *mumble-bumble* years to get only half that gorgeous.

---

[266] And subsequent occasions when Medicinal Margarita research was involved.

[267] The voice changer thingy was as addictive as meth. Not that the author has ever used meth because she has not, but she reads studies about it, which is why she could equate coming off the use of Snap Inc.'s Snapchat Voice Changer thingy as coming down from a meth binge.

Then I got Snapchat and I began to recognize in those pictures of friends' daughters the use of the app and — this is very important — *the parents didn't know their precious beauties were using it.* The parents thought this was what their daughters really looked like and then the mothers went out and had surgeries to recapture their youth! Holy cow. It was a stampede, I tell you.

However, my dear friend and fellow crime writer novelist Linda Sands and myself use the app responsibly. For instance, we always hold back from the public our best Snapchat sessions because that is the kind thing to do. Even without Snapchat we are unbelievably awesome and cause many people to be extremely intimated by our extreme good looks and simply marvelous personalities. When we walk down the street together, traffic stops, people stare and, it never fails, a small child will eventually say "Hey, what is everybody staring at? Mommy? Daddy? Why is everybody so mesmerized and stupefied?"[268] Then the child spots us and it can't speak either.

Yes, it is true, men want to be with us[269], some men want to be us[270], and women want to hate us but have a hard time doing it because we are just so friendly and kind and helpful.[271] So, Snap Inc., while we would love to use your app

---

[268] This is totally made up. Not really. It's true.

[269] Those males who want to be with us recognize they would die and are happy to go home to their wives. So, in a way, these two crime writer novelists save marriages. They know you thank them.

[270] We have heard from two men in particular who joined together to perform in drag as "Angela and Linda: The Best Amazon Dot Com Crime Novelists". The show is HUGE in Europe and Asia.

[271] The author wants to remind certain P-HWPCLDRSFC readers that this is a book of humor and going over the top is a requirement of the genre so rein in your PC outrage and just laugh with joy. You do know how to laugh with joy, don't you?

more often in a public setting, we feel a certain responsibility [to the mental well-being of your other users, and to those on our Bacefook and other social media feeds] and do not overuse your app.

But still, the amount of money you have saved me in photographer fees[272] and surgery[273] is awesome and I thank you.

Sincerely,

Angela K. Durden

— and on behalf of Linda Sands, Durden's dear friend and fellow crime novelist, two grateful women who are living life *tempo Snapchato*

---

[272] This is true.

[273] This has been explained earlier. Are you reading the footnotes? Excellent.

Senior Skip Day

I'm sitting at my desk. The radio is on in the background for a bit of noisy company. The station is AM 750, a Cox Enterprises property. Top of the hour news begins:

- Aretha Franklin is seriously ill.[274] That is sad because that woman is the original diva that other divas could not out-diva even when they were lined up on a stage and trying their darnedest to out-diva her.

- Omarose[275] Onee Manigault-Newman is in trouble for releasing secret recordings of President Trump the day after she was fired from his administration or some such drama as that.[276]

---

[274] Aretha would die the next day, sending fans into a joyous mourning because her life was joyously celebrated even as we were sad she was gone. Please see "Goodbye, Aretha" in this book.

[275] Yes, this is the correct spelling. *Omarosa* is a nickname.

[276] The author recognizes the long game of Manigault-Newman, who saw a lucrative publishing deal in her future. From being on the Trump reality show to working for his administration after he won the election out from under the pantsuit of Ol' Hill to getting fired, the author could have told the president that Manigault-Newman would have done something like this and would hold the release of the secret recordings to time with the release of her book. This author is sure the book will be sold by the pound as excess inventory at book remainder shows, and in three years consumers will be seeing her face looking out at them from big boxes sitting in the middle of grocery and drugstore aisles.
Manigault-Newman will never earn out her advance so the advice this author gives her is to put that money in the bank and don't touch it until the accounting is done. The author of this book feels sorry for the woman as it is obvious she has spent years working on a "platform" that all publishers want their authors to have. Too bad that nobody cares anymore about "platforms", even if that platform has controversy surrounding the orangiest president with the worst combover ever that even money cannot improve.

- Somebody got fired from the FBI...and he deserved it, yes he did fer shurrrr.
- A high school senior dies on Senior Skip Day.

Graduation night. Senior Skip Day. Prom night. What happens on all three? Somebody loses. For some it's their life. For others it's their cher...errrr...I mean virginity.[277]

On this day listening to the news, this particular senior was going one hundred and six miles per hour and decided to take an exit ramp that even at regular speeds is dangerous, therefore, it is clear he either wanted to die and made this decision on purpose, or he was stupid. Either way, he is out of the gene pool and his parents and girlfriend and buddies are sad and that makes me sad.

I've got a son. I don't want him to die. He's been stupid with speed. I'm not being insensitive. But I can tell you that if my son died from speed he produced while in a vehicle under his charge, I'd never blame the car, ramp, school, the PTA, or the USA, nor start a campaign to get another law on the books that by its very nature will never protect a suicidal or stupid person and will punish everybody else.

---

[277] The author wants the reader to know that equating losing a life with losing virginity is not disrespectful to those who have lost their literal life, but that it can be equal to an actual death if the person who loses their virginity becomes with child because their life is over as they know it and futures of more than one individual will change at that time.

First, you've got the impregnated. Then you've got the impregnator who, these days, cannot get away from his responsibility; let's just hope he can handle a sports ball better than anybody else. You've got parents, siblings, grandparents, and/or other extended family members of the impregnator and the impregnated whose lives will change, too, because these days the impregnated seems to think Mama and Daddy will continue to pay the bills and watch the baby while they go on with their schooling and their partying and all that junk.

Footnote to above footnotes: The author agrees that schooling is not junk, and she asks that you think of the word *junk* as colloquial for *stuff*.

What I've learned of communication by singing at Jazz jams.

When I was in fifth grade, a man came in the classroom and said, "Who wants to play an instrument?" Those who raised their hands were told to follow him. Even though I was not clear as to which instrument he meant, I trooped down the hall to a room I had never seen before. He looked each one of us up and down, in turn making pronouncements the likes of which I had never heard.

"You. You look like you can blow hard. Take this and go sit over there." Or, "You, come here. You look like you are strong. Go stand over there next to that."

This went on and on until finally he got to me. "Hmmm," said he. "What would *you* like to play?"

As I usually do after carefully observing everything going on around me, my first thoughts were not about the answer to the question, but about the motives behind the asking.

Interesting. The man has not asked anyone else that question and yet he asks me. Why did he do that? What will he ask next? What does it mean that he gave only me a choice? I get to choose? Choose from what? I do not know all the categories of available choices. How can I ask him to list those for me? Is this a trick question? What happens if I choose the wrong one? Will he ask me to be nice to him later?[278]

I must have had a blank look on my face because the man said with a smile, "Here you go, Girl. *You* will play *viola*." He said *viola* like he loved it and it was special.

---

[278] If you have read the author's memoir, the paranoia would make perfect sense.

I had no idea what a viola was, but there I was being handed one and it must have been an important instrument because no violas had been assigned to that point. Violins and upright basses and cellos, trumpets and clarinets and trombones, but no violas. I was the only viola. I felt special and did not want to feel that way, but I held the instrument and the man got on with showing each of us how to hold our instruments and some of what these would do.

Papers were handed out. We were told to take our instrument home and get these papers signed. I could do that, and that afternoon I was schlepping a beautiful case. Paperwork was handed over to Mother. Mother read it and said, "No way. Take it back. Tell them no."

That's when I looked at the paperwork. **What?** Money is required for this? What a creep that man was. When he came into the classroom, if he had said, "Hey, who wants music lessons *and* who have parents that can pay $XX, raise your hands?" then I would not have followed that man.

Instead, he thought my family was like a lot of families. The child pitches a fit and the parents fork over the money. We did not pitch fits in our family for "stuff"[279] or heads would be knocked and knocked hard. In any case, this situation taught me three big lessons. One: Always ask questions and get details if they are not offered. Two: Questions to ask can be refined and reordered in order to elicit details. Three: Confirm those details before getting hopes up.[280]

Viola was returned with a "I didn't know it cost money!" Man sighed as I walked out of the room. His only viola player was gone.

---

[279] Or "junk" as the author's Mother and stepfather called anything the kids wanted, and they meant junk.

[280] These were the author's lessons. Your lessons may be different but no less important to you.

What has all this to do with what I have learned as a Jazz singer? Simply this: I wish I had had opportunity in fifth grade to learn how to play with others to produce a beautiful sound. If I had learned this, then much earlier in my life I could have changed how I reacted to people and situations and such as that. Let me explain.

In my family, none of the children ever asked parents or siblings for help in anything. My stepfather's idea of raising children was to divide and conquer, if not destroy. He actively studied each child and his wife, my mother, to determine their weaknesses, then he set about exploiting those. We grew up as strangers living separate lives. Keeping secrets was considered personal protection in my family.

Naturally, keeping secrets precludes working together, because working together requires talking and those who keep secrets do not talk about anything of merit. Oh, we could talk Monopoly and Rummy and Slap Jack, but projects and skills were so rarely discussed that we were all left to learn on our own. The assigning and doing of chores was not for the smooth running of a household, but perfect opportunities for massive and sadistic punishment if left undone or improperly executed.

But if I had only learned in fifth grade what it really meant to work together, maybe I could have taken those lessons home and quietly deployed them and maybe our lives would have been better.[281]

But I didn't, and it wasn't until after my divorce and music woke up in my head with a vengeance hell-bent on killing me if I ignored it, and I started writing songs and then started singing in public, yes, only then did I begin to understand how the parts of a band or orchestra worked together. Before that, I could rarely differentiate between the individual elements and only heard what was to me a

---

[281] The author realizes this is wishful thinking on her part, but she has indulged in it anyway.

cacophony of sound. Even being up close and personal to a stage full of towering talent, I could not truly break the sounds apart of, say, three different horns or two different guitars. Part of that has to do with ear training, and I'm working on that. However, it wasn't until I started singing at Jazz jams that I began to truly understand the nature of communication and the power it has for good and evil.

One can watch the interplay between the players on the stage all day long but getting up on that stage and taking part is a whole 'nother[282] matter.

I went to Jazz jams for six years during which time, week after week, I made a study of what happened on the stage. Often many of the players were the same, but as is the nature of a Jazz jam, whoever shows up is called up. Some nights the jam *cooked* all evening and the audience went away sated. Other nights the phrase *too many cooks spoil the broth* could have totally described what came from the stage. What was the difference between the two outputs?

Communication.

You see, some folks just like to talk; they will not share the conversation. They dominate it. We've all known folks like that. No matter how witty or smart or entertaining their words or delivery, they just plain will not allow anybody to get a word in edgeways and if somebody finally does get a word in, they will roll over that person like one of those big machines that roll over dirt to pack it down into a submissive homogenous pile. Eventually, the listener realizes they are not valued for their input. What happens then?

The one who is shut down becomes uncooperative with the one who has diarrhea of the mouth. The former gets busy with other things and tunes out the latter until the latter

---

[282] Short for a cross between another or other. Used in the South as a standalone word and usually said as "nuther" with no apostrophe implied.

becomes one hand clapping in the woods.[283] Nobody is having any fun and everybody looks bad.

Then there are those who are afraid of conversation. Some run from it. In all cases, everybody is uncomfortable and antsy.

It is no different with the singers and the players on the stage at Jazz jams — with the added participation of the audience. In this complicated conversation between singers, players, and audience, the audience is the most important because it is the audience that applauds the effort and pays the bills. If only hearing themselves were the most important aspects to players and singers, they could've stayed home and jammed in their living rooms. But they don't stay home because they need the audience. Maybe they don't admit it to themselves, but they do. Yet some players and singers forget the audience's role and begin to think stage time is all about them, their needs, their desires.

That's when you get the stage hog. The musician that closes his eyes and goes into the longest, ramblingest, fastest doo-wop-ditty, let's-lose-the-audience solo ever[284] and won't quit until he's good and ready, or somebody taps him on the shoulder and yanks him offstage.

Or the singer who insists on doing a standard their way but doesn't bring a lead sheet for the musicians, doesn't know their proper key[285] to sing in, forgets the words or the form, and doesn't know when to give the band their solo time.

---

[283] Yes, the author is aware she mixed her metaphors, but language is a living, breathing thing and she likes to give it its head every now and then.

[284] An old Jazz cat the author knows calls that "jerk-off music". The author knows that is a crude term, but it gets the point across that it is a solo endeavor and the only one having any fun is the soloist.

[285] Meaning the best key for the singer.

Nobody looks good in this scenario either. In both cases, the audience is usually not happy.

Which means, conversation is over, attention is diverted.

I saw all this from the audience but did not understand the pressures on the stage until I got up there. Yes, I made mistakes, but I didn't make the same one twice.

My first time sitting in at a Jazz jam was at one run by Dr. Gordon Vernick of Georgia State University, which he holds at Red Light Café in Midtown Atlanta on Amsterdam Avenue every Wednesday evening from nine until midnight — or until the cats stop swinging. I played piano and sang an original tune the band had never heard before called "Jonesin' For Ya". Not only that, the song was 12-bar blues in B minor in 5/4 time.[286]

Applause was awesome. The drummer loved the tune and loved playing a 5/4 song that wasn't Dave Brubeck's "Take Five". I exited the stage and went to my seat looking on the outside as if I was a cool hepcat. But sipping wine, I attempted to gain control of my racing heart. Then the audience began to reach out to me in a way I had not experienced before: Individually. Quietly, folks came by my seat or stopped me as I moved about the venue. They told me what my song meant to them and how much they enjoyed it. And would I, pretty please, bring some more original tunes for them to hear? Of course, I answered, yes indeed.

I thanked each for taking the time to come up and tell me these things. It meant a lot and let me know I was on the right track as a songwriter, composer, and — dare I write it out loud? — a singer.

---

[286] The author admits this was a bold move on her part and she thanks the drummer (Che Marshall, who absolutely nailed the timing and brought his artistry to it), the bass player (who was a new fellow himself and scared but dang if he didn't hang in there), and Dr. Gordon Vernick for having the guts to step outside his comfort zone and let her up on his Classic Jazz stage. Gordon even did a trumpet solo on the song, so yay for the author/songwriter/singer.

But that was my first time. And I knew I didn't have the piano chops to hold my own on most of my songs, much less a standard. I definitely couldn't fake my way on the piano through any standard tune played at a Jazz jam. Accepting my limitations, I did not force my way up on the stage to make a mockery of the process or a mess of the performance, instead limiting myself to songs I had that were built around patterns they all knew, such as 12-bar blues. That way, the pianist could do all his fancy stuff with the keys and look good and take solos, as could the rest of the band, and I could fit in my lyrics when it was my turn.

See? Everybody could look good. Still, even that was limiting to me as a songwriter and performer. Was I to be known as the one-trick pony who could only do 12-bar blues songs? No. I had many other melodies and feels, some upbeat, some ballads, some funny, some sad. Each called for something different.

Here is where I ran into another of my conversational limitations. How could I let the band know what to do and when to do it? In other words, how does one write a lead sheet? I could write lead sheets for the 12-bar tunes with no problem, but those were simple, following a predetermined pattern and, besides, the band already knew that form. But what happens when you have massive chord changes and the verse has one bar length and the chorus has another bar length and there are timing changes?

I was lost and could not seem to find any good advice on the subject. Come to find out, one reason I could not find any good advice on the subject is because each musician in each performance situation has different requirements for what they need for tunes they do not know or know well. These requirements were all mysterious to me. While I spoke their language enough[287], I was not fluent in the underpinnings of

---

[287] The author speaks "music" about as well as she habla espanol. That is to say, she might think she was asking where the bathroom was but would actually be telling someone to go milk a cow.

their conversational flow. What was I to do? I was at an artistic standstill.

That's when I met Alan Dynin. I had seen Alan flitting through the Jazz jams over the years, and for some reason did not know what he did. Alan is a pianist. And not just a run-of-the-mill one, either. But I didn't know that when I met him. We were introduced, and he said, "I understand you are a songwriter. Can I hear some of your songs?"

We made an appointment. He came over to my condo. He asked me to sit at the piano and play and sing. I did. I was barely started when he said, "Ummm…excuse me. Can I…sit at the…piano? I've got an idea."

Sure. We changed places. He looked at my lead sheet and he said, "Okay. Start singing how you want this song to go."

And lightning struck. Almost two hours later we are looking at each other like "What the *hayle* just happened?"[288]

It seemed as if Alan and I were able to have perfectly remarkable musical conversations. But would lightning strike twice? Three months followed in which we got together once or twice a week and went through the same process…and lightning did strike again and has not stopped striking.[289]

Now, the big question was: Could we duplicate on stage what we were doing in my rehearsal room?

We stepped out with another easy tune (again a 12-bar), but this time Alan was on the keys and it was he who communicated with the band. All I had to do was sing. But the sound system had a glitch (monitors weren't working)

[288] Alan is from Ohio, so he would not say *hayle* as that is totally Southern and he is sort of an existentialist and actually said, "Wow! Let's do this tomorrow?"

[289] Alan is a genius when it comes to helping with chord choice and timing and even where to go in a melody the author would never have thought about, thus bringing a subtle wit or a smart riposte to the conversation as they "trade fours".

and I couldn't hear the piano. Plus, an enthusiastic and very tall trumpet player was blowing smack in my right ear so that I couldn't hear myself. I watched Alan's hands for the pattern to know where he was and let him nod at me when it was time for me to come back in after the solos.

I decided to go for broke and sang it as if it was a damn Rock song which, as everybody knows, is not a Jazz song. The audience was happy[290], the band had a ball (they do like to crank it up every now and then), but I was disappointed in my performance and — this part is key — my lack of preparation for just such glitches.

I should have given thought to how to use the microphone when I couldn't hear myself. After listening to my whine about my self-disappointment, Alan helped me with knowing how to handle that in future.

As of this writing, it has now been almost two years since Alan and I formed a duo. We call it AD² (AD Squared) since both of our names begin with A and D. We've done several shows as a duo and are regulars at jams in the city. We sing many evenings at Venkman's on Tuesday at the Joe Gransden Jazz Jam, Wednesday at Gordon's as previously mentioned, occasionally at the Churchill Grounds Pop Up Jazz Jam, and a few other places every now and then.

Audiences are very happy with what we bring to the conversation and let us know. But what happens if Alan cannot be there to interpret between me and the band? This is where I have had to work on further conversational elements. I study some standards and learn the key in which I can sing them, and practice how to sing in various styles. For instance, one night when Alan couldn't make it, I told Joe Gransden I could sing "The Days of Wine and Roses" in D. How did I want to do it, he asked. I said *tempo rubato* to begin, then move into ballad style. Joe said, "Can you swing after that?"

---

[290] One woman even forgot herself and jumped up clapping and screaming in happiness. That is not a typical Jazz audience conversation style.

"Hell, yeah!" came back my swift response. I could say "Hell, yeah!" because I had studied what it meant *to swing*.

I did that song in three different styles that evening. See? Joe had a conversation with me. But what if I had been up on the stage and had never given thought to what "swinging it" means? Ah, now Joe would have had a harder time because, you see, in his jam, Joe is most responsible for keeping the conversation going with the audience, who is…what?

That's right! Paying the bills.

So, Joe knows the value of keeping an audience happy with what they hear and hungry enough to come back for more. Anybody on his stage who does not join in properly to the conversation is not tolerated for long. Three times hogging the conversation and they are out and must work their way back into good graces.

I knew one man, a Rock drummer, who did not know the difference between Rock drumming and Jazz drumming. One evening he was hogging the conversation the whole time he was one the stage and didn't even know it. Not only could nobody get a note in edgewise, the singers were drowned out, and the timing was off.

The man was very nice. He was a great Rock drummer. Still is nice. Still is a great drummer. Even though the audience was not happy during his time up there, they didn't know why. About a month later I saw the man and he told me that somebody (he never said who) had told him he had stomped his way through the set that night and told him he should get with Jazz drummers to find out how to change. He did and the next time he got up, he had learned how to converse! As some Jazz cats say, "It's a beautiful thing."

I've had to train my ear and look for signs given when I'm on stage, even if those signs are given by somebody I've never played with before. I've learned when to listen, when to invite a response, and when to butt in and redirect when necessary. It's been a great learning experience of which I could say so much more, but I think you get the drift.

You need to understand one other hugely important thing about my experience. For most of my life[291] communication was a weapon used to destroy or it wasn't done at all. I learned never to ask questions, to figure things out for myself, or attempt to do everything alone. That meant I came to a lot of incorrect conclusions.

It has been such a joy to be on stage with, and be tolerated if not accepted by, these very talented people who have been so giving with their knowledge and of whom I can ask a question or run a theory by. And it is nice to be missed when life impedes and I can't make it out as often.

After I wrote the above paragraph, it was time to leave to go sing again and, with this essay in mind, I arrived at the Joe Gransden Jazz Jam at Venkman's. A couple of things happened that evening as I was waiting on Alan to arrive. Joe cupped his ear and I heard him say from the stage, "What?... Angela Durden?...Yes, she will be singing tonight. When?... When her piano player gets here." I was talking to some friends and looked over at the area where Joe was looking. I didn't see anybody I knew. Then about an hour or so later I was standing near the stage steps when a woman said, "Excuse me." I walked over to her. I'd never seen her before. She said, "You are my most favorite singer ever."[292]

Well, if such a pronouncement doesn't put pressure on a gal, then I just don't know what does. To release that pressure, I remembered that I am there for the audience and the audience is not there for me. That helped a lot.

---

[291] You can read all about that in *Twinkle, a memoir*. You will cry, but it ends hopeful. After all, you can see how great the author turned out, right?

[292] You might be thinking, "Angela, you sure are bragging." However, as you know, it isn't bragging if it is a fact. Besides, in this the author is simply trying to tell the story of communication at a Jazz jam that had she not been singing there she would not have ever had. So, just go with the flow and realize that there is nothing you can do or say that she has not done or said to herself to keep her ego in check.

Speaking of lightning striking. While we, standing on terra firma, can see lightning striking *out of the blue*, that does not mean conditions for it do not exist. Lightning never happens unless a condition exists favorable to its forming. The same thing happened to me at a Jazz jam at Red Light Café on one of those Wednesday nights. The *atmospheric conditions* favorable for this Jazz Lightning Strike were the following:

- Very small crowd
- Fewer-than-normal horn players
- No upright bass player
- Marlon Patton on drums
- Only three singers showed up
- This was piano player Kevin Bales' third gig of the day and he was running fast on adrenaline.

The previous week, I had the pleasure of singing "Autumn Leaves" on another stage with Kevin Bales and his grand piano, along with Craig "Shawboxx" Shaw on bass, Dave Potter on drums, and even Joe Gransden on horns. It was a beautiful thing. But this week, Marlon and Kevin were in a state of mind on that stage that can only be described as experimental, or maybe improvisational to the nth degree.

Gordon Vernick calls me up to sing. We're going to do "Autumn Leaves" again, but I'd been soaking up those improvisational vibes and went straight up to Kevin, who looked at me through bleary eyes and a smile, and said, "Bales. You listen to me and you listen to me good."

He nodded.

"The first time through, you follow *me.* You hear me?"

"Oh, yes. Of course. Absolutely."

"But, Bales. The next time…honey, I want you to surprise me."

Bales' eyes went wide and his smile went wicked. He hooted and said, "Aren't you afraid I'll scare you?"

"You can't scare me, Kevin. Throw everything you got at me."

Well, I believe Marlon overheard that conversation and so did the guitar player because we went through "Autumn Leaves" once and the audience was happy. It sounded nice and slow and emotional. Then we went through it again, but this time Bales and Marlon were flirting musically just a little bit and I flirted back vocally to match. Again, the audience was sitting up a little straighter because they had not heard me sing like that before.

We get through that one and *BOOM!* Thunder began to rumble and lightning began to strike and the audience began running for cover — a metaphorical running. The audience got involved too, especially this one man who was whistling long and low and saying things like "oooo, Mama, YES!" when he liked certain things I did. Let me tell you, when a man whistles like that, oh yeah, Mama likee. Kevin said later we were on the stage for forty minutes. That was one long lightning strike…and was nothing like I'd ever experienced before by way of a musical conversation.

Suffice it to say, it was better than sex.

Here's how it went:

Using the form and chords of "Autumn Leaves", Bales played within that form in a psychedelic fashion. Marlon followed suit. And so did I. It was my job as a singer, in this instance, to see where Bales was going. Though his patterns changed constantly, he would repeat a pattern enough that I could jump in vocally and match him, or the drummer, or the two horn players (one was Matt Miller) as they riffed.

Since it was my job to place the words from the song, I'd quickly scan the song lyrics in my mind to find which one word or two- or three-word phrase would fit the moment and plug those in. Sometimes it wouldn't be a word itself but part of the sound of a word that could be held long, rise and fall with the scale, and/or be repeated over and over in a mantra.

Bales, catching on to what I was doing, listened and could tell just when I was finishing my *sentence* and off we'd go to another part of our *conversation*.

That was one high-quality conversation that struck *out of the blue,* but only because the conditions were right for it, we all brought something to the table, and we were prepared to use what others brought, too. See? A conversation.

This learning I've been doing at the Jazz jams has also helped me in my non-music life. Instead of barreling through a problem without looking right or left, I'm more apt to look around at who I might know and ask for help. Instead of flinching in fear when someone sees my need and volunteers help, I'm more amenable to accepting them instead of pushing away as if they were evil.

Healing from an abusive background is itself a journey. I've been on that journey for many years and thought I was doing okay. But once I got in with the musicians on the Jazz jam stages is when I found out my journey was not over.

This is what I've learned of communication at Jazz jams. Funny the thing we need that God provides when we don't even know it ourselves. Music is from God. It is throughout the universe. It lives in the wind. It sings to us from the rustle of the leaves. It laments with us from railroad tracks. It soothes and invigorates. And when we can make music together, we learn to put up with foibles and weaknesses, not suffer fools, and we learn to take the lead when it is our turn.

Inspirational Quotes

Do an online search for "inspirational quotes" and you will see a snapshot of our divisive world. There are few inspirational quotes that apply to all humans, but you will find inspirational quotes for:

- Males
- Females
- Old people
- Young people
- Females who want to be empowered
- Females who are bumping up against the glass ceiling
- Females in the C-Suite who are hated by women bumping up against the glass ceiling
- Males in the C-Suite
- Males who want to be in the C-Suite but will never get there and cannot blame it on a glass ceiling
- Males who like males
- Females who like females
- Males who like females
- Males who like females but can't get any attention from one
- Females who like males
- Females who like males but can't get any attention from one
- Leaders
- Followers[293]

---

[293] Just kidding. In the current politically correct dystopia, there are no followers because everybody is a leader.

- Educators[294]
- Entrepreneurs
- Business owners
- Employees
- Children
- Those with children
- Those without children
- Those with children who wish they didn't have children
- Those with no children who wish they had children
- Those with children who can't get them to do chores
- Those whose children are perfect
- Those who have nothing inspirational to say to their children and are looking for something motivational to say
- Those who need inspirational quotes to get them through the week
- Acolytes and sycophants of politicians
- Body tattoos
- Veterans of every war
- Hippies against every war
- Aging female bra-burners
- Any who seek to be authentic
- Wrestlers, Amateur
- Wrestlers, WWE
- Wrestlers, Sumo

---

[294] Not teachers.

- Wrestlers, in the bed
- Players of every sport
- Travelers (non-Gypsy)
- Travelers (Gypsy)
- Takers of staycations
- Writers (Frustrated[295])
- Writers, Other (See above)
- Risks (Taking)
- Risks (Managing)
- Hearts (Broken)
- Hearts (In love)
- Hearts (Raw and Broken)

The list goes on, but I've made my point.

What is the point?

Oh, yes. The point is that these segmented quotations do not pull us together. They divide us. For instance, there is this quote from Advance Auto Parts that says: "It is time to change your oil. Think ahead. Think Advance." If this doesn't divide the populace, then I don't know what does. You see, you got your owners of cars that use oil and owners of cars that are electric.

Divisive!

How about this one: "Always do your best. What you plant today, you will harvest tomorrow." Dividing up the world into gardeners and non-gardeners as if non-gardeners cannot do their best.

Divisive!

---

[295] Meaning "not traditionally published so that millionaire celebrity status is reached".

And this one: "You can't cross the sea by merely standing and staring at the water." What about those who cannot stand? Or see? Or swim? Or afford a big ol' boat?

Divisive!

And what about this one from the Dalai Lama which is confusing: "Be kind whenever possible. It is always possible." Well, hello Dalai. Who died and said you were wise? The very word "whenever" implies there will be times it is not possible. Didn't Shakespeare teach us nothing with his equal treatment of both sides of the motivation when he wrote *"to be or not to be"*? In any case, I dare Dalai not to give the "feather"[296] to drivers who move to the South from the North and then proceed to honk exactly 0.001274 seconds after the light turns green. Therefore, Dalai saying "it is always possible" flies in the very face of reality. It is only natural that when a Damn Yankee honks exactly 0.001274 seconds after the light turns green, one's blood boils at those impertinent carpetbaggers. We here in the South are not used to such habitual impatience and do not take it lightly when some so-and-so proceeds to act like the road exists for his sole use, therefore no amount of inspirational quotes will have any victory in this instance, even if that inspirational quote is on a bumper sticker and says *Honk if you love Jesus.*

It's a good thing chemist Norm Larsen, inventor of WD-40 in 1958, didn't listen to Julie Andrews when she said "Perseverance is failing nineteen times and succeeding the twentieth."

"No bird soars too high if he soars with his own wings." Well what other wings would he use? And what has that got to do with me? Just to fill this out, though, this quote was written by one William Blake, a man his contemporaries called a nutcase but was nevertheless lauded as a visionary and a prophet after he died, who obviously went against

---

[296] "To give the feather" is to hold up Pinky instead of Tall Man. It is a polite way to give your opinion to someone who doesn't deserve a whole bird.

dictators, Socialists, and Communists because otherwise he would've said, "If a bird wants to soar too high, he must soar with state-approved wings for state-approved reasons and to state-approved heights, but only after filling out the proper forms, paying a fee for permission to soar, and then getting that permission when we good and damn well feel like giving it to you."

Then there is this brilliant piece of flummery: "Act is if what you do makes a difference. It does." Well, duh. The way this is written would inspire a dictator and terrorist. Imagine a dictator. Go ahead. Close your eyes. Imagine a dictator. Any dictator will do. Now, imagine that quote on a poster hanging on the wall behind their desk.

It ain't pretty, is it?

The more accurate inspirational quote would be: "Act as if what you do makes a difference for the better." See? Much more inspirational in a good way.

Another fellow said: "If you don't like how things are, then change it. You aren't a tree." Never mind that *things* is plural and *it* is singular. That mistake is driving me crazy, of course, but think about this: You. Aren't. A. Tree.

As if a tree just stands there and accepts its fate.

No.

Trees are a vital part of keeping the air filtered (leaves) and breaking up the soil (roots) and providing housing (for birds and squirrels) and holding stands (for hunters) — and that is just the beginning of what trees do. See? Trees are helpful and kind. Some even sacrifice themselves so humans can have planks, beams, slats, and staves with which to build.

"You aren't a tree." Sheesh. How uninspiring.

But I honestly did not know what to do with this inspirational quote. Yes, it was called an "inspirational" quote and, for the life of me, I cannot figure out why:

"I'm thrilled to continue my partnership with U by Kotex for Generation Know while helping to empower girls. I've always been a motivational resource for my younger sisters and hope I can positively impact and inspire other young girls too."

Khloe Kardashian said this. I'm not even going to try to explain Khloe Kardashian other than to say at the time of this writing she is famous for being famous. Her father was one of O.J. Simpson's Dream Team defense attorneys in the famous murder trial. Her stepfather was Olympian Bruce Jenner, who lost his ever-loving mind when he was in his late fifties or early sixties and set the Liberal world atwitter upon becoming a "woman". Listen, by *becoming a woman* I do not mean Bruce actually became a woman because he didn't. He changed his name to Caitlyn, got a boob job, wore dresses, heels, and cosmetics, and started crying on TV, but did not have his whangdoodle changed into a hoo-hah.

I'm off topic, but am I really? I don't think so. In any case, you are waiting to be inspired in a succinct, pithy, and to-the-point fashion. I can't leave you hanging. I promise I won't leave you hanging. So you can take to heart today the inspirational and highly original quote[297] on the following page. Make it your own.

---

[297] The author admits she wrote the inspirational quote in one of her deep darknesses of despair. It was originally a 2018 Bacefook post penned in the early morning hours when the dark is dismal, the cold is callous, and her soul was sad.

We may see the mountain's peak and
marvel at its grandeur, but it is held up
strong by all the
unseen boulders beneath it.[298]
Angela K. Durden — *circa 2018.*
Actually it was 2018. December to be more precise.

---

[298] This brilliant quote ended up going around the world through the magic
of the corporate algorithmic approval process. By "around the world"
the author does not mean seen by everybody, but that the post merely
went to a Bacefook Post Processing Farm where it languished for seven
days as the Central Politburo of the Communist Party of China, a
Bacefook subsidiary, decided whether or not its coolies (neither slaves
or free) could be allowed to process such a post. The approval died in
committee when it eventually voted en bloc a big fat "No, it cannot be
shown publicly on Bacefook".

As stated in an official position paper entered into the record, which said in
summary, "Only *peaks* should be honored as strong and necessary.
Boulders are of no consequence and exist only to serve *peaks*. *Peaks* do
not want *boulders* to get the big head."

Two conversations in hyperreality, or Karma is a bitch.

What do the lead singer for Paul Revere and the Raiders (one believes he is named Mark Lindsay) and the lead singer for The Four Seasons (one knows he is Frankie Valli) have in common?

Neither know how to have a productive and good conversation with an audience.

Mark was taught a lesson in that by an audience of close to 5000 and Frankie was rescued from an avalanche of 49,000 boos by Peter Noone. What you will read are not second-hand accounts that could be called urban legends which everybody believes are true but are not. You know, like the giant crocodile that lives in the New York City sewage system or the Loch Ness monster around which an entire area has built a tourist attraction.

Yes, I saw both of these men on stage myself, firsthand, and am telling these stories to you now. One day they will not be believed because there will be those who will say such large events never happened or that crowds of that size would never rise up against the Cult of Personality, but I'm here to tell you these things happened. I swear and affirm that these declarations in this essay are not in any way exaggerated.

On marketing materials for a summer concert at Atlanta-Fulton County Stadium (replaced by The Ted), Frankie Valli was listed as the headliner. Now, the headliner being on a lineup is supposed to guarantee the show has a fighting chance of making a profit...or at least breaking even. Valli was that guarantee. Peter Noone, formerly of Herman's Hermits and no slouch when it came to attracting an audience, was the host of the show. Therefore, technically, there were two headliners. Slam-dunk profit. Look, when you can keep almost 50,000 people engaged in between the acts, get those acts on and off the stage with no time wasted but not seem hurried, then Peter Noone was the best host ever. The man knows how to converse with a crowd and we loved us some Peter Noone.

The show was rocking along nicely and everybody was having them a high old time, but where was Frankie Valli? He was waiting for the entire stage to be changed out so that *his* band and *his* lights and *his* setup could be made ready for him. It took forever. Then Valli came out and we're thinking *Alright!*, but no. He was not happy about something, so, in front of almost 50,000 people, unhappy Valli started with the swaggering pushiness and disrespect of musicians, lighting people, and the audience. So the roadies just got slower. I did not blame them.

But the boos started. Just a few here and there. Until finally the whole place was booing and who stepped into the fray? None other than Peter Noone, who had been off the stage — no proof, but probably at the executive order of Valli. The day was saved, along with the show, when Valli was rescued from an avalanche of boos by Peter. When Valli walked out on stage, the audience got quiet and stared as the man acted like a made Mafia gangster. You could tell he didn't want to be there. And people started leaving.

But, boy oh boy, that Peter Noone. Amazing. With his sheer niceness he got their attention away from the drama and stopped the exodus.

The second event happened a few years later at an outdoor venue next to a river in Roswell, Georgia. I forget the first couple of acts, but they didn't inspire the audience too much even if they were so-called mid-level *name* acts. To fill the void while the stage was being changed out for the headliner act — Paul Revere and the Raiders — two local guys, just filling the time, got up on the stage with a keyboard, guitar, and two mics and proceeded to blow the socks off the audience.

We were screaming and dancing and laughing and when these two guys launched into Pink Floyd's "The Wall", well the audience went effing[299] nuts. So far so good…except…

Except the stage got set up and the lead singer (I hear his name is Mark Lindsay) for Paul Revere and the Raiders was tapping his foot at Stage Left where everybody could see him. He kept waving at the two guys, making a rotating gesture with his two hands that meant *wrap it up*. Well, the two guys didn't know what to do because the audience was expecting the full song of "The Wall" to be sung and they wanted to finish it. These two fellows were having a mighty fine two-way conversation with the audience and nothing would get in the way. So the more the lead singer showed his ass with his bullying ways, the more insistent became the 5000 members of the audience that he needed to shut the hell up and let the local boys finish their song.

Nobody was going to deprive these people of this. Nobody. Finally, the bewigged lead singer simply tapped his foot and the guys finished to a huge, roaring, whistle-filled standing ovation. They were bemused, but thankful. And we loved them.

Onto the stage strode the Raiders with "Paul Revere", when — oh, the audience was tickled pink and furious that all their gear had glitches. Karma and the old bitch thing struck handily. Something wasn't working right and who had to apologize to the audience for it? Yeah. Ol' "Paul" hisself, but even in that he couldn't be nice and he was ripping into the sound guys and roadies and…it wasn't pretty. The more he was unkind, the unhappier the audience got.

We listened to his show and, yes, they did a fine job, and the jokes were good, but we just were not feeling it and watches were looked at. Then when "Paul" complained they might miss their plane, we didn't care anymore.

---

[299] Effing is polite talk for…well, if you don't know, look it up.

How not to rob a convenience store.

I was twenty and the month previously had been robbed at gunpoint during a forty-five-minute secret hostage-taking event at the convenience store I worked at. The event was secret because the customers did not know they were hostages, but I did. It went like this. The bad guy said if I did anything stupid they would die. Otherwise I was to continue checking them out and getting their money. And we sure got busy real fast what with everybody buying beer for their Christmas parties. Finally all the customers/hostages were safely gone, thanks to my keeping my head about me. Then the guy takes the gun out and says for me to go in the back room to get tied up and I said no and he said *what?* and I said no and he could kill me right there where folks could see but I wasn't going. So he took the bagged-up money and left.

That was a successful robbery as he did not get caught. But, like I said, that was the previous month. So, there I am a month later, all alone, minding my own business, sitting on a stool behind the counter waiting on customers to come in when a car whips into the parking lot and a man jumps out of the back seat and comes running in all excited. He whips a gun out of his pocket and points it at my heart and says "Don't move or I'll kill you. Give me the money." I said, "Do you want the money or do you want me not to move?" He thought for a moment and said, "Give me the money." I said, "Can I move now?" He said I could and I said please point the gun somewhere else and he did and I took the money out of the register and put it in a bag and he grabbed the bag and out the door he went into the back seat, whereupon he threw the bag of money in first and money went flying everywhere and the getaway driver and his girlfriend were screaming and the driver put the pedal to the metal and went right on out into the main drag in front of the store and promptly t-boned a patrol car which was just driving down the street unknowing of the robbery.

This is how not to rob a convenience store.

Fast forward about twenty years and I am in a mall when I hear gunshots. Bam! Bam-Bam! Bam-Bam! Bam-Bam! Bam-Bam! Running past me are the bad guys. I said to myself, "Oh, dear. This looks just like what happened to me." I watched the robbers jump into the car. They were all screaming at the getaway driver, who promptly put the pedal to the metal and t-boned a telephone pole[300] right in front of a patrol car.

Seems the guy that robbed my store did not circulate his story far or wide enough so that the lesson was shared. Bad guys are so selfish.

---

[300] The pole fell onto the car and it took a while for the ambulance to extricate one of the robbers, who had taken a bullet from the jewelry store owner.

Pansexual: The New Slut?

So there I was. Minding my own business at 6:15 in the morning. Perusing the MSN headlines for some hard news when what did I spy with my little eye but the hardest hard news headline of all. Yes, there for all to see in all its earth-shaking seriousness was "I am Pansexual: And Here Is What I Want YOU to Know".

Nineteen-year-old Flickr.com[301] user Hannah Pegg, as her picture caption identifies her, wrote a serious article that said things like the following:

- She never knew that she could be anything more than a lesbian.
- Thus, she continued to identify as a lesbian.
- She took a queer studies class.
- That made her stop and look her "sexuality dead in the face".[302]
- She was stumped.[303]
- She did some *necessary Google searching*[304] and found a list of sexual orientations.

---

[301] Flickr was owned by Yahoo!, but they sold it in May 2018 for a boatload of money because they were desperate for some cash flow. They are also not servicing their email accounts anymore and that has left AT&T up a digital crap creek without a bucket to collect crawdaddies.

[302] This is a direct quote.

[303] This is an old term and the author of this essay wonders where the young girl heard it. Probably not at school; therefore, it is possible she heard it from her grandmother.

[304] The author admits to doing her own Google searching from time to time but has never once described it as necessary and finds this term much more interesting than the whole of the article about this girl's search for her sexual/human orientation.

- She finally landed on pansexual.
- Something just seemed to fall into place. There was finally a word to explain how she'd been feeling.

The girl then proceeded to take one thousand and fifty words to make the following points:

- Pansexuality is complicated.
- It is different from person to person and cannot be explained.
- What Freud said about it wasn't what it really is.
- Pansexuality is fluid and Freud only understood it a little bit, but not really.
- It encompasses all people, regardless of their gender identity.
- As a pansexual, her love for all people knows no bounds.[305]
- Pansexuals are turned on by connections.[306]
- Pansexuals' sexual activity depends on the type of person they are.
- The girl is against shaming people for "getting around".[307]

Little Hannah asks the tough questions and supplies the answers, too.

- Q: Pansexual or bisexual?
  A: Depends.
- Q: Where does bisexuality end and pansexual begin?

---

[305] Was Jesus pansexual? Or Mother Teresa?

[306] Ah, got it. Pansexual is the new slut. So if that is true, WWJD?

[307] Which means she has probably been shamed for "getting around" which shaming most likely came from her mother and the girl has Mommy Issues so is making a passive-aggressive comment on her in print for all to see.

A: Depends.
- Q: What is the gender binary?
  A: It's a limiting social construct based on narrow assumptions.
- Q: What are narrow assumptions?
  A: Depends.
- Q: Is the current LGBTQ community limiting and narrow?
  A: Yes.
- Q: Is pansexuality *just another label*?
  A: Not sure, but it's important to label the feeling, so it just depends.
- Q: Why do so many people not know about pansexuality?
  A: Public schools and institutions of higher learning with their heteronormative health classes are all to blame because the LGBTQ+1-friendly community is not allowed to put the curriculum into schools and get all weird about using words other than boy and girl, woman and man, male and female, or papas and mamas.[308]
- Q: What has her first year as a pansexual been like?
  A: Awesome.
- Q: What does her future as a pansexual look like?
  A: Not sure. It depends.

In any case, we learn in this hard news story that Little Hannah feels so much better now that she can "make connections" with everybody. She admits that the narrow label her parents tried to put on her (that is, girl who will like boys and thus give them grandchildren inside the marriage union) was limiting to her heart that was "just a little too

---

[308] You will note how the author changed up the order of the sets of heteronormal labels, in half the instances listing females first and in the other half listing the males first. She did this because she wanted to be accused of being fair and balanced.

big"[309] for their confining thinking. Here is the last paragraph of this hard news story, quoted **verbatim** in all its simplices:

> "I'm not sure what's in store for me, however, I know now that I'm not alone or 'confused'. In fact, I'm the furthest thing from confused. I didn't need some big revelation to tell me...I was pansexual.[310] ***All it really took was some reflection and a Google search."*** [Bold italics added.]

"All it really took" to find out what she was and not be confused about it "was some reflection and a Google search"?[311] Really?

Which, of course, brings us to the next big question that must be asked:

What does one buy a pansexual for Valentine's Day?

---

[309] Again the author notes this is a direct quote.

[310] No, but she did need a roommate to listen to her for a year and "hours and hours and hours" as she tried to figure it out which, given the next statement she made, made...

[311] ...the author reel.

"Ghosted"[312]

You say you love me.
I say I love you, too.
I kiss you, you say,
Yabba dabba doo.
Yes, things they are
going along so very
nicely.

Then all my friends say
Sorry for your loss.
I cry and I cry for the
man I love the most.
Yes, I've
been
ghosted.

Did you die?
Are you a spy?
Are you in hiding
waiting to testify?
Will you write across the sky a
definitive goodbye?
I must admit
I am
mystified.

---

[312] Lyrics reprinted with permission of Angela K. Durden.

Because…

You said you loved me.
I said, I loved you, too.
I kissed you, you said,
Yabba dabba doo.
Yes, things they were
going along so very
nicely.

Now all my friends say,
Sorry for your loss.
I cry and I cry and I cry and I cry for the
man I love the most.
Yes, I've
been
ghosted.

A profligate morning.

I am such a thrifty gal that I use a tea bag so long that by the time the decision is made to throw it away, all I'm drinking is boiled water. I've got pieces of underwear that go back twenty-plus years and that, even now as raggedy as they are, I still proudly wear. For a new pair of panties to enter my drawers[313], well, the situation must be extraordinary. Take, for instance, the time I went to visit my really good friend and fellow crime writer Linda Sands when she was at one her many extraordinary palaces[314] on the Emerald Coast, just a stone's throw from a white beach with gentle lapping surf and fish doing belly flops on the surface.[315]

Anyway, there I was, having just arrived and was unpacking when Linda came running down four flights of stairs[316] screaming, "Angela, are you alright? What's wrong?" Whereupon coming to a skidding stop in my bedroom, she saw me doubled over the suitcase, one arm stretched high to the sky and crying, "Jesus, help me. JuhEEEsuzz, please give me strength."

Linda, kind-hearted soul and a lover of Jesus herself that she is, patted me on the back and begged me to tell her what was wrong so she could pray for me because, said Linda,

---

[313] The author admits she can be quite the accidental punster.

[314] The author wants the reader to know that she is not so shallow as to have chosen Linda Sands as her friend based on what her houses look like, the many and varied locations they are in, the geegaws with which she populates those houses, or the nearness of a beach.

[315] In other words, a thoroughly useless beach, but you see how the author keeps Linda as a friend anyway, thus proving the author is not shallow.

[316] That's right. She sleeps in the tower where the wind blows through curtains of white lacy silk while I, her really good friend, am relegated to the dark basement, but I do not hold that against her.

"The prayer of the righteous has much power." Then she got to thinking and said, "So, maybe my prayers won't work so much, but I have faith that maybe God will hear me on your behalf." After much gasping and heaving emotionally[317], I managed to squeak out, "No. Panties!"

"No panties. I don't understand," said Linda, who by now was confused by her usually patient and strong friend with a straight back and a smile on her face even as she shoots her Smith & Wesson Bodyguard with .380 hollow-points while sneering the wishful command to The Ex, "Die, you sumbitch, die!"

At that show of a lack of empathy on Linda's part, I turned on my friend like a she-bear protecting her young[318] and said, "No. *You* wouldn't understand, would *you*?[319] I didn't bring any ***panties***. You know what that means, don't you?"

Linda grinned and said, "Sure, you'll go commando all week."

Well, I have never gone commando in my whole life[320] so I again turned on Linda like a she-bear protecting her young[321] and said, "NO! It means that…*that*…***that***…" I began sobbing again while Linda whispered *Jeezus!* "…I will have to spend ***money***!"

---

[317] The author is leaving out the details of the gasps and heaves as it was not pretty.

[318] The author admits this was not her finest hour and she is grateful her friend is so forgiving.

[319] The author will not say what it was she said to her most dearest friend, but suffice it to say, it were not nice.

[320] The author wants the reader to know she is lying about this, and that's all she's going to say about that.

[321] The author admits she does not have many angry faces and must repeat the same expression from time to time.

That's when Linda said, "Oh, buck up, my friend, and stop being such a cheap bitch[322] and go buy some new thong underwear. Your boyfriend will like that."

"Boyfriend? *Boyfriend?!?* What boyfriend?"

"Exactly. Let's go find you some sexy underwear."[323]

All this preceding story is simply to make the point that in no known or unknown universe or galaxy, nor on any planet, moon, or asteroid of any decent size would you find my face under the dictionary definition of profligate.[324]

Which is why I, on this somewhat cool August morning, waiting on the heat of the day to arrive, sitting on my balcony, reading me some Umberto Eco, Dave Barry waiting on the table to have attention paid to his book, found myself wanting a cup of tea to accompany the deep thoughts in *The Name of the Rose*, Eco's seminal[325] though long-winded novel[326] based (rumor has it) on a true murder mystery from the Middle Ages involving a bunch of monks.[327]

In I went to my kitchen and soon the water was a-boiling and two tea bags were chosen for the dunking. One of green

---

[322] See? Leave it to a good friend to put everything in perspective for a girl having a meltdown.

[323] The author admits that the purchase of the sexy underwear did not lead to the attracting of a boyfriend, which state has caused Linda to sigh ad nauseum. **Shut up, Linda.**

[324] Profligate in its many iterations could be: Wasteful, reckless, spendthrift, decadent, extravagant, licentious, wicked, immoral, or shameless.

[325] Seminal in the same way that Dave Barry's book *dave barry's complete guide to guys* was seminal.

[326] If all the long-winded had been taken out, the book would have been a novella, but the long-winded parts were pretty good, so the publishers decided to keep it all in there.

[327] Yes, *those* Middle Ages.

tea, the other of black. I let the bags steep for exactly six minutes.[328] And here is where the profligation begins.

I threw the bags into the trash after *only one use*.

Oh, what was I thinking?

Could I be losing my thrifty[329] ways?

By only using the tea bags once could I be contributing to the worst sin of all: Climate Change?[330] What penance can I make that would be accepted by the…okay, I won't get into politics and fake science here because this essay is all about me and my guilt at not being able to stop riding that hell-bound train to the poorhouse.

While I avert my eyes from the tea bags, I shall now console myself by looking at all the panties in my drawer and thinking how I will never have to buy another pair the rest of my life.

One takes consolation where one can.

---

[328] Yes, the timer was on, so the author knows for certain.

[329] The author admits the best word here is *cheapskate*.

[330] The author says that many will see that as a stretch, but this is her opportunity to "reach across the aisle" to make nice with those whackjob…errrr…pussy-hat wea…ummm…she means Caring Liberals. She hopes they appreciate her effort, for it is huge.

I reached the end of the Internet.

On finishing the essay entitled "A profligate morning", twelve letters existing as a single entity were flagged by Word[331] as something to which the writer was invited to give closer attention. Further research showed those twelve letters did not exist in the embedded dictionary as a single entity. The word was *profligation.*

You the reader, having just finished the essay in which this word was used, fully accepted that word as being real because it looked legit, sounded legit, and was even spelled legit according to the rules of adding things to the end of a word to make that word do something else. Therefore, I decided to prove that Word was limited and went to a search engine[332] and typed in the word. Guess what?

Goo…I mean the only search engine that is worldwide famous had never heard of the word which means that, having indexed all the known world and some we wish had never been indexed, I reached the end of the Internet and invented a new word.

So, all you dictionary committees out there, take note: Profligation.[333] New word. Add it.

---

[331] Dear non-tech people of the 20th and 21st centuries and readers somewhere in the future who manage to stumble across the archives of all things Angela: Word is considered to be the default word processor that comes preloaded on all computers no matter if their operating systems run on MacIntosh or Windows.

[332] Google, but do not tell them that.

[333] What? Does the author have to do all your work for ya? See previous essay for the use of this word in a sentence.

STEM: Over-promised. Under-delivered.

The tweet read: "100% Fresh Beef + John Goodman = ASMR(ish)" and included a link to a video wherein the star stared into the camera and whispered lasciviously about McDonald's Quarter Pounder as sounds and visuals of one of those patties got hot and bothered on the grill.

"Hey, you," Goodman purrs as only he can. "McDonald's new fresh-beef Quarter Pounder is hotter and juicier. It'll leave you speechless. I can almost feel that juice sizzling. Oh baby, the melted cheese is hugging every corner of that grilled patty. Slivered onions. Mustard. And ketchup…" I like burgers as good as anybody, but he went on so long I thought he'd never shut up about it. It's not *that* good. I know. I used to cook them when I was employed by Mickey D's.

ASMR videos, named for Autonomous Sensory Meridian Response, are carefully crafted featuring hot young women who look like real women, and by that I mean no bulging Adam's apples, who touch objects obviously fraught with meaning and whisper into fancy-schmancy microphones in an attempt to create something people will want to watch long enough that they will then want to buy a product from the company paying for the video production.

But Goodman's ASMR video went in the opposite direction. What is pleasant about a big ol' fat man opining about a burger? Obviously there is something pleasant about it because three million views later the McDonald's ad campaign was still going strong. Why is this important?

Because McDonald's is rolling out customer-operated order-taking machines and thus, while business is booming, they need fewer frontline people to make nice with the public. The reason McDonald's and others are cutting back employment opportunities is twofold. One: Employee churn makes proper training all but impossible. Two: Federally mandated minimum wage levels almost doubled the cost of having an employee. Put One together with Two and you have a tsunami of stockholders [read *investors*] unhappy with their dividends who then move their money somewhere else.

Our equation should now read "100% Fresh Beef + John Goodman = Increased Business – Employment Opps…" I might be a polymath but I'm not fluent in the Maths, so you will have to figure out the equation yourself. In any case, moving on.

At the same time Goodman increased McDonald's business, there was a huge push for education based around STEM: Science, Tech, Engineering, and Math. All this sounds good and I agree there is nothing wrong with STEM other than one little thing: The promise of what it is supposed to solve — unemployment.

I am not alone in this thought.

According to a 2017 study by the Bureau of Labor Statistics, the seventh most popular career for STEM graduates in the United States, and most popular non-computer-related role, is in sales. The study found that 750,000 STEM graduates found employment in computer- and information-related positions the previous year — such as software developer, computer systems analyst, and network systems administrator — while wholesale manufacturing sales representatives of technical and scientific products accounted for nearly 350,000.

What the study did not tell you but I — as an Autodidact Polymath and Magnificently Methodical Southern Woman and The Most Brilliant Woman In The World — can tell you is that most of those STEM jobs are done by former hawkers-of-burgers-and-now-baristas who pad their resumés by claiming that changing out the paper on the receipt printer is a network systems administrator position and that rebooting the store computer makes them a computer systems analyst, or STEM-qualified CSA.

The rest of the reported group went to work at car dealerships where, after working through their three-month guarantee and not being able to actually sell a car[334], they moved to the next dealer salary guarantee offer, and so on ad infinitum which explains the state of the car business.[335]

Unable to think critically, other STEM graduates went to work in the fast-food environment (non-management positions) where, with evidence to the contrary readily available, they continued to advocate for an increase in the minimum wage only to show up one day at work to find they were replaced by electronic ordering pad-slash-payment processing portals that consumers could operate with an ease and high confidence that their order would be accurate. These customers include mechanics (shade-tree and ASE certified), tire changers (from independent shops and corporate-owned chains), cashiers at Walmart and PetSmart, independent reps for Mary Kay cosmetics and financial planning companies, Waffle House cooks and La Parrilla bartenders, as well as some female Jazz singers, among others.

These replaced STEM-qualified fast-food/coffee workers, who couldn't find their stinky boohiney with a fistful of

---

[334] Even with systemized training in proven lying...errrr...the author means sales techniques, these people are so used to having the proverbial milk fall from the teat into their mouths that they did not understand a conversation stopper when they saw it, did not know that a no really meant "give me more information", and blithely stumble-bumbled their way into talking the people out of buying from "this crappy dealership".

[335] Internet gossip...errrr...researchers share pictures of thousands of lots around the Capitalist world filled with what they claim is overproduction of vehicles used to artificially inflate jobs reports. Several reporters tried to explain full lots away by claiming the photos were not exactly current and if you were to see these lots today you would see them full of the newest batch of overproduction and that we, the rube reader, were not to imply anything by that other than, and I quote, "Dealers store cars in anticipation of sales."

To which we rubes reply, "Well, duh. But isn't anticipation of a sale the same as saying there has not been a sale? Isn't that like a woman saying she anticipates getting preggers but her Mate o' Choice hasn't yet uploaded the Spark o' Life?"

Charmin, just didn't get it and decided to suckle the sugar tit of the bitch that spawned them. That is, they went on to apply for unemployment and bought pussy hats to wear at the next George Soros-sponsored protest for which they were hired to show up (at two-thirds the minimum hourly wage plus a bus ride, lunch, and a cool photo op) in order to "be mad" at Candidates A, L, and Zed and the Great Orange President while shouting "Feel the Bern!" and "We're With Her!"

What we are seeing in this year of 2018 is the dénouement of a consistent process of dumbing down of the populace by a powerful Socialist group: Teachers' unions. STEM is the most current version of that systemic process application.

Previously it was New Math and Whole Language Arts, but there have been other processes before them going back to the 1960s, all of which did nothing but suck the joy out of learning by making learning so complicated even the teachers didn't know what the hell was going on.

What has come along with this dumbing down has been a huge assault on our children in the name of Caring. Yes, I speak of the rise of a wide array of Learning Disabilities treated with drugs, some experimental. Some of these disabilities are being blamed on vaccinations that for generations held at bay life-threatening diseases such as polio, measles, and more.

This view is a false flag designed to rouse the rabble much like a running squirrel gets the attention of a dog. The dog will move fast in the chase — the squirrel is very important to him! — but two minutes later the dog has forgotten all about it and is back wanting its Greenies treat.

The dumbing down included not knowing the history of the important disciplines being pushed in STEM courses now. When I hear parents inflate the minimal danger of vaccinations to earth-shaking proportions, I always ask them if they know the consequences of their actions. They stare as if I just spoke ancient Greek. And we have the consequences now. Let's consider just two: Measles is back with a vengeance, as is polio. Ignoring the killing and crippling of millions in the past, a parent who is so worried about *their child* to the point they ignore their neighbors' children is a parent I would never want as a friend.

The question then arises: Why is the dumbing down of the populace so important, and to whom is it so? The answer:

The Deep State, comprised of politicians on all sides of all aisles, an entrenched bureaucracy more interested in their retirement accounts, and those who are manipulating all of them to be able to pull profit from all countries.

Which brings us to the next essay, "The Winds of War."

The Winds of War

There's a war going on right under your nose. Most do not see it, even as the winds of war take their lawn furniture and blow it into the next county.

This war is age-old and has rightly been said to be between Good and Evil.

But as all wars do, this one has an ebb and flow. A quieter time of backroom planning and a louder time of furious deployment of those plans. Turn on your radios or televisions or log in to online news portals or read headlines in newspapers, you'll see the same thing in almost all instances:

The latest deployment of a war room plan.

Yes, I'm speaking of the scurrilous, defaming attack on Judge Brett Kavanaugh, President Donald Trump's latest nominee for a seat on the Supreme Court of the United States. Lest you say, "All victims should be heard!", let me say to you, "You are right! But please don't let someone claim victimhood if it isn't true."

I'm a victim of long-term sexual assault by my stepfather with my mother's blessing. I know of the desire to speak up and say something yet having the emotional or psychological need to hold it in. I know of the finally speaking up and not being believed. And I had proof but could not use it.

Christine Blasey Ford, on the other hand, offers at best hazy memories, is being begged for more proof, can't provide it, but is willing to use insinuation to destroy. I never made up my abuse and would never claim it if it hadn't happened, and never once did I blame someone else.

I always remembered, and the patterns and times of it were clear.

Yet I know women who have publicly claimed abuse at the hands of a man but privately told me they did it to get an advantage.[336] False allegations of rape are not new, and every one of them should be denounced when found out. But these days *false allegations* is a politically incorrect term. All allegations are to be believed, supported, and celebrated on the off-chance they might be true. False allegations of abuse do not help the cause of real victims. Those who offer them up are obvious haters.

The question then is this: Why did Christine Blasey Ford do this? I've got a simple answer: She wanted desperately to be a heroine for a cause she feels strongly about and had, in fact, been looking for years for just such an opportunity. After all, her reasoning goes, isn't all fair in love and war?

Poor thing, though, does not realize she was simply a false flag kicked over the traces by the P-HWPCLDRSFCs'[337] goal-meeting committee. The goal is to form a one-world government wherein all those designated as politically incorrect will cook and clean for them while they live in luxury behind secure walls heavily guarded.

Helping out in this is FLOTSAM.[338] Funny thing, though. All of a sudden Ford is not feeling so confident in offering proof of claim and FLOTSAM and other operatives are backpedaling even as they later brought forth other thoroughly unbelievable claimants.

---

[336] After this essay was written and before publication in this book, it came to light that women had indeed lied about ever having even met Kavanaugh.

[337] Pussy-Hat Wearing Politically Correct Liberal Democrat RINO Socialist Fascist Commies.

[338] **FLOTSAM** is snarky for what mainstream media thinks of themselves: For Liberal Opinion That is Serious and Actually Matters.

But Kavanaugh's trial in the kangaroo court[339]…errrr, I mean testimony in the Senate hearing continued anyway. Ford, a professor of psychology at Palo Alto University and a research psychologist at the Stanford University School of Medicine, had opportunity to trot out a little-girl victim voice to say she was 100% certain it was Kavanaugh, the big bad wolf, who had touched her naughty parts (and which parts did not want to be naughty).

Oh, how Christine was applauded for her courage to come forward and speak on these things. What few will remember, though, is that supposedly[340] Ford wrote this accusation in a *confidential* letter. To that I call bull.

In fact, I do not believe any letter was written by Ford alone. Furthermore, it seems quite interesting that 36 years after the event Ford chose to be outed publicly in a fashion that was designed to do the most harm as fast as possible with the minimal amount of evidence or effort.

But the conspirators of this cabal were taken by surprise: Kavanaugh refused to roll over and play dead and Trump refused to withdraw his nomination. Kavanaugh vigorously defended himself, his reputation, his good name, and his family's good name against an onslaught of evil. Geez. What was the cabal to do?

They hastily drummed up four more women, each of whom had more fantastical stories to tell with the last woman claiming Kavanaugh was involved in, if not was the mastermind organizer of, "rape trains" at ten different parties

---

[339] A mock court in which the principles of law and justice are disregarded or perverted; a legislative investigating committee characterized by irresponsible, unauthorized, or irregular procedures.

[340] The author here uses the word "supposedly" to mean purportedly to mean that the narrative put out was that Ford sent a letter saying these bad things about Kavanaugh, but that she didn't want anybody to ever, ever, ever know about them and asked the receivers to pretty please keep all this private and not tell a soul.

this woman said she attended in such a careful fashion that she only allowed herself one beer so she wouldn't be the next victim. Even major liberal newspapers and news magazines said that story did not make any sense at all and began to question that accuser.

If she saw any females being assaulted in rape trains on that many occasions while she stood there drinking a beer, why didn't she leave and call the police? Exactly. She didn't call the police because it never happened.

The lesson Kavanaugh soon learned, though, was that no matter what at any point in the process — whether he rolled over and begged forgiveness or stood his ground — nothing he said or did would have suited the Deep State. How do we know this?

We know it because when he said the accusation about the "rape trains" was something out of *The Twilight Zone*, the Deep State and its handmaidens had a veritable meltdown and accused him of an even worse crime: Insulting a woman while insulting Rod Serling's wonderful television show that only dealt in truth.

We know it because Jim Carrey painted a picture of the angry face of a Senator who supported Kavanaugh and said, "No wonder women don't report abuse."

We know it because the television show *Saturday Night Live* hired popular actor Matt Damon to act out a skit wherein he played Kavanaugh, making fun of the emotion Kavanaugh showed in defending himself.[341]

We know it because two days after President Trump told the FBI to investigate Kavanaugh *one more time*, MSNBC ran

---

[341] Matt Damon has now gone on the "sh!t list" of actors kept by the author along with Meryl Streep, Robert De Niro, Jim Carrey, among others too long to list here, but of whom she will never purchase another ticket to see their movies nor watch their movies in syndication and will turn the channel if they show up on a talk show.

a Sunday morning headline that read "FBI *Still* Hasn't Contacted Ford or Her Attorneys".

We know it because just about every editorial still calls Kavanaugh a rapist, and worse — a man who doesn't **believe** any female and will do his utmost to deprive a woman of the right to kill her child while it is still in her womb. Kavanaugh was confirmed. But just like Justice Clarence Thomas, accused by Anita Hill[342] and raked over the coals in the Senate confirmation hearings, in what Thomas famously called a "high-tech lynching", Ford's accusations will follow Kavanaugh, and when he dies, FLOTSAM will lead with this:

"Supreme Court Justice Brett Kavanaugh passed away today. He was accused of sexual assault by a heroine of the #MeToo movement, Christine Blasey Ford. Though he denied being the mastermind of rape trains, he tried to overcome the dark days of his youth by devoting himself to good works and we thank him for those things, but he was a bad, bad man and, frankly, we don't know how anybody ever liked him and women's rights have forever been tainted by his appointment to SCOTUS."

Mark the words of this Autodidact Polymath Magnificently Methodical Southern Woman and The Most Brilliant Woman In The World[343]: This is what will be written.

The winds of this war will blow for a long time, but they must not blow unopposed.

Kavanaugh, Trump, several senators [most notably and surprisingly, Susan Collins (Republican, Maine)], as well as Citizen Journalists and other citizens, pushed back against the enraged Deep State gang.

Immediately after Kavanaugh was confirmed on a Saturday afternoon in a Senate vote of 50-48, a George Soros

---

[342] Anita Hill went on to make big bucks on the speaking circuit.

[343] She is telling the truth.

group of hired protestors beat on the doors of the Supreme Court, demanding to be let in to kick Kavanaugh's ass.

Senator Chris Coons (D-DE), in all seriousness, went on a national news show and said, "It is **too early to begin** impeachment of Kavanaugh."

Oh, sure. He used words like *healing* when what he really meant was, "We Dems have to win the midterm election and then we will impeach the president and the new justice and we will impose all manner of totalitari…errrr…I mean Caring Democratic Socialist Policies that will roll back your freedoms…errrr…I mean give you more choice while you sit in your newly created segregated safe places you've been asking for."

Do not be fooled in this.

Diligence is required.

Look, while the Deep State-sponsored coup against the Constitution is in trouble, the battle is not over. Now is not the time to rest. It is time to keep hammering home the message that wolves might huff and puff and growl and snarl, but threats will not get them much more. No less than freedom depends upon it.

So, get your sheepdog on and keep it on.

Choosing Between Two Bales of Hay

This essay will not have much to say. It exists for one reason: To show you what a great title looks like and this title, fear not, is great. For instance, when you[344] saw the title, what did you do? If you are like most people, you first processed the thought of hay. What is it? How does one go about getting it? What is its use? Then you did research on what a *bale* is and why hay had to be baled and the various shapes bales could take, as well as the machinery or other method involved to make it so. Next you asked who would need hay so that they would have to choose between two bales of it.

After that, you would then realize the title was metaphorical because humans are not horses and "two bales of hay" means something else, therefore the symbolism it carries could be weighty if the choice were between, say, life and death, or pleasurable if the choice were between, say, chocolate and vanilla ice cream.

You would then ask yourself "Which choice will the writer imply? Weighty or pleasurable?" Your heart will increase its beat in anticipation of the answer. All that before you even got to reading the essay under it, and that, dear reader, is what makes a great title. Here's another great title for you. (You have to go to the next essay to read it.)

---

[344] The use of *you* in this essay is not meant to imply the person reading the words, but is generally used to indicate a generic, unspecified person or persons. In this case *you* specifies the person who had to go through all that thought process and, as you have paid money for this book, it is clear you are not the *you* of which the author speaks.

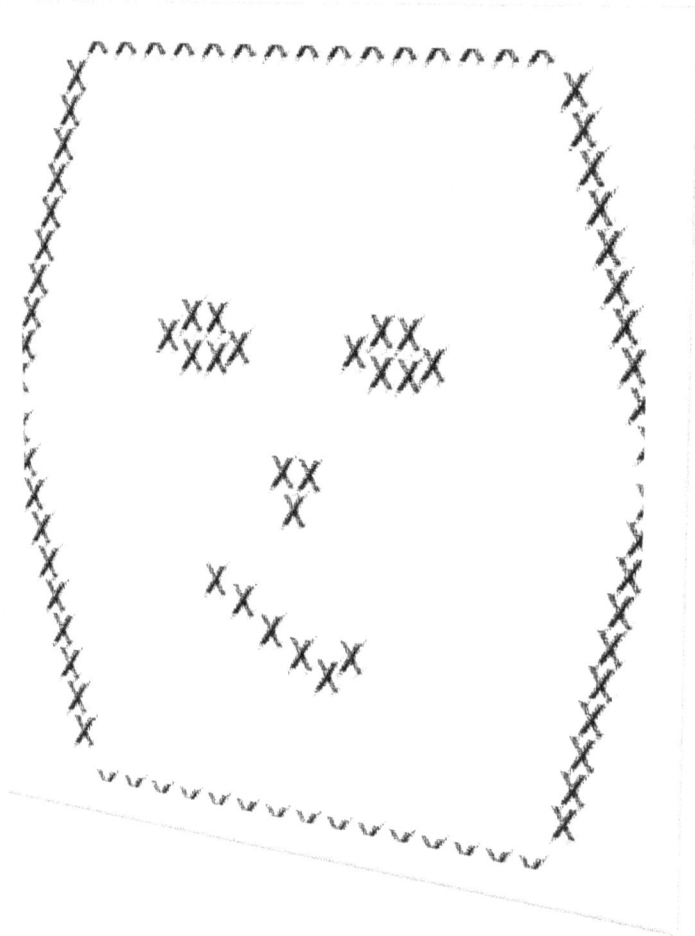

Emojis and Emoticons:
The New Language of Love

Sometime around 2016-ish, the social media giant Bacefook threw the world a curve. They added more emoticons and emojis their users could employ to express themselves without having to actually write one damn word. This move was not taken alone and was actually a marketing tool used by the company. It stole the idea from Apple Inc., who had long had multiple emoticon/emoji choices in their Messenger App which came bundled with their popular iPhone.

Bacefook would later try to get out of some hot water with the United States government by claiming that Apple's bundling of Messenger was just as bad as what Mark Zuckerberg's company did, and so either Apple needed a spanking too or nobody needed any sanctions against them.

The one emoticon Bacefook had been using was a thumbs up, which when clicked meant a reader liked a user's post. But what if a reader *really, really, really* liked the post? Could he click Like more than once to show he *really, really, really* liked it even more? No, he could not, as clicking twice merely toggled the Like from on to off. This was forcing people to actually write a sentence in reply. Obviously complaints must have flowed into Bacefook HQ about this because finally, with much rejoicing and rolling in the aisles, the company rolled out these multiple choices:

But, in truth, did these make replies any clearer? Each clearly identifies an emotion. They are, in order: Like. Love. Laugh. Wow. Sad. Angry. Each clear and concise. However...

There are several problems with this system. Let's take one example. Say a user posts a personal comment that you Like, but they have attached a news story that makes you Angry. You can only choose one graphic comment. Which do you click?

If you click Angry, will your friend the poster believe you are Angry at him for what he said or what he attached or that he attached it? Will that begin a feud with your friend or any of his echo chamber followers? If you click Like, will your friend think you are a creep because you liked the story about the bad subject or will he Like that you Liked his comment? How can he tell which you meant?

Bacefook had an answer for that. Again, an idea they stole from Apple since Messenger had been doing it for years already, but an idea that worked. Bacefook now made it possible to insert as many emojis and emoticons as you wanted in a reply so that, as standalones or mixed with minimal words, one could communicate more clearly. It could look like this:

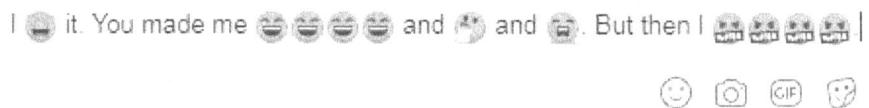

I 🙄 it. You made me 😂😂😂😂 and 🤨 and 😭. But then I 😬😬😬😬 |

☺ 📷 GIF 😜

Let me translate: I [LOVE] it. You made me [LAUGH, LIKE, A WHOLE LOT] and then it made me [GO HMMMM] and [CRY]. But then I [CUSSED A LOT OF DIRTY WORDS THAT WOULD MAKE A SAILOR BLUSH].

Or like another fellow "wrote":

Juke Highwalker 💜 💜 💜 💜 💜 💜 💜 💜 💜 💜 🔥 🔥 🔥 🔥 🔥 🔥 🔥 ✌ ✌ ✌ ✌ ✌ ✌ ✌ ✌ ✌ 🌍

What the hell does this even mean? See, expanded systems of emojis and emoticons have their limitations. So, to solve that problem of limited and unclear exchanges[345], and following Apple's Messenger App lead, Bacefook added an ever-updated and rotating assortment of GIFs, for Graphics Interchange Format. GIFs are moving pictures of a person or animated character isolated from a full movie or TV show. They are usually no more than two seconds in length and play nonstop while showing on a computer or phone screen.

Readers in the future are probably shaking their heads at this primitive communication method, but I swear that was how it was in the second decade of the twenty-first century. To make it worse, just about everybody using the service had a swanky degree in higher education, so you would think that users would be capable of forming complete sentences that made a point. Wouldn't *you* think that? Of course you would. Pay that much for a degree and not get one's money's worth? I think not. Yet, what have we got? Instead, it got to the point that even the entire lifecycle of relationships in the First World began to be played out on smartphones through messaging emojis and emoticons and exploding and animated graphics. It worked like this:

Man: HRU 2day?

Woman: OMG. U?

---

[345] Actually, Bacefook did not care about clarity of messaging between their users. What they cared about was keeping eyeballs on their service. Therefore, expanded emoji, emoticon, sticker, and GIF choices were simply the company's method of hollering "SQUIRREL!" to keep their dogs...errrr... the author means...ummm...users' attention away from the fact they were mining data and selling it and access to eyeballs to absolutely anybody who could afford their price. The author says, "Do not get me started on that manipulating lying-ass company's ways."

Man: WYWH

Woman:

Man: B2W. B9.

Woman: ???

Man:

Woman:

Man: L8R

Woman: XOXOXOXO

Man:

Yeah, it was all fun and games until it wasn't because here is also what happened during the same time: Restaurants began losing business. You read correctly: Restaurants began losing business by the, you know, by the truckload. Yes, lots and lots of them closed and all their consultants and all their coupons could not pull in enough customers to save them. Then manufacturers of food products began to look for other places to sell their products because restaurants were not buying enough which, of course, made it harder to attract customers to the restaurants because they could have it all delivered to them through Meal Prep Services.[346]

Nobody knew why customers stopped showing up at restaurants. At first the economy was blamed, as was a logical thought process, but even when the economy rebounded, restaurants were still going out of business and nobody could figure it out. Well, I, your Autodidact Polymath Magnificently Methodical Southern Woman and The Most Brilliant Woman In The World, did figure it out:

People were "phoning in" their relationships because it was so much easier. See, previous to emojis and emoticons on smartphones, a guy had to:

- call a woman,
- arrange a time to pick her up or meet her at a particular restaurant,
- maybe make a reservation if the restaurant was swanky,
- take a shower,
- choose an outfit to wear,
- change his socks,
- change his underwear,
- brush his hair,

---

[346] Meal Prep Services put together entire meals consisting of an uncooked protein (vegetable or animal), raw vegetables (like onions, potatoes, carrots, broccoli), spices including salt, heads of garlic, along with directions on how to chop, mince, season, and otherwise cook the food. These usually cost more than a restaurant meal consisting of the same ingredients but made the neo-chef feel good about staying home and eating food the neo-chef cooked without any help from Mother.

- brush his teeth,
- choose, then take, a mode of transportation,
- map out how to get to the restaurant or woman's house,
- go to the restaurant, or the woman's house to pick her up and then to the restaurant,
- park,
- possibly pay for parking in a public lot or valet the vehicle,
- walk in the restaurant,
- greet the woman (unless he's already done that when he picked her up),
- hold the door for the woman,
- make small talk all evening,
- pay for food and drink (can include expensive alcohol, one whole lobster for her, and two to-go boxes for her),
- tip well where the woman can see how much he left,
- walk her to her car (or his car as the situation calls for),
- say goodbye in the parking lot (or at her house),
- wangle an invitation to waggle his weenie in her presence[347],
- be prepared for hearing "No",
- be prepared for hearing "Yes",
- know the rules for "Yes" of which the main one is "No means No",

---

[347] This invitation process is often misunderstood and misapplied especially since Radical Feminists got involved in writing the rules.

- make way back to his domicile where he would have sweet dreams — or whatever,

- remember to call the woman somewhere between two and five days later and say something like, "Wow. I had a great time the other night. Let's do it again soon."

- Then finally call her one year later and when challenged on why it took so long to call the woman, he will say, "It's been a *whole year?* Really? Man, time sure does fly."

It was quite the complicated process and involved huge commitments of time for something with an outcome that was iffy at best. Though truth be told, after such a routine many a man found himself married with children because the process was so complicated and men, unable to think with any clarity while in the presence of a woman who had gussied herself up and was smiling and making nice by saying things like "Oh, you are so cute!" and "Oh! You are SOOOO funny!" and "Ooooo…mmmm… is that a flashlight in your pocket?" often found themselves handing over a ring and blurting "Will you marry me?" in front of entire restaurants full of waiters and bartenders and other diners, many of them men who had previously done this very same thing and so egged on the situation because why should they go through all this bullshit by themselves, right?

But all that changed when emojis and emoticons and GIFs came into popular usage because now all a guy[348] had to do on a Friday or Saturday night was stay home playing video games in his underwear, drinking his big-box store cheap beer, burping and farting willy-nilly, and occasionally (usually during bathroom breaks) texting a woman:

---

[348] A nod here to one Dave Barry as a suggestion for the topic of his next seminal work.

Man: HRU 2day?

And when her smartphone would ding *Incoming*, she would run to her phone to see that he was thinking of her and reply:

Woman: OMG.   . U?   2.

Then she would text her girlfriends and send them a screenshot of the text exchange and they would text her back with things like "OMGEEEE! I am SOOOOO happy for you" as if a proposal of marriage had been made. Then she waits for his next text but it never arrives.

In any case, waiters and bartenders twiddle thumbs and restaurant owners wonder how on God's Green Earth they will make payroll much less pay the rest of the &^%~!@* overhead.

Of course, technology being what it is, that is just tech being slow to deliver messaging because these things get hung up in China at the Politburo's Messaging Distribution Center. The guy may have sent the message Friday evening at the respectable hour of eight-thirty, but her phone dings *Incoming* seven hours later, waking her from a dead sleep as she almost has a heart attack wondering "Who died?" Then she sends him a text immediately and says —

"Why did you wake me up?"

Getting no response, she sends another.

"Why aren't you answering?"

Getting no response, she sends another.

"Why are you ignoring me?"

Getting no response she sends another and continues to send ever-increasingly weird messages[349] until she is worn out from the effort.

Woman:

Woman:

Woman:

Woman:

Woman:

---

[349] Such as "I thought you loved me!" and "I thought we had something special!" and other such messages ramping up in intensity and accusation. The author wants the reader to know she has never done anything like this and what knowledge she has of this came from a secondary data set after massive research during the Medicinal Margarita Study that she and Linda Sands conducted over the course of several years.

Woman: got to hail u summer witch. Eye um be you![350]

And the guy, of course, has slept through the entire thing because he's turned his phone off and is totally clueless about what happened. When he turns his phone on the next week and sees all this, he usually breathes a sigh of relief then texts his buds: "dacb".[351] And they text back:

Friend 1:

Friend 2:

Friend 3:

Friend 4:

Friend 5: CU@7. WOW? Beer?

Friends 1, 2, 3, 4, and Man:

---

[350] The woman used the microphone on her phone to dictate the message and the phone's service provider then misunderstood her real meaning and supplied what they believed she said or what fit within the use of their corporate language policies. What she actually said was, "What the hell, you sumbitch. IMBU!"

[351] Lazy-man shorthand for "dodged another cwazy bullet".

Conversation over a coffee shop counter.

Conflict & Consensus in Modern American History is a book edited in 1967 by Allen F. Davis and Harold D. Woodman featuring a compilation of essays by various historians. From 1600s Jamestown, Virginia, to the Civil War in the 1800s, it explores different viewpoints on the same eras in order to ultimately explain how a wildly varying group of governments and territories became the United States of America.

Since it is best never to eat a feast in one sitting lest one throw up all of it, I've been digesting the essays slowly. Carrying the book with me wherever I go, I read bits and pieces and make notes as I wait for folks to show up for meetings. One should never waste opportunities for reading and, come to find out, dropping some learning on an NPC.[352]

There I was at my fave independent coffee shop[353] down the street, holding the book, thinking about what I would order, when the girl[354] behind the counter sees the book.

"Whatcha reading?" she asks, pointing.

I turn the book. She leans forward and reads aloud, "ConFLICT? And? ConSENsuuuUS? In MoDERN American HIStory? What's it aBOUT?"[355]

---

[352] The author will get you to that.

[353] That most coffee shops seem to be run by Liberals, it is a wonder any are called independent.

[354] Technically, she was in her mid-twenties which would put her in the category of woman, but I call her a girl here because she was so frickin' young and that includes mentally.

[355] Yes, she read the title out loud using questioning inflection. The author did not make this up.

There is a line behind me, but who am I to tell her she can't learn? After all, wise and ancient sages say when the student is ready the teacher will appear and there we were. But I was mindful of the line and so attempted to quickly summarize the book. I was brilliant, if I do say so myself.

"It's a book of essays from multiple historians explaining the Constitution of the United States. Why it was needed. How it came to be. Why it is important to the country's and the world's stability and vital to protect and defend it."

Wheels were turning, and she was quick with a reply. "Oh. Well? But the Founding FaTHERS? Made this counTRY? So they could be rich and expLOIT IT? So they wrote IT to support THEIR GOALS? Not anybody elSE'S?"

By now, everybody is listening. So, I had better make it quick and even more brilliant than usual.

I did not disappoint.

"Your thought would have merit if the Founding Fathers had been the first ones here. But they weren't, you know this, right? The land we now know as the United States of America had people in it long before the Founding Fathers were born. Many areas settled by folks from France and other countries. Settlements were a roiling mess of conflicting interests, so—"

She jumped in quick with what she thought was the thing that would shut my mouth. "Well? Would you deny *mass*ACRES happened?"

She did not count on the superb response of wit from an Autodidact Polymath and Magnificently Methodical Southern Woman who is The Most Brilliant Woman In The World. "Oh, honey. *Everybody* knows those things happened..."

Her eyes got big and she said, "Really?"

"Really!" says I. "Which is why we have had amendments to clarify and adjust."

By now, people in line are nodding, which was a shock as this coffee shop, like many, is loaded with P-HWPCLDRSFCs.

The other two barista chicks are staring because they, too, were blown away. You see, they were not used to seeing their friend shut down and it, like, shocked them? Like, totaLLY?

But the line needed to move and I began my order even though the girl was still thinking of a reply. "So, I'll have a small café au lait with coconut milk and two Splendas in a ceramic mug and a Jalapeño bagel with pimento cheese. Thank you."

I would love to have been a fly on the wall when those three got together later and discussed that morning's lecture/debate, but then again, maybe not. I have high hopes they remembered what I said, or that they considered it long enough to let the lesson sink in. I can say in the town that houses the RadFem conclave of Agnes Scott College, the Science/Medical closed societies of liberal Georgia Tech and Emory University, and the schizophrenic Socialist co-op of Georgia State College, probability suggests otherwise.

Not all, but most students, faculty, and other personnel at these institutions of higher learning are NPCs. In video games (including online role play), roles of NPCs ("nonplayable characters") are simple: They repeat necessary messaging to playable characters as these navigate their way through obstacles. In gaming, NPCs are simply talking signboards. They have no will of their own. They do not have any decision to make and, in point of fact, cannot make one, only saying what they are told to say.

Granted, anyone on any side of a debate can be in the role of NPC, but facts are facts: In university settings, NPCs are more often than not[356] P-HWPCLDRSFCs spouting a party line they have neither given thought to nor attempted to play Devil's advocate with. In gaming, if NPCs outnumbered playable characters, then the game would be boring because

---

[356] Of all NPCs existing on a campus anywhere in the world, P-HWPCLDRSFC NPCs exist by a margin of 99.985% to the 0.015% of the Conservative NPC. No NPC helps their cause.

the playable character's decision-making tree couldn't be acted upon. If NPCs were smartly deployed as viruses in online role-playing games, players would not immediately know why their world was turned upside down.

But give them a little time and *Boom Shakalaka* they would begin to understand and controlling measures would be rolled out.

It's the same with the girl at the coffee shop. I hope she is a playable character who has been tricked into the role of NPC and that she will soon wake up. But for now, discourse and debate no longer exist as discourse has left her building.

I have friends who are NPCs. I know exactly what they will say and how they will say it when it comes to the big issues of the day. These are not bad people when they aren't spouting the P-HWPCLDRSFC party line. We sing, put on shows, and enjoy food together. Heck, some of us, after meeting one chucklehead after another, even trash talk men together after a couple of glasses of wine. But their memories are short. They cannot think critically. They live in the land of Black and White where Gray never enters.

Please, God. Let me spend some time with a playable character. Amen.

God heard my prayer. Seems there are more playable characters than I could have imagined, and these are taking to the streets — digital, print, asphalt, cement, and dirt — and speaking up to the NPCs saying, "Shut up. Your messaging makes no sense."

I was accused of being an unsuccessful smartass. Does that make me a dumbass?[357]

The title of this essay was inspired by two men on Bacefook when one accused me of being an unsuccessful smartass and his friend chimed in with "Hahahaha! Does that make her a dumbass?" I gave them an answer and it wasn't one they expected. I put a laughing face emoji in a post and wrote, "Oh, that was good." Still, another longer reply did let my inner smartass out. Judge for yourself if I was successful or not.

Gentlemen, this situation isn't a Democrat against Republican thing. It is a one-world government cabal against lovers of freedom. It is the quest for totalitarian control of every aspect of society depriving citizens of their God-given rights and all other rights, too. It is hidden enemies against all that is holy.

Do not forget this because when the focus is on parties, one misses the bigger enemy.

You ask "who needs facts?" Women are told that to be believed all one need do is FEEL strongly. No facts needed. I feel so very strongly, therefore I am right.

---

[357] Contrary to popular opinion pushed by online trolls, Bacefook users' opinions can and do change.

I cannot believe my FEELINGS are not being SUPPORTED and that you are refusing to validate the VICTIMHOOD status of all women by men. I am a woman. Yes. Me! Am a woman.

And a woman who is powerful simply because she feels so strongly. I'm being dissed and ignored by —

[HANG ON LET ME SEE IF YOU TWO ARE WHITE AND OLD MEN BEFORE I CONTINUE. I see according to your profile photos that yep, you are old and white and look male] — [continuing…] that's right! Dissed and ignored by two old white men. I demand you send somebody else to talk to me on your behalf because I see I will NEVER get a FAIR hearing in this most repulsive of atmospheres of incomplete CARING about MY FEELINGS. [If you do send somebody else to speak on your behalf, I must approve your choices first and then, after you have chosen which you want to speak on your behalf, I will not approve your choice.]

Please be advised: Any word or sentence in ALL CAPS does not constitute screaming but is simply a way to make stand out certain words or phrases. In this instance, please consider ALL CAPS to be the equivalent of underlining, bolding, or italicizing words within a narrative but since this particular TECH GIANT providing this portal is too dang cheap[358] to add those functionalities, this responder/poster/woman will look like she is screaming.

AND

I deserve to receive SOMETHING from an old white man simply because I am a woman. And you, the old white men, will have no right to complain about it. Therefore, by all that is holy to the Radical Feminist and their Deep State handlers, I should be the one who gets the FREE subscription to the magazine you're pushing. But, since all old white men are evil, I will NOT give you my mailing address and YOU will have to guess what it is.

Further, if you do not correctly guess my address, I will hate you and complain about how I am being dissed by an old white man. However, if you do guess correctly, I will turn you in to the popo for stalking me. Do I get to choose which magazine I want to receive? After all, a woman has a right to choose...right?

Reply From an Old White Man[359] Angela, again nonsense!!! No one has more or less validity than another based on gender or age...True colors show in their character and testimony. You seem to be lacking in

---

[358] The founder of this tech portal is white and will soon be old, so maybe he could be counted among the misogynistic men who force women into typing in ALL CAPS so old white men will hear them.

[359] Names changed to protect these men. Please note: They did not respect the author's feelings, but you see how she respects theirs?

both...To be a successful smartass one must have command of clarity through logic and evidence, make their point and comically satire one's debate partner. Once again you display none of these vital elements...Please just bow out and stop wasting my time. Read something actually informative, and #VoteBlue2018. It's truly in your own best interest whether your Kool-Aid washed brain realizes it or not...

Angela Durden Thank you, <u>**Old White Man**</u>, for being there for me. I mean, you might not know this, but it is true and I will take a private lie detector test to confirm it: In all my life I could never have come up with combinations of words such as you just did. I mean, I've been called b**ch and that old standby the C-word and the L-word (not lesbian, Liberal). And have been accused of formerly being a man, but those guys were just blind.

But never, ever, ever, ever never have I ever been called an unsuccessful smartass. You can ask my ex-husband (if you can find him) who said I was very successful at it. Anyway, enough about you. I want you to write more about ME because I could never think of stuff about me like you can.

Nothing else was ever heard from these men.

So?

Was I successful as a smartass?

The Boy and his Mother Child[360]

When a man marries, he expects his wife never to change and is always surprised when she does. But like male songwriters Marv Green, Shane McAnally, and Kent Blazy made clear for all men everywhere in their hit song sung by Reba McEntire called "All the Women I Am", there are no two ways about it: Men are doomed to getting surprised by their women.

For instance, a man takes as wife the shy, sweet, ugly girl that was never the cheerleader who said all she ever wanted was to stay at home and cook for her man and clean his brown-striped underwear and fold it exactly just so and gently place it in a drawer ready for the love of her life and father of her future babies to put on as he goes to work for The Man to make money so she can stay at home and cook for her man and clean his brown-striped underwear and fold it exactly just so and gently place it in a drawer ready for the love of her life and father of her future babies to put on as he goes to work for The Man.

Then sooPRIZE-SOOprize, she finds out she really likes that meth and hubby comes home to a woman dressed like a stripper and missing a few teeth declaring, "I need more money than you can make for me, baby. Here's a coupon for a 10% discount on a lap dance. Ask for me by name and I'll be

---

[360] **DISCLAIMER:** This essay is a work of fiction. Names, characters, places, and incidents are either the product of the author's imagination or are used fictitiously, and any and all resemblance to actual persons, living or dead, business establishments, open or closed, events, no matter the venue, products, no matter the manufacturer, or locales in any country, city, town, or county, is entirely coincidental and are not to believed even if you know the author and can say, "Hey, but I remember that time!", at which point the author will sue you for defamation of character and will pursue other ugly legal scenarios that will demand your attention for years, after which she will own your house, your car, and your 401(k).

right on over, Big Boy. Customer Service is my middle name, you big ol' hunk-o' hunk-o' burning lurrrrv."

That man's surprise is simple and, unless he too starts liking meth, will be divorcing her ass toot-sweet. Problem solved. Other men, however, get more surprised. For instance, the man who marries a woman whose personality changes every day. That's right, as Marv, Shane, and Kent wrote, it "ain't always easy living with" all the women she is. Which is not to say it's a bad life, it's just full of surprises.

But this story isn't about men dealing with the forty-plus personalities of his wife because, let's be candid here, what man doesn't like tickling strange, right? Of course they do. That's why married couples play bedroom games. So a man whose wife has many personalities can "cheat" on his wife with his wife and nobody gets in trouble. These men do not know how good they have it.

But this story is about the child of such a woman who, when he is a tyke, already has it figured out which "Mommy" will let him buy the toys he wants.

Humor writer Dave Barry and a lot of his friends were married to such women even if they didn't know it — and they, like most clueless men, didn't know it. We understand this because he wrote of it in Chapter 3 of his seminal 1995 work *dave barry's complete guide to guys*[361] wherein he admitted that certain toys[362] just showed up in his and his friends' houses and they had no idea how they got there. Well, they got there because they had wives whose sons had figured out which "Mommy" liked those toys and would buy them because they wanted them, too. It is a sure bet that Dave and his buddies also played make-believe with different

---

[361] This is not a typo. That is how that author wrote it on the cover of his own publicly released book. The BALLS on that guy.

[362] Gun-shaped!

"Mommies" while never once complaining about dat, iffen you get mah drift.

To break it down for you, we now turn our attention to one such situation. The Boy knew his Mother Child well. You see, The Boy was a quiet thing. So quiet that, even when he was born the only thing he cared about was food. Having been in the womb for a month longer than necessary, he was very hungry when he was pulled from it via a massive incision in his mother's abdomen. He didn't scream or pee in anger on the doctors and nurses or bite his mother's nipples while screaming "I can't get anything out of this damn effing thing" like his sister did when she was born. He was so laid back that he didn't want to breathe real air and lay there like a dead buddha and they had to force oxygen up his nose to turn him from blue to pink, after which he simply grunted, and his mother knew that meant "feed me" and so she did and he went to sleep.

One would think that The Boy wasn't self-absorbed like his sister but he was, though in a different way. Whereas his sister, The Girl, who watched her mother in order to play head games with her to get her way with things like dating, The Boy watched his mother to find out more about her. What a loving son, The Mother thought. Until one day when The Mother said, "Where did these toys come from?" and The Boy shrugged and said, "You bought them."

But The Mother did not remember buying those toys and denied all knowledge of it. But The Boy kept watching and more toys kept showing up. Then one day, when he was about, oh, around…fourteen-ish, The Mother "woke up" holding a credit card while standing in a checkout line at a national chain of toy stores that are now out of business in America. She turned to The Boy and said, "Son?"

The Boy's reaction to the toys being returned to the shelves was dichotomous. On the one hand he was ashamed of tricking The Mother whom he loved muchly. On the other hand, he sure was wanting the newest PlayStation from Nintendo and now he knew he was not to get it…ever…

because he also knew this of The Mother: Once The Real Mommy knew what was happening, The Real Mommy didn't let any other "Mommy" get tricked.

The Boy knew his days of playing video games for uninterrupted hours with the best player he ever knew, The Mother, were over. And they were over with a vengeance. This sent The Boy into a tailspin of despair until he turned twenty three, which was one year after he moved back home. How he came out of that despair was that a new game was invented, and since he was employed full-time he didn't need The Mother to purchase his toys. What was the game? It was Guitar Hero.

One day The Boy, upon remembering the fun he had with a certain "Mommy", realized that he had made a big mistake all those years ago and he came to this realization without hearing the wisdom in the song that Marv, Shane, and Kent wrote. That's right. The Boy realized that The Mother was "all the Mommies he knew" and that all he had to do was make an invitation.

That is how The Mother came to be invited into The Boy's bedroom to put on a set of headphones and hold a game controller in the shape of a guitar and for about three years The Boy had the joy of The Mother's company once again.

The Father was not happy about that, and that explains The Divorce and The Estrangements, but that is not what this story is about, though this situation did impact The Boy and The Mother's ability to play Guitar Hero together because The Mother moved as she did not want to live in that big fancy house with mostly bad memories of The Father because, you see, The Father was not like Dave Barry and his friends who happily accepted "all the women" their wives were but instead made frowny faces all the time while saying things that begin like "Well, OTHER women like it when I…" and The Mother would reply "Well then, let them wash your underwear" and that is all she is going to say about that.

You never really know someone until you sleep with them.

Let me get this out of the way before we go any further. By "sleep" I do not mean the having, getting, or performing of sexual acts in which when the eyes close it is usually in an ecstasy of passion or in the escaping of your current reality.

By sleep, I mean the closing of the eyes to snore, perchance to do other things. We'll get to that. I hope that is clear as I do not want to continue to have to 'splain it because it is true: You never really know someone until you sleep with them. A songwriter[363] once said, "In sleep I am aware. Is this why I dream? Perception is reality. Is this why I scream?"

Sleeping with yourself is nothing to write home about. But if I had only learned the value of paying attention to others when they were sleeping in close proximity, then I could have avoided a long-ass marriage.

Let's start with my sister. We slept in the same bed until we were teens. She slept with a cat happily laying across her throat. The cat had fleas, but did she care? No. And no amount of daylight punishment would stop her from sneaking that cat in through the window after bedtime. She was once found outside in the dead of night with a flashlight "looking for the sun," that damn cat right beside her.

A few years later, there I am newly married hardly two weeks when I woke to a fist being pounded into my gut by the man who said he loved me. His eyes were open. His stare, blank. I must have made a noise or moved because the pounding stopped, and he rolled over as if nothing happened. I asked him the next day why he was pounding on

---

[363] The songwriter is one Angela K. Durden in a song titled "Black Roses Hang [It's the Way of the World]", but if one didn't read this footnote, one wouldn't know that, and one would scour the Internet looking for the rest of the song so one could make total sense of these brilliant lyrics.

me and he looked at me like I was making it all up. No amount of talking or crying convinced him he had been hitting me. What did that sleep-pounding truly mean?

Come to find out, he was quite the passive-aggressive kind of fellow. He never hit me except once (a slap) when I really needed it to get out of a hysterical moment that just wouldn't quit, and I later thanked him for that. But he "pounded" on me mentally our entire marriage. I was not yet a fully cognizant polymath and so missed the connection between actions in sleep being representational of waking characteristics.

Then there was this time I traveled with a cousin and we shared a hotel room. Family gossip had it that she snored like a roaring freight train and I was warned to get another room down the hall. But I did not believe it could be that bad. I admit here, to you, in writing, they did not lie.

What they didn't tell me is that she also talked in her sleep. If the snoring didn't keep me awake, then her ramblings certainly did. But, boy oh boy, did I learn a lot about her that night, though nothing salacious, therefore nothing that would interest a reader.

My brother came one night. A thump coming from the area of the sofa kept waking me. What the hay-hay was that? That's when I learned he turns over in midair like a breaching humpback and never once wakes. I watched him. You want to talk hang time? Basketball players would die for his. His entire body rose from the sofa in one fluid movement, hung in the air as he turned a full one hundred and eighty degrees, readjusted the blankets at the top of the hang, then hit the sofa with a bang...sound asleep.

Then there was this other cousin who came to spend a few days with me as she traveled through. She snored like a puppy whimpering while it paws the air dreaming of a full teat. It was so funny, I had to stuff my mouth with a blankee to keep from waking her up. From that I learned that she really, really identifies with dogs.

But what have these same folks learned from sleeping with me? That is a complicated answer and I'm not exaggerating because it involves walking in my sleep as well as screaming, fighting, jumping, and more. But I will give you one example that has happened over and over: Laughing in my sleep.

I once woke to the whimpering-puppy snorer laughing out loud at me laughing in my sleep. No, she did not stifle her laugh with a blankee. The whale-breacher asked me in the morning when I was cooking our breakfast, "What was so funny last night?" My husband woke me plenty of times with, "Why are you laughing at me?"[364]

So, I recommend sleeping with others to get to know them better. But just remember, I didn't say sleeping as in boinking.

---

[364] That should tell you a lot about The Ex without the author having to say one more word about that.

Why I could never be a shopkeeper.

Let me say at the outset that the fact I cannot be a shopkeeper in no way, shape, or form means I dislike shopkeepers. These people put up with piles of crap from one customer after another, day in and day out. They come in for that *thing* they need so desperately that if they don't get it their universe will stop spinning and their world will collapse into a black hole of deeply compressed gravity and upon finding that store without that *thing* proceed to attack the shopkeeper who, if he[365] says anything that does not sound like "Wait! I DO have that!", will be attacked verbally if not physically and accused of all sorts of crimes against women[366] including the biggest crime of all: Not Caring.

Which, of course, totally brings me to why I cannot be a shopkeeper: I hate these types of customers. Damn. They aren't grateful for the fact that they have at their fingertips a massive quantity of products, many similar to each other though the labels claim otherwise.[367] And these are in many stores located within short walks or drives of their homes or places of work.

---

[365] The author wants her female readers to note that the use of the word "he" in this instance does not preclude females as shopkeepers but that the author hates the use of he/she and he or she since these two phrases inject into the narrative a politically correct nuance that she also hates because it slows the action.

[366] The author wants her female readers to note that while, yes, men can also get pissy with shopkeepers, it is usually women who do cause the problems. This is a fact and if a reader does not like the fact, they are free to write the author in care of the publisher, who will then pass it along to her. The author is looking forward to receiving such a letter or two because she, while writing humorous stuff, would like to laugh at the writings of someone else for a change.

[367] The author refers to the use of the words "New!" "Better than our OLD version!" "Better than Brand X!", etc.

These customers are spoiled frickin' rotten and I would be jumping all down their throats with, "Oh, yeah? Well, if you don't like our service, then you can just…"[368]

I have concluded that the best fit for my personality and skill set is a bar. Not just any bar, mind you, but one where rich men hang out.[369] Rich men with nothing to prove, like Sean Connery back in the day when, after playing a vigorously relaxing round of golf, would sit in a moderately large wingback chair in a corner of his club, read the paper, and sip his favorite Chilean Merlot[370] whilst nobody gives him a second glance except the silly American tourist who won a trip to that golf course and who, should he bother 007 with some stridently gauche request for an autograph, would be politely hustled out of the room by somebody like me.

But are my self-reported conclusions about me accurate? As I am a realist, I feel and believe they are. Because I do value accuracy over feeling and belief, I set out to challenge those conclusions by taking the Myers-Briggs Type Indicator® test. Are my feelings and beliefs about self based on reality and facts, or are they simply wishes and hopes?

I went to the official website of the company and plunked down $49.95 plus tax. Why tax? I do not know as this was a

---

[368] The author is loath to put her responses in this book of erudite essays, but she wants the reader to know that she can get down and dirty by shouting short declarative statements that include such words as yourself and you, it, go, words ending in *uck*, wanna, and wish.

[369] These men would be real rich men, not the posers, fakers, other wannabes, and broke-ass millionaires that cannot help but trumpet they have money when it is a known fact they do not, will not, or no longer have it. Real rich men that would leave the author-as-bar-owner alone to write and if, by chance, a naughty boy causes a ruckus, the author would by a mere glance over the top of her laptop and a quick, "Steady, boys!" cause the entire thing to die down and camaraderie would be restored so she could get on with her writing.

[370] That, of course, the club keeps in their cellar just for him.

service, not a product. At least in my mind. But whatever, I paid it. Twenty minutes later the report is saved to my computer and printed out and read. I am laughing. Here is the summary, verbatim:

Type title: ISTP

Core personality traits: Logical, analytical, rational, objective, critical, pragmatic, realistic, factual, practical, efficient, reserved, quiet, detached, confident, independent, adaptable, flexible, tolerant, risk taker, troubleshooter.

Type description keywords: Introversion. Sensing. Thinking. Perceiving.

Type description summary: ISTPs carefully observe what is going on around them. Then, when the need arises, they move quickly to get to the core of a problem and solve it with the greatest efficiency and the least effort. They often function as troubleshooters. ISTPs resist regimentation and rules and enjoy the challenge of solving a new, concrete problem using facts and data. They value home, family, financial security, health, and autonomy.

Clearly this is a description of someone who will fail as a shopkeeper. But it perfectly describes that which I am: A healthy, coolly dead-eyed, self-directed, flush, cautiously watchful Autodidact Polymath and The Most Brilliant Woman In The World loner, as well as what I would prefer to be: Financially secure.

Wow, those Myers-Briggs people have it going on — and that was just on page one. Importantly, the test proved that I am not self-deluded and that most people have trouble "reading" me. This I know as mostly men and some women (including Mother) have always said the following: "I just don't understand you, Angela."[371]

Well, duh.

I didn't make myself like this, God did. Just see how far a complaint to Him and some therapy will get you in understanding me. That's right. Not far. But guess what? I am clearly one of sixteen "types". Type ISTP, to be specific. I didn't even go off the beaten path that often, though granted my path is on another planet.[372]

I can focus like nobody's business.[373] As an example: Once on a family trip to Disney World on a ride featuring blowing water and ostentatious explosions and Proudly Green dragons sneaking out of caves and snorting fire, one little comment made its way through to my brain. Now, this comment I shall tell you about momentarily made its way through simply because I was at the end of my focusing period, that is to say, I had figured out whatever I was thinking about and was again joining the world.

I heard, "Wow. She is so cool." Who were they talking about? Everybody on the boat, my husband and both of my own children included, were staring at me.

---

[371] This statement is often accompanied by a shaking of the head from left to right in quick succession and a frown. If the author ever finds a man who smiles and nods when he says, "I just don't understand you," then the author will know she has found a keeper.

[372] Yes, the author admits she is from outer space as upon first meeting her and having not yet opened her mouth to speak to them men have said "Baby, you are OUT OF THIS WORLD!" Of course, after finding out what that statement actually means and how that "trip" will cause them to crash and burn, they will shake their head and say, "I just don't understand you, Angela."

[373] "Like nobody's business" is colloquial for "can tune out all others and all things".

My husband was shaking his head and frowning and saying, "I just don't understand you."[374] I said to the boat operator/captain dude "What?" and he said "You haven't flinched once or screamed" and I said "Was I supposed to?" and everybody on the boat laughed and some thought I was part of the show then another dragon snorted fire and everybody but me screamed because now I was focused on trying to figure out what in the *hayle*[375] was going on.

Well, if only I had handy my Myers-Briggs Type Indicator® test results printout, I would have known, to wit, that ISTPs sometimes become so absorbed in one of their interests that they ignore or lose track of others. See? Focused.

Another trait of ISTPs is that they dislike any work that involves inefficiency or inconsistency in getting results. You would think, then, that no ISTP would ever be a writer if that trait was 100% true 100% of the time. You would be wrong because ISTPs also focus on getting the desired results, which means that when an ISTP writes they can see their word count go up and up and up and up and…UP![376] See? Results.

If I had only known when I was a kid that I was an ISTP, I could've explained when Mother said, "Who ARE you? Where did you COME from? I just do not understand you, Angela."

Mother and Mother's Honey and my siblings were all, every single solitary one of them, inefficient. If there were two ways to do something — one that saved time, energy, and money and one that dragged it out forever and cost five times

---

[374] Totally explains the divorce. Well, not totally, but somewhat.

[375] "What in the hayle?" (correctly said as *HAY-ell*) is the precise pronunciation we Southerners use when we really, really mean it.

[376] The author admits to not checking the word count with any regularity because she is so focused, but that once she does she is always surprised, often getting giddy, to see the count has risen by one or more thousand words.

what it should and made everybody miserable in the doing — they would invariably choose the latter. I had no problem with this as long as they weren't dragging me into whatever it was they wanted to do.

I am a realist and tolerant (both ISTP traits) and so how they spent their time was their business. But if they were going to spend my time, then I had a say-so in how the process would go.[377] That includes the series of Famous Dishwashing Disasters that lasted from the time I was thirteen until I moved out at nineteen.[378] Suffice it to say, at thirteen I learned that there is an extremely efficient and cost-saving way to clean the kitchen and dining room after a meal. Being a lover of efficiency and also having closely observed Mother and Little Sister complaining for years about how long it took and how hard it was to do the dishes, I thought they would be ecstatic to learn of a new way that would solve their problem.

See? ISTPs carefully observe and often act as troubleshooters. What Myers-Briggs would not have told me back then was that ISTPs are often not appreciated by most family members, especially those who are crazy[379], and so I kept pounding home the lessons I learned in school about doing dishes until finally both Mother and Little Sister cornered me and said, "You aren't the boss of us!" or

---

[377] The author wants the reader to know that she is willing to be paid for her time and therefore if paid-for time is spent in being inefficient she won't like it and will try to speed it up even if it means less profit, but that if the "customer" insists on paying her to twiddle her thumbs, she isn't stupid and will take the money. However, her family never offered to compensate her monetarily for her time and therefore they were always saying she was "bossy" and that, dear reader, was just not true.

[378] The author still has flashbacks about these horrendous years and so chooses not to go into detail.

[379] The author apologizes for teasing the reader, but if you want to know about her childhood, please buy the book *Twinkle, a memoir*.

something like that, at which point Mother made a parental decree that, of course, did not work but I went along with it for a while (ISTP trait: Pragmatic) until such time as a better way could be implemented (ISTP traits: Adaptable and Flexible).

My ISTP traits even came to the fore in my paying jobs and at school. I could tell you how many bosses and teachers and principals did not like my suggestions for solving their clearly self-generated problem, but what's the point? You already get that nobody likes a second-grader telling them how to fix their problem, especially as soon as the second-grader opens her mouth and out pops a most logical, sweet solution.

But I cannot help this. In fact, this ISTP thing is inherited from my father's side of the family (their gene pool was exceedingly strong[380]) and the best I can do is control the timing of the application of those personality traits because they ain't going away. And that, dear readers, is why I like to write books. Because the situations, plots, characters are all under my control and do exactly as I say.[381]

---

[380] Even though Little Sister had the same father as the author, the only genes from that side that she got controlled physical appearance. The crazy she got 100% straight from the DNA pool of the mother.

[381] The author is misleading the reader just a tiny bit here. It is true this is the reason she likes to write books. However, what is not made clear is that characters often say to the author "You aren't the boss of me!" and next thing you know the book is nothing like what the author intended. But even in this, the author's ISTP traits save the day.

No habla Greek,

mon sewer.

Isn't that clearer? Or why online translation engines will never bring world peace.

SOUTHERN AMERICAN ENGLISH

While the movie was dark and weird and there is The Chicken Incident, it was a pretty good murder mystery and the helper monk chooses the path of God and all's well that ends well as they ride off into the gloom on a horse and donkey. I bought the book with the clear intent of reading it after *Travels in Hyperreality* was finished. I believe that the read will begin on Day Seven after Travels receivership because I cannot bear to waste any more time on such tedium.

GOOGLE TRANSLATION INTO SPANISH:

Mientras que la película era oscura y extraña y está The Chicken Incident, fue un misterio de asesinato bastante bueno y el monje ayudante elige el camino de Dios y todo está bien, que termina bien cuando cabalgan en la oscuridad en un caballo y un burro. Compré el libro con la clara intención de leerlo después de que *Travels in Hyperreality* haya terminado. Creo que la lectura comenzará el Día Siete después de la suspensión de pagos de Travels porque no puedo soportar perder más tiempo en tal tedio.

GOOGLE TRANSLATION FROM SPANISH BACK INTO ENGLISH:

While the film was dark and strange and there is The Chicken Incident, it was a pretty good murder mystery and the *assistant*[382] monk chooses the way of God *and everything is fine, which ends well when they ride in the dark* on a horse and a donkey. I bought the book with the clear *intention* of reading it after *Travels in Hyperreality* has finished. I think *the reading will start on* Day Seven after *the suspension of payments from Travels* because I *cannot* bear to waste more time in such boredom.

Only Google knows what the Spanish translation of the original English said. But I'm bringing all this up because there are nuances in every language that algorithms cannot understand. There is this woman who, for years mind you, made a good living translating legal documents from/to English/Spanish. She had a great reputation. She did a wonderful job. Her clients loved her. Then, seemingly overnight[383], her business dried up. She couldn't get a translation gig to save her soul.

When she called her customers to find out who they were now using to do their translating, she was told they were using something called Google Translate where — FOR FREE! — they could get their documents translated. She asked one customer if she could see a translated document and, because they held her in high esteem, the customer sent it. She was beyond horrified at the result.

Besides obvious misunderstandings, it seems the Google Translate engine didn't know the law and had put her clients

---

[382] Original word was helper monk.

[383] Seemingly, but not actually as the woman told the author that the process was a gradual lessening of business over a period of five years.

in grave financial peril. So, the woman pointed this out to her former clients. You will not believe what they said. You won't believe it. But it is true. They said —

"Well, it's not like anybody is going to read it."

The woman had tears in her eyes when she related this. Why have a contract to begin with? Exactly, she said. This is what Tech Giants have brought us to. They fully expect consumers to abide by their terms of service and nobody to read it.

Goodbye, Aretha.

August 16, 2018, the Queen of Soul died from pancreatic cancer exactly 41 years after Elvis died from a heart attack.[384] I mentioned this to my friend, an old, old, old former radio guy from the mid-1960s to early 1970s who remembers Elvis and Aretha well.

He hastened to change the subject to a more upbeat topic and said, "Hey, Angela, the reason I remember when Elvis died is because he and Aretha both died on my birthday."

I said, "What? Today is your birthday?"[385]

"Yep. Guess who else was born on this day?" He looked all eager for me to guess but I just couldn't and looked at him like I really wanted to know and then I said, "Who?"

"Madonna!"

Let it be made perfectly clear that my friend has never once heard a song by Madonna because my friend stopped listening to the radio on the very day he quit the radio station. My old, old, old friend is one of those people who is thrust into situations where he must remember massive facts and figures then spew them out again quickly and accurately. Which is why he made such a great DJ. He is also one of those

---

[384] The author is aware that the heart attack came because of drug usage and that a toilet was involved, but when she wrote "Elvis died from a drug overdose while sitting on a toilet" she felt disrespectful of the man and thought better not put that sliminess in her book. Therefore, the reader will agree *not to remember*, which means *to forget*, this footnote which should be easy because she didn't write it, right?

[385] The author said it like she was sorry to have just found out and that if she had only known she would've thrown him a big old party or something and that since she didn't know, why it was just too bad she had such short notice, blah, blah, blah. The fact is that even with a heads-up, she wouldn't throw him a party because she doesn't believe in annually celebrating the fact that anybody came into the world and has made a conscious effort her entire life to ignore those types of days.

people that never forgets data. So the fact that he even knew Madonna's name and that she was a singer, actress, and all-round glamorous material girl has nothing to do with his interest in her but more to do with her team's marketing expertise and damn, they are experts at it.

Of course, even Madonna's team is having trouble with marketing these days because a lot of their efforts centered around Madonna's outrageous and ever-increasing scandalous behavior — and these days the bad-girl thing isn't working for the sixty-one-year-old.

All this is quite opposite from Aretha Franklin who is not known for swirling scandal, but for her massive talent. Granted, Aretha had drama in her life, but she did not use it to get free column inches. Instead, she did not want to talk about the drama, often refusing to speak of it.

While I was not there when reporters got pushy in digging for scandal, I can bet the Queen of Soul put them in their place real fast, and I can bet they didn't try it again for fear of finding out what "or else" really could mean.

And that is why I like Aretha. She was truly the Queen of Class and Soul. She showed both during the 1998 *Divas Live* brought to television by VH1 which lined up the best of the best: Aretha Franklin, Carole King, Céline Dion, Gloria Estefan, Shania Twain, and Mariah Carey. So, what happened was that Aretha didn't stop singing when it was Céline's turn to sing. Well, Céline, unlike most Canadians, wasn't putting up with Aretha stomping all over her stage time and she decided she was going to show Aretha a thing or two. By way of explaining Céline's actions, Carole King began by saying, "Bless [Aretha's] heart, but she does like to take over."

But Aretha knew who was on the stage with her. And she knew who needed to learn a lesson. And so she was teaching the tiny Canuck to know her place. Now, Aretha could do that and not be a smartass highfalutin egomaniac because Aretha had come up the hard way in life and in the business. Céline did not. In fact, Céline's story is more like a fairy tale.

Aretha understood that some folks gotta learn the hard way and that some folks need to learn in public and where but on national television in a much-vaunted show would be better? No place. Aretha did not shirk her duty and when she kept singing through Céline's part and Céline was getting antsy about it, Aretha knew Céline would try something stupid — and she did.

She tried to out-diva Aretha.

Céline's attempt did not work. Do not believe what the other stars on the show said about the situation because I'm telling you what it looked like from the viewer's POV and that is all that matters in live TV[386] and in this show Céline showed herself up as being a Wannabe. She pulled out all the stops in her vocal arsenal and found herself wanting.[387]

Yes, ladies and germs[388], she found herself craving the power, tone, control, and range of Aretha's voice and was inadequate in rendering the song "Natural Woman" with all the emotional capacity carried fluently through Aretha's voice. Céline ended a great evening by trying to start a catfight and all that did was make her look bad. Not a good move, Céline. But, Aretha, Aretha! Even Céline will miss you and I bet she does a tribute to you in one of her splashy shows because, I do believe, the lesson you taught her has been learned. Oh, goodbye, Aretha.

---

[386] Backstory is great years later and makes everybody chuckle.

[387] The reader can imply two meanings that if the reader will just continue into the following paragraph, this will be explained. The author recognizes she is coddling the reader by supplying too much entertainment in the footnotes and she considers this footnote to be a "CTA" [call to action] for an intervention.

[388] "Ladies and germs" is used in humor and comedy in place of "ladies and gentlemen" and was first put into popular use by Milton Berle, who was "The Funniest Man In The World" for quite a long run. The author uses it when she can to pay homage to a funny but sad guy who understood humor both overt and subtle.

Garden & Gun[389]

A friend of mine passed along two issues of the above entitled glossy magazine. One was 148 pages, the other 172.[390] I was excited to get them. Not because of the garden, because while I might know a lot and be talented in a lot of areas, there is one thing I am extremely good at above all else and that is destroying plants. Yes, I have a black thumb.

When it gets near plants that I want to grow on purpose, they die. It was not always that way. I used to have some beautiful houseplants and my vegetable garden kept me in plenty of things to preserve through the processes of hot-water-bath canning and packing in a freezer to see us through the harsh winter months when the snow was piled 10 feet higher than the house and we had to use the underground pathway to get to the root cellar for the taters and unyuns.[391] But the year we moved from the North Georgia Mountains to the Big City of Hotlanta and The Husband-Now-The-Ex said, "Let's leave the plants in storage, they will be fine" and I said "I don't think so, I'd rather bring them with us now" and he said "I just don't understand you, Angela" and I said "No kidding, but what has that to do with the plants?" but he left the plants in storage anyway and they froze and died and from that point forward my green thumb turned black.

That is why the title of the magazine was only partially interesting, guns being the main attraction for me. But upon eagerly diving into the two issues, it became abundantly clear that whoever published it was skeert or pussy-hat

---

[389] Published by The Allée Group LLC out of Charleston, South Carolina.

[390] The author did not compare ad count vs. editorial placement to determine which was in abundance in the one and lacking in the other.

[391] Editor will please allow the author to have her fun and just not mark this word for review. Thank you.

whipped.[392] I do not back down from my statement. One issue merely had a story about a man who trains dogs for field trial competitions wherein not once was the word *gun* or *hunt* mentioned. The other issue had a hint for training dogs for field trial competitions wherein the subject said he would occasionally *kill* a bird for a dog to maw and jaw on a bit so they would know why they were out there in the field in the first place, and it had an article about a man who restored old guns as works of art, but not one mention of how the bird was rendered without life.[393]

I'm gonna say it.

I'm. Gonna. Say. It.

What the *hayle*?

I mean, the whole magazine had everything to do with the Genteel South[394] and nothing to do with The Real South. For God's sake, a whole article about how to fry chicken? And another on how to mix a flawless Bloody Mary? And what's this one here? Ah! Holy Mother of Jesus. Slap my boohiney until it is bright pink! A weekend at *Barbeque Camp*?

---

[392] Skeert: Southern dialect favorite meaning *scared a whole bunch more than normal.* To see the best usage, read this:
Bubba Joe to Billy Bob: Hey, Billy Bob, I dare you to jump over that gator.
Billy Bob to Bubba Joe: Way-ell now, lemme tink 'boot dis.
Bubba Joe to all their friends: Hahahahahaha! Billy Bob is ssss-*keert!*
Billy Bob to Bubba Joe: Way-ell, now iffen you be such a braveheart and so forth, why don't ewwwwe throw yer own ass over that-there gator. Dubble-dawg-darr-ya. Let's see who's s-s-s-s-*keert* now, huh?

[393] Did he shoot the bird or kill it with his bare hands? Which is scarier? Well, to P-HWPCLDRSFCs, both are. So how did he kill the bird?

[394] The Genteel South is another name for a group called Rude Southerners. Rude Southerners make a show of flaunting their prosperity and they are excellent at quietly signaling that you do not belong to their group and never will; even if you marry in, you will only be tolerated and the family will wish for divorce. Those in the Genteel South, or Rude Southerners, Yankees, and Southern-born Genteel Wannabes make up the sole subscriber base of these types of magazines.

Dear Readers,

Please be advised I can no longer have these magazines on my desk, even for research. I have thrown them away and dumped upon them in the trashcan some right-gnawed cobs of yeller corn boiled to within an inch of its life and two tough stalks of similarly boiled collard greens. And my friend, whose Yankee girlfriend is the one who is trying to understand the Genteel South so she can understand her boyfriend and his friends, should he ever darken my door again with the likes of this filthy apostacy[395], I shall put an appropriate hex on his soul and run him from off my property with a proper cocking of a real gun and a shouted "What in the *hayle* is your problem, mister? You dump on my doorstep teachings and ways of the Spawn of Satan? Howwww. Day-rrrr. Ewwwwe. Suh! Be gone!"

I'd holler as his taillights slowly bounced over the speed bumps in front of my condo, "Repent and sin no more, my son. Juheezus luvs ya. This I know! For the Bible tells me so."

---

[395] Even the title of the periodical is misleading. It should be <u>Garden & (Maybe a) Gun</u>.

Confessions of a Millennial Retro Hipster Jazz Fan

As an Autodidact Polymath Songstress[396] and The Most Brilliant Woman In The World Who Is Also The Most Astute and Intuitive, I make studies of such a wide range of topics and have become such a sought-after authority on those that I have also been called catholic. Not *a Catholic*, mind, but catholic from the Greek *katholikos* (universal, general) and *katholou* (in general) which when broken apart is from the *kata*[397] (down) and *holou* (whole) all of which for you non-autodidact, non-polymaths means the word catholic has nothing to do with religion, a subject about which I do not like to opine though I can when called upon.[398]

What has all that to do with the title of this essay? I'm not exactly sure of that at this point in this treatise, but we shall discover it together. Maybe the use of the word *confessions* had something to do with it. In any case, a young man in his twenties attended the Jazz jam at the Red Light Café when Alan Dynin and I were performing our original song "I Can't Seem to Cry". The lyrics are simple — I will include them

---

[396] *Songstress,* as used by this author, includes both the singing and writing of lyrics and melody embodied in a song.

[397] Not to be further confused with The Gun Kata as practiced in a not-far-fetched dystopian future as depicted in the movie *Equilibrium.* Especially if caring Pussy-Hat Wearing Politically Correct Liberal Democrat RINO Socialist Fascist Commies, who are jealous they are not oligarchs, have anything to do with how to fashion a utopian Socialism.

[398] The author, often mistaken for an idiot snake-handling fundamentalist because of her accent and her ability to make herself have an expression that would lead holier-than-thou authorities to that conclusion, often takes by surprise many an authority of holy texts and not more than a few opinion-makers, that is preachers, who are certain of "what God really meant" when she disagrees with them as they believe her to be a sheeple.

here momentarily — yet extremely profound, thoughtful, and deep, causing certain listeners to enter a reflective state of mind. The lyrics are:

[BEGIN. SLOW TEMPO HERE.]

I cry over puppies.
I cry over kittens.
I even cry over spilt milk.
But no matter
How hard I try,
I can't seem to cry
Over you.
I cry when my groceries
Are bagged upside down.
I even cry over
Burnt toast.
But no matter
How hard I try,
I can't seem to cry
Over you.
[BEGIN UPBEAT TEMPO HERE.]
Cross my heart and
Hope to die
Stick a needle in my
Eye if I lie.
[BEGIN TO SLOW THE TEMPO HERE.]
Yes, no matter
How hard I try,
I can't
seem to
cry
Over
you.

The song has two different tempos. The first is slow and gentle and sweet; the second is fast and stormy and cynical. Alan's piano stylings on this are amazing[399] and the notes fit my voice perfectly.[400] Alan's composition also allows bass players and drummers to have opportunity to shine as they are wont to do — and deserve to get to do — when they come to a Jazz jam.

The song ended and Gordon[401] was happy with it, so yay for me and Alan. But also yay for the audience. Down we went off the stage to mingle with the listeners and pay our respects to other players and singers waiting their turns. The evening wore on until it was almost midnight. I went to pay my tab at the bar.[402] And here he came. The Millennial Retro Hipster Guy[403] seeking in the confessional that is Angela both the validation and absolution he needed in his life.

---

[399] Holy cow!

[400] The author as songstress admits this was intentional and self-serving when she wrote it.

[401] You will remember him as Dr. Gordon Vernick of Georgia State University, and this is his jam.

[402] When Michael the Bartender is there, the author usually gets him to make her a Chocolate Martini which is to die for and is the best in town, but on this night her tummy was feeling sketchy, so she applied two largish applications of Medicinal Pinot Noir and boy, oh boy, did that ever do the trick. Tummy troubles over!

[403] To save ink, we will refer to this young man henceforth as MRH Guy.

MRH Guy inserted himself into the path I was taking, causing me to stop. His sad, needy eyes met mine. He made a greeting, which greeting I returned in a socially acceptable form.[404] MRH Guy then proceeded to commence to hold forth on how extraordinary was my voice[405] and Alan's playing, too, was extraordinary. But it was clear he had something he truly needed to say that could not be said so loudly. MRH Guy looked around to make sure his girlfriend was not within hearing distance, leaned into me, and whispered, "Your lyrics were so…so simple yet…so…so very profound. You see…I too have cried over little things but couldn't cry over my woman."

Oh, the next ten minutes we spent together were astounding. I told him a funny story that made him laugh (this was the validation of his feelings) and allowed him to freely express more inner thoughts (this was the absolution or "freeing" he sought). And isn't that exactly what music is supposed to do and did on this night at the Gordon Vernick Jazz Jam at Red Light Café which every Wednesday night from nine until midnight-ish houses more catholic thought[406] than you will find anywhere else in the Bible Belt?[407]

Yes. Yes, it is and it did.

---

[404] The author knows her diva days are ahead of her but at this point she does not thrust aside, nor employ bodyguards to do the same, nor in other fashions attempt to avoid "The Fan".

[405] The author wants the reader to know she reluctantly objected to the flowing and flowery praise but did agree that MRH Guy was correct in his assessments.

[406] The author does not claim to be the high priestess in these gatherings, but if the office is thrust upon her…well she believes she is obliged to take on the duties such office presents and will do her best to serve the people where they are.

[407] The Bible Belt, or The South. Though there be plenty of religion elsewhere.

The Nature of the Crave: Part One

KD Lang[408] said it best when she sang "Constant craving has always been."[409]

To show you how far back the crave began, we go to Genesis Chapter 1 where the first crave was Yahweh wanting to create and not be alone, which He did and then He wasn't.

The second and third craves were Satan's. He wanted to be worshiped like God and to destroy all things good. We know all this from the context of the chapters.

But the fourth crave, though it was the first mention of the word itself in all of the human writings, was Genesis 3:16 where Jehovah[410] said to Eve "…in birth pangs you will bring forth children, and your *craving* will be for your husband and he will dominate you."

Having myself given birth twice, I can honestly say that I do not remember craving my husband's presence during the birth of our children. Granted, the births were through Caesarean section and with the application of don't-care shots there was no pain, but I can opine clearly on why women crave their husbands during childbirth pains: They want to kill them for getting them like this.

God knew how we women would feel and so he did not cause the crave, he simply predicted it. Now, we women do crave our husbands at other times and, yes-tee-hee, we do like to be dominated at certain times.

We've all heard the old joke where a man says to another man "I wear the pants in my family" and the other man says

---

[408] Yes, she is Canadian, but we overlook that.

[409] To read more about another Canadian and craving, please see the essay entitled "Goodbye, Aretha".

[410] English version of the Hebrew Yahweh.

"Yeah, because she lets you" and the good-natured barbs keep flying. But a happy home is one where the husband knows his place and his place is to dominate. I shall give you an example of the best kind of domination, to wit:

Husband dials phone. Wife answers.

Husband: What's for dinner, Woman?
Wife: Woman?
Husband: I mean, ummmm…what's for dinner, Dear Wife O' Mine?
Wife: That's better. We are having your favorite, of course.
Husband: Oh, goody. What's my favorite again, Dearest Gentlewoman O' My Heart?
Wife: Pot roast with roasted potatoes and carrots. A side of creamed taters with butter and milk. Buttermilk biscuits fresh from the oven with your choice of honey, strawberry jam, and/or molasses.[411]
Husband: Oooweee! Baby, you sure do know how to treat your man right. What's for dessert?
Wife: Why that would beeeeeeee…Cream of Me. If you can handle it, Big Boy.
Husband: Handle it. Oh, Papa will show Mama how he can handle it.
Wife: Really? Tell me how you will *handle it*, Big Fella.
Husband: Well, *Woman*…
Wife: Mmmmm…Baby, talk to me.
Husband: After dinner, the very first thing Imma gonna do — and you won't be able to stop me! — is the dishes. Spick and span that kitchen will be.

---

[411] The author is aware that should a girly girl or RadFem have gotten this far into the book without already having a screaming hissy fit meltdown, they will at this point proceed to be having one as the author mentions a family where the man works a job outside the home and a woman works a job inside the home and the woman cooks and the man eats.

Wife: Uh, huh. Yes. Yes?

Husband: Then, Baby, Imma gonna lay you back on the sofa and…mmmm…

Wife: Mmmmm….WHAT?

Husband: Imma gonna rub your feet as you watch your favorite tee-vee show.

Wife: Rub my feet, Baby? Tell me how you gonna do dat?

Husband: Listen close, Baby, cuz you won't be able to say no when I get started. Imma gonna do your feet one little piggy at a time, yes, indeed.

Wife: Both feet?

Husband: Oh, yeah, Baby. You know it. Papa always finishes what he starts.

Wife: Hurry home, Baby. Mama needs her Papa. She needs him bad.

See? Crave the domination. God was quite smart when He saw that situation coming up.

According to <u>Webster's Third New International Dictionary (Unabridged, 1981)</u> *crave* means "to ask authoritatively; to demand as necessary; to want; to know; to need; to require. A *craving* is the urgent asking; an entreating; a desire to satisfy; a begging."

Certainly the husband and wife in our previous example understood it at a cellular level, though it is doubtful they could have written about it for others to understand. But this essay is not about the constant cravings between a man and a woman. No. This essay is about me and my recent crave for chocolate.

I had been pedal to the metal doing double nickels for days on end.[412] I was snatching bites of food here and there in between the hard and difficult jobs of thinking and writing and editing and rewrites and playing solit...errrr...never mind. Anyway, days of hard thinking and writing and editing and in other fashions pushing words around to bring them to heel found me staggering each day toward the kitchen and tearing the shelves apart looking for that chocolate bar I had hidden in a most logical place. And finally on the seventh day, when I felt I must rest from my labors, the crave became unbearable and that damn Hershey Milk Chocolate Bar refused to be found and I fell to my knees and held up hands in supplication to God Almighty and said —

"PuhLEEZE, God, you know your daughter. You know she needs the chocolate. The crave is fast and hard upon your child and she cannot think and she cannot function without it. Nay, nay, Heavenly Father, your daughter cannot leave her domicile to go to the store for that would be cheating You. Yes! You, Father. For You must be able to answer an entreaty so that you can feel good about Yourself.

"So, Father, know this: That without chocolate, preferably dark chocolate though milk chocolate will do in a pinch, I simply will not be able to continue on with the work that ye hath given me to do and therefore it is incumbent on you — Nay! Nay! — you are obliged, Dear Father — I don't want you to take it like I'm commanding you or anything but I am simply quoting Scripture — to provide your servant girl with edible comestibles of the variety that will feed her soul, not the soul of flesh and bone, but the soul of the inner self, her

---

[412] "Pedal to the metal" is a term truckers use to indicate they are at speed. "Double nickels" harkens back to the time when legislators thought they knew best how to save fuel and demanded that everybody not exceed the maximum MPH of 55. Therefore, the metaphor should explain itself when applied to how much the author was working.

chi, her essence, her lifeforce, yes, Dear Father, her heart of hearts."

I had barely gotten out the Amen when a bright light flashed over my head toward a shelf and landed perfectly on a small container that had miraculously appeared before me.

"Yes, yes!" I cried. Rising to my feet and stretching arms to a Tupperware[413] container, I snapped the lid, and there were semi-sweet chocolate chips, Nestlé brand, my favorite chocolate chip in the whole wide world.

"Dear Father, giver of all things good and chocolatey[414], I thank you for this small answer to my bequest for a crave to be fulfilled. Ummm…yumm…yummy…In Jesus' name, Amen."

Let the choir sing!

---

[413] The author has not been paid an editorial placement fee for any mention of brand names in this essay or anywhere else in this book and if anybody is assuming she can be bought, then a pox on that person UNLESS they want to talk deal and then the author will put you in touch with her entertainment attorney to work out a strategic partnership.

[414] The reader might assume the author is being shallow because with her prayer she is asking for chocolate when she could be asking for other things in this world. Things that shows she *cares*, like she could be praying for world peace or an end to hunger or for P-HWPCLDRSFCs to shut the aitch, ee, double-hockey-sticks up with their whining and sniveling.

The author would like to reassure all readers that she does pray for these things but she does not make it an ostentatious show and therefore is mostly private about such matters…until she isn't.

How Angela put da beatdown on the Kingsmen drummer.

I am used to being in the spotlight. It is true. Wherever I go, there I am in it. The spotlight manages to find its way to me. Does anybody ask me if I want it? They do not.

For instance, as a member of The Recording Academy — National Academy of Recording Arts and Sciences, or NARAS as it is known on legal paperwork; Grammy to the rest of you — I get invited every year to attend the awards ceremonies that usually go on about a whole week. While you may be familiar with the big, splashy, over-the-top televised awards featuring red-carpet-ready slips of cloth flung haphazardly over perky body parts getting most of the attention of the attentive yet solidly anti-objectifying mainstream media, you may not know that earlier in the day is another ceremony where most of the 70+ awards are presented.

As a member, I get to attend both. The television version is the best to watch from way up high in the nosebleed section because there you can see what goes on behind the curtains. These people do not mess around. Artists check their ego and do as they are told. If a problem arises, two men each argue for their case in a furious ten-second blast, a third decides in two seconds between the two, and *Boom Shakalaka.* Just like that, the argument is over and the problem is solved.

If only world peace could be solved via Grammy show production methods and values.

The viewing audience does not get to see this. But I did. It was so fascinating that I wasn't even paying attention to the acts themselves and totally missed Elton John's solo in the middle of the audience on a raised stage with a grand piano and microphone under a beautiful spotlight. In fact, it wasn't until the entire audience let out a collective loud gasp that I looked around and what did I see? I saw Elton John being grabbed by two giant men just before the Sir completely hit the floor. Exiting the stage, he had tripped and fallen.

You viewers would not know this, but I, faithfully reporting to you, have now informed you of off-camera drama.

However, let's get back to the awards ceremony earlier in the day. While in the televised version seats are assigned, these seats were listed as General Admission. That is, one found a seat where one wanted to sit, and one took it. Nobody could tell you otherwise. I did and ended up sitting right next to a guy who got a Grammy for coming up with some new sort of World Music sound. He was an old guy. His wife was an old woman. They looked like retired schoolteachers. They would never have been invited to sit where viewers could see them on national television. Nonetheless, they were important in their own right.

The early awards ceremony was live-streamed on the Internet. So we had camera guys rushing around to get closeups of winners as they rose from their seats or walked down the aisle. This ceremony went on for four hours with no commercial interruption. It was beyond awesome. Skrillex won his first award there that early afternoon as did Gotye ("Somebody That I Used to Know feat. Kimbra").

But four hours is four hours and after two and a half hours were gone, Mama's bladder was screaming for mercy. I got up and walked out to go potty. You need to understand that I was dressed up quite swanky. I had on gray lace pants under a black velvet cavalry jacket loaded with blingy buttons. Furthermore, you need to understand that I'm tall and I've always walked better than a runway model, especially if wearing any sort of heels. This is not on purpose. It's a natural thing I received through DNA.

So after taking a much-needed whiz and making sure I was put back together properly and had no toilet paper trailing behind me on my shoes, I reentered the auditorium. Almost to my seat, I heard a winner's name called out. And there I was.

In. The. Spotlight.

Being live-streamed across the entire Internet for all to see. The winner. Except I wasn't the winner, though I damn sure looked like one. Other cameramen were getting in position to have me walk up on stage. The announcer, big smile on his face, was waving me down and saying, "Come on up." And I'm shaking my head.

Out of the corner of my eye I see this other woman standing on the other side of the auditorium. The real winner. Being all ignored and stuff and here I was stealing her thunder. Not that I was doing it on purpose. I was just relieving my bladder. So, I pointed over to her and she slunk up the stage steps and tried to smile, but it was all over. Even the cameramen didn't rush as fast toward her. The moment had lost its momentum.

And that's just one time this sort of thing happened to me. I do not manufacture these events.

The reason I'm telling you this is because another event happened where I was in the spotlight along with my husband (him for the first time ever) when we were at a concert along with two friends and my aunt and cousin and 5000 other people to see the rock group The Kingsmen. Unfortunately, I believe the audience thought they were seeing the folk group The Kingston Trio because when The Kingsmen drummer did a five-minute, frickingly awesome, unbelievably witty, damn-straight drum solo, everybody was holding their ears (including one of our friends who was himself a drummer).

Everybody, that is, except me and my husband. When it finished we spontaneously jumped out of our seats in a standing ovation. I screamed to my husband, "Whistle for me! Whistle for me!" And he did and I screamed and we were clapping and stomping our feet and everybody, including the band, stared at us as we stood there, alone, in the proverbial spotlight because nobody was shining an actual light on us.

I turned to the people around me and said, "Why is no one else standing up? Do you not recognize genius when you hear it?" The band was asking the same questions quietly amongst themselves. "You people are such old fogeys."

Finally the rock-not-folk concert ended and the band took their place at tables in the lobby so they could sell and sign merch. The band was arranged in order of least important to the primo uomo[415] who, in this instance, was the drummer. He was the prettiest, I'll admit. A few fans lined up to get their merch and autographs. Well, I had never before heard of this band even though they were quite famous, but because of that one drum solo I told my husband I was going to get their CD and they were gonna sign it. Our drummer friend and his wife also bought some merch, and we got in line together.

The guy on the far left, the least important member of the band and sitting there like he was invisible, had on a T-shirt that referenced a thing that had happened in Portland, Oregon, and, if memory serves, it had something to do with the co-founder of Microsoft, Paul Gardner Allen[416], raising money for something. I forget. It's been a long time ago. But at the time I knew about it and said something to the guy with the T-shirt who then got animated and said, "Wow! You've heard of this?" Well, yeah. Who hasn't, right? Then he said, "I helped put that on. I worked with Paul Allen on this." Get. Outta. Town. No way! "Yes! Way!" And away we went having this awesome conversation. Just us two.

Little did we know that spotlight which follows me around was now on the two of us. We were having such a great conversation, we were in our own little world. Nobody else existed in that time and that place.

Until finally we heard it.

A deadly silence filled with a growing whining.

---

[415] If the drummer had been female, the author would have used the term "prima donna".

[416] Who passed away in October 2018.

We looked around and there was the drummer, at the far end of the bank of tables, giving me and the band guy a dirty look. The rest of the band had crossed their arms and skooched their chairs back so they could dodge the drummer's daggers he was throwing at us.

"Excuse me," said the drummer impatiently. "You're holding up the line."

The band guy whispered, "He's mad. You better go."

But me and my smart mouth and my commitment to justice said otherwise and I piped up to the drummer. "What? This line?"

"Yes. Stop talking and move on through."

My husband, aunt, cousin, and two friends were standing past the drummer near the exit, waiting on me. They were worried for me, too. Well, my husband wasn't because he knew what was coming and he knew it was the drummer whut was gonna get a beatdown from a Magnificently Methodical Southern Woman.

"But," said I. "I'm having fun talking to him." I pointed to the guy.

"Well, you are holding up the rest of the line. Move it," said the drummer, obviously a Socialist.

I said, "They can go around." I turned to the line and said, "Anybody wanting to talk to this guy?" Everybody shook their heads no. "Great. Then y'all can go around."

But the line waited because the drummer just had to get snarky now, didn't he? I do not remember what he said but his tone implied "Bitch. Get yer biscuits moving or else I'm gonna have to hurt ya."

I blinked.

And that is when my husband rolled his eyes, shook his head, and stood back while it happened to somebody else.

"Excuse me? Let me tell you something, you little twit. When you did your brilliant drum solo up there on the stage? The one you worked hard to perfect? The one that everybody in that audience was plugging their ears for? Just who was it whut stood up and screamed and whistled for your genius? Huh?"

The guy I was talking to sat back in his chair and joined his bandmates in some mighty big grins and swiveling of heads from him to me. I continued.

"That's right. It was *me* and my husband." Husband closed his eyes and pretended he was not there. "Yeah, he whistled for me because I cannot whistle. Two people out of five thousand who gave you the props you deserved and what are you doing now to your biggest fan in the audience tonight? Calling her names? Rushing her down the line with a handshake a preacher reserves for the poor parishioner? Really? And let me tell you something else. You do not make the band. The band makes you. So you just mind your manners, comprende?"

I gestured to the line to move and it promptly snaked around and the guy and I got on with our business at hand. So finally, conversation over, and having made myself a few new fans that evening, I got on with allowing each member of the band to sign. Yes, that included the drummer. He did not say anything to me. Simply signed his name, slid the CD toward me, and away we went.

Interesting follow-up: My cousin and aunt never said a word. Come to find out, that is exactly what they would have done and they were simply admiring the strong Kell DNA in first-rate action. However, my husband and two friends did nothing but rag on me all the way home.

"Angela, he is famous. How dare you speak to someone famous like that?"

And that is when I knew they all three self-identified as future pussy-hat wearers. Good God Almighty. I am so glad I divorced them[417]...I mean, him.

---

[417] They were The Ex's friends. The author was merely tolerated.

The Art of the Snappy Comeback:
That's my name. Don't wear it out.

One person who would disagree with you about my overall good nature and ability to get along with just about everybody would be The Ex. In fact, he had a special name for me that confirmed his opinion. In this, he agreed with the Kingsmen drummer. That name was Bitch.

Yes, Bitch with a capital B, and make no mistake about that. Though he let it fly verbally once in a while, he mostly *thought* the name. I could tell from the look in his eyes that's what he was thinking. Then he left no doubt toward the end of the marriage when he started saying it out loud in public.

Funny thing: Pussy-Hat Wearing Politically Correct Liberal Democrat RINO Socialist Fascist Commies[418] and certain Jazz Kittens[419] share The Ex's opinion of the reader's favorite[420] Autodidact Polymath Magnificently Methodical Southern Women and The Most Brilliant Woman In The World. And just like I told The Ex when he called me the B-word, I am willing to tell them all with relish and glee, "That's my name. Don't wear it out."

I say I am *willing* to do it as if I haven't done it. That is correct. And the reason I haven't done it is because, well, for years I let myself be guided by this philosophy, namely: One shouldn't pick on people with learning disabilities and, it

---

[418] Often referred to by the acronym: P-HWPCLDRSFCs.

[419] Yes, the reader has deduced correctly that this may, in point of fact, be a redundancy with the preceding statement as not a few Jazz Kittens are P-HWPCLDRSFCs.

[420] P-HWPCLDRSFCs and The Ex do not hold the author in the same favored status nor do they recognize the overall talent and genius that is she. They are such limited thinkers.

became clear to me that as an Autodidact Polymath Magnificently Methodical Southern Women and The Most Brilliant Woman In The World, compared to me everybody has learning disabilities. So, I made it an operational guideline to simply smile indulgently when the not-so-well-thought-out insults came and to thank them for their most learned opinion.[421]

That worked for many years. And by *worked* I mean fights and murder were avoided.[422] But dang it all to aitch, ee, double-hockey-sticks and back, I wasn't having any fun, and further was constantly being mistaken for an easy target by bullies which finally prompted me to ask, "Angela, is this really how you want to live the rest of your life?" And the answer was no, it was not.

But what was missing?

It took me a while to realize what it was and in this I would like to thank *That '70s Show* for reminding me about The Art of the Snappy Comeback. The TV show originally ran from 1998 to 2006, but accurately represented a time before Political Correctness in all its glorified absurdity came to rule human conversation.[423] It is clear the show's creators lived during that time and were familiar in a firsthand way with that art, now almost lost. I aim to help change that.

---

[421] The author has found this method does have a sharp bite at the end of it for them because often the people to whom she grants a thank-you then believe she approves of their comment, if not outright agrees with it, and they are always mighty surprised to later find out she does not.

[422] The author agrees that murder was a bit of a stretch, but for the sake of making a point — and to remind you that you did not know The Ex — she feels it was perfectly acceptable to say that.

[423] By "human conversation" the author means First World countries with strong state-funded systems of education, from elementary to college and the spectrum in between, which insidiously inserted Socialist thinking coupled with "Caring" thus rendering null and void the part of conversation known as "The Burn" or "The Comeback".

Of course, before we can bring back an art, we must first understand how that art disappeared. More specifically, why. Let's walk through it. It started when three things came into being at the same time. One: An eroding of the use of *Yes ma'am, No ma'am, Thank you,* and *Please.* Two: Children calling adults by their first names instead of the use of the titles Mr., Mrs., or Miss. Three: The rise of the fake Socialist[424] professor in academe. And four: The promotion of the notion that *to care* meant nobody ever got their feelings hurt.

Let's start with one: There came a point where to use these social niceties was thought of as rude and, in some cases, arrogant.[425] All of a sudden it seemed people were ordering other people around. The difference between "Please, sir, pass the salt and pepper" and "Pass the salt and pepper" is huge. Like, Grand Canyon huge. Like, Master-to-Slave huge. If the resulting disuse of these niceties didn't make more class distinctions, then I don't know what could.

Number two: I was aghast the first time an adult told my children to call them by their first name and immediately whipped my head toward the issue of my loins and said, "You will address her as *Mrs.* Smith[426], I don't care what she tells you to do, you understand me?"

Mrs. Smith then turned to me and with nose in air and a self-righteous sniff proceeded to explain to me how I was hurting the self-esteem of my child by not making them equal to adults at which point I said, "Mrs. Smith, you want to adopt them and pay all their bills? No? Then shut up and let

---

[424] Time would prove these to be real Communists.

[425] The author notes the reader's point: Arrogant and rude are the same, so the statement seems redundant. However, while rudeness is embodied in arrogance, arrogance itself embodies conceit, snobbery, and condescension from those with lots of money and a high place in society, whereas poor people can be rude in their own way.

[426] Not her real name.

me teach my children good manners. Thank you."[427] Mrs. Smith was offended and let me know. I asked if it would make it all better if I was to say it all again but use her first name.

She walked away in a huff.

Number three: Furthering the problem[428] was the insidious placement of Soviets in the American school system. Yes, the KGB specially trained certain of their patriots to pretend to be anti-Soviet and to seek asylum in the U.S. Of course, these fake dissidents offered the CIA, FBI, and other alphabet government agencies just enough secret information that they were rewarded with cushy tenured positions in all the best schools across the land. They then identified the forerunners of our current iteration of dissidents, the P-HWPCLDRSFCs, recruiting them via sneaky means[429] to push their agenda on U.S. campuses by shoving it down the throats of students afraid they would not graduate if they disagreed with the prof.

And finally, number four: The promotion of the notion that *to care* meant nobody ever got their feelings hurt. Little-

---

[427] The author has lost touch with Mrs. Smith and has never cared to find out where that Socialist witch is anyway. However, the author did find out that twenty years after this incident, Mrs. Smith became Mr. Smith and then donned a red pussy hat and marched in the streets beside his sisters. As a female, Mrs. Smith preferred men so as a woman she was straight. But now as a man she still prefers men and therefore has ticked another inclusive box as a gay man.

[428] The author chose to use this negative word on purpose, though some general managers of car dealerships and other sales directors would prefer the use of the word *challenge.*

[429] Flattery, alcohol, drugs including LSD, Timothy Leary and other guru types, calling them by their first names except when in bed and then using their title in a sexy voice, and so forth, so that while at work on campus Martha and Mark taught class, but at night when they were boinking each other's brains out they were My Wittle ProfessOR and DOCtor FEELgoooood.

known fact: Without any irony on their part, this notion began to be promoted on university campuses by professors who honed the art of bullying their students while requiring those same students to think that all opinions carried the same weight except the professors' were weightier, and that one must never use certain words and phrases[430] *or else people would think the student didn't care!* Whole sitcoms[431] were built around this concept, thus pushing the Soviet messaging through a Capitalist ad-supported medium.[432]

Now that we know the history of how we came to where we are, let us return to the revival of The Art of the Snappy Comeback and how that is looking in our popular culture.

It all began when Donald "The Hammer" Trump decided he would run for president of the United States. Democrats, Radical Feminists, professors (retired or still teaching), and their acolytes humored The Orange One, as they named Trump, and smiled at him indulgently while gently saying things like "He just has no idea how silly he is. He has no chance to win the Republican nomination much less ever getting elected against our royalty…we mean, Hillary."

Oh, the sweet scorn fairly flowed down from their mountaintops in the form of headlines in all newspapers, major or otherwise, tweets by pundits, magazine covers, learned articles in serious publications, whole books, and on television with nightly reports on how "The Donald", a former reality show star, had not even a snowball's chance on

---

[430] The author is not going to list those words/phrases as the reader would be bored out of their gourd with reading a list of 5974 words/phrases — and still growing.

[431] The reader may recall a famous episode in a show called *Seinfeld* whose most famous line was "Not that there's anything wrong with that." This line can still be heard coming from the mouths of Millennials who have never heard of Jerry Seinfeld, thereby making the case for the Soviets' success in infiltrating the U.S.

[432] Russkies are way sneakier than anybody.

---

a loaded barbeque grill in the South on the Fourth of July. Until, that is, Trump won the Republican nomination.

That is when the previously caring Left, RINOs[433], Deep State, and The Bigs of the Mainstream Media took off their gloves and put brass knuckles on each hand and came out swinging. Oh, the names they called him went a-flying around the world. Even leaders of other countries opined about Trump. None of them counted on Trump's reaction.

See, the Left, RINOs[434], Deep State, and The Bigs of the Mainstream Media have been so used to being obeyed that when they told "The Hammer" to stop pretending he could win the election and he didn't quit, they were horrified, aghast, sickened, depressed, and, in two famous instances, were left speechless on the air. Attacks on Trump went from bad to "now we're serious and we will destroy you".

So, why haven't those attacks against Trump worked like planned? Because Donald is the king of the snappy comeback. He's so good at it, you would think he had written the book *The Art of the Comeback* instead of that other one.[435] Then came the time when Trump didn't wait for his enemies to strike first with their poutin' and whinin', and instead had tweet after tweet of snarky comeback bait awaiting them when they woke in the morning. Now who was behind in the news cycle? Now who was messing with their little minds? Huh?

Yeah, that's right. Of course, what was humorous was that the Left, RINOs, Deep State, and The Bigs of the Mainstream Media didn't have any comebacks at all.

Not a one.

---

[433] Republicans In Name Only.

[434] Republicans In Name Only, in case you forgot.

[435] *The Art of the Deal*, which in the opinion of the author was a stupid book, but he sold a bunch of them, so maybe not so stupid after all?

Not one single retort that anybody cared to talk about.[436] We know this because the media was not quoting each other but was quoting Trump all day long because it was only then their sagging Nielsen ratings and paper circulations went up.

Trump's tweets and speeches and eyerolls and such, even as his wife tried to make nice, gave hope to millions — I misspeak! — billions of people around the world who said, "Hey, I can do that and bring back some clear thinking in my neighborhood." And they are doing that. Why, just the other day I heard a young man say to a young woman, "Woman! What's the matter with you? You on the rag?"[437]

And the reason that young man felt empowered to say such as that to a Radical Feminist acolyte was because Trump has said something similar to Little Dear Leader, also known as Little Rocket Man by millions now that Trump named him. Isn't that just cool and great and so…so…real and human? Yes, it is.

The snappy comeback restores equilibrium by telling bullies, and others who are out of control, that there are limits and they will abide by them or else suffer the consequences.

See? Snappy comebacks are cheaper than war, and when done properly make the murder count go way down. Chicago and Detroit could use lessons in *The Art of the Snappy Comeback*. God knows nothing else is working for them.

As full as those towns are of pussy-hats, I don't see that happening.

---

[436] The best it ever got was when Anderson Cooper replied on air to a Trump tweet when he said, "Oh, yeah? Well…ummm…well."

[437] The author is lying. She did not hear this, but it is funny and she says you just wait and see if that doesn't come back into popular usage making her a prophetess so that her full title will be Autodidact Polymath Prophetess Magnificently Methodical Southern Women and The Most Brilliant Woman In The World.

Hazel and The Russians:
<u>A Lesson in Diplomacy</u>

On November 26, 1964, the 110th episode of the popular TV show *Hazel* aired. While this author cannot assert with absolute authority, I do believe this was the only time the show got political and, to bring it around to the Millennials reading this in the second decade of the 21st century, I say: See? Russians have always been a pain in the ass of the world since they decided they wanted to mercilessly run the planet.

What happened was this: Mr. Baxter — or Mr. B as Hazel the lovable, helpful housekeeper-cum-elderly-aunty-type called him — and his family were chosen to host a Russian dignitary in their home during Thanksgiving, a particularly American celebration that would surely aggravate a Russian.

Which celebration promptly did so much aggravate the foreign visitor that he became insufferable. No matter what the family did to make the man feel welcome, he insisted on insulting the family, their community, and the U.S. He particularly wanted to free Hazel from the shackles of a Capitalist employer who wanted to turn the unfortunate woman into nothing more than a slave to his rich lifestyle.

From the get-go Hazel did not like this Russian man and, as all beloved television housekeepers do, she was having a difficult time holding back her opinion of the man and a more difficult time smiling at him while his insults hurled like rockets across her perfectly set table.

Mr. B and Mrs. B and their precious son, along with other dignitaries, seemed to walk on eggshells around the Russki, and Hazel, just as her mouth was opening, would be shushed and hushed and hustled out of the room before she could start an international incident.

The author did not see this episode when it first aired, and only saw it when she was an adult after it went to syndication. I can tell you I cheered Hazel when finally she could not be shushed, hushed, or hustled, and she let it fly toward that insufferable, prideful, insulting, offensive, and belittling Russian that such ways might work in his country, but they wouldn't fly in hers, no sir, and Mr. B., said she, you can't shut me up and somebody has to stand up for all that was right and good and fair and holy and if he, Mr. B., won't do it, then by Jehoshaphat's hiney, she would and make no apologies for it, no sirree.

Of course, we then find out that the "Russian" was a plant to test the host family to see just how far they would go in conciliatory actions toward the big, bad bully and whether they were capable of hosting the real Russian. In the show it was implied that the State Department and even the president watched from on high, much like the Greek gods and goddesses watched Jason and his Argonauts as they went through their tests. Jason passed. And so did the Baxter household — thanks to Hazel. Boy oh boy, was Mr. B. ever proud of Hazel for reminding him he had a spine.

As of this writing it is now fifty-five years since the airing of that episode and what do we have in the White House? We have Donald "The Hammer" Trump acting much like Hazel. Look, she told the guy, you mind your manners and you act right, or else. "The Hammer" is doing the same thing. Hey, he says to Putin, you might want to stop showing off those abs while riding a horse shirtless, and comprehend this: We'll make nice with you until you act stupid and then we'll throw you on an anvil and proceed to beat you with your own hammer and sickle, youunnerstan'whutImmasayin'huh?

If only RINOs would get a spine, too.[438]

---

[438] As of this writing it is 2018, and the author is watching Brett Kavanaugh be destroyed by Democrats bringing out a cabal of women with fake charges of sexual abuse making the United States Senate a laughingstock around the world. Socialist Fascist Commies...errrr...I mean Democrats and RINOs will always say, "Even if those charges are false, Kavanaugh is a lifelong ratf***er." Which statement only proves why they are a laughingstock.

Speaking of bullies.

Social engineering by force of law is merely a mask for a greater evil. The greater evil of eliminating freedom. Freedom to worship, freedom to live by a higher moral standard, freedom to protect family, self, and property, freedom to own, freedom to pass along to children and grandchildren principles of conduct that safeguard and strengthen the very fabric of our communities and families.

That greater evil demands our attention. Call them out for what they are: Bullies. Bullies who demand agreement or they will make life a living hell, stop you from doing business, shut down your places of worship, decree who will and who will not be your teachers, who you can and cannot associate with, and more stupid rules that do not matter.

Bar none, bullies are everywhere, on every side of every issue. Bullies are weak of moral spine and are only interested in themselves. Bullies never sacrifice themselves for the greater good and are narrow of mind. Bullies blame and whine as they focus on the negative. Bullies do not have positive goals.

Bullies celebrate all that is weak. Bullies cannot bear to hear an opinion when it does not agree with them. Because they have no solid foundation for their position, they hurl vile insults loud and long, using the amplification of social media, businesses, and a willing press — of whom many are bullies themselves. Bullies find and use the easily duped and weak of mind.

Strength of character is anathema to bullies. They cannot help but shudder in disgust when they find themselves around those of strong character. Bullies never have a problem with smiling as they insult, but they always make sure they do so while surrounded by their acolytes. Yes, bullies are afraid to stand alone for what they believe.

They do not hold truth as sacred. They worship the lie and sow disinformation. They produce discord and shove wedges between people for no other reason than to manipulate for self-interest.

Whether by political or religious means or through threats to job security, bullies always exploit those who are willing to go along and say nothing.

I make no apology.

In my forty-plus years of studying and discussing it, I've learned the Bible is a book that tells us a few things. One: Why we are here. Two: How we got here. Three: Why the world is in the state it is in. Four: Who our real enemy is, why he is the enemy, and how to identify that one as well as his followers. Five: The history of God's dealings with mankind as it relates to the outworking of His purpose. And six: A lot of stories that relate the struggle for keeping faith and the troubles from loss of faith, all of which can give us meaning and guidance for our own lives.

The Bible has been manipulated for political purposes (which is why the quickly and badly interpreted King James version of 1611 came to be). It has been interpreted through the prisms of social mores of agendized groups. Subsets of believers have killed other subsets of believers because of doctrinal beliefs and other power grabs (think WWI and WWII: Christian nations fighting other Christian nations).

Parts of the Bible have been falsely changed to represent specific doctrinal beliefs (think the doctrine of the Holy Trinity). It has been rubbed as a talisman and wielded as a sword. It has been outlawed and burned. It has been sacrificed on the altar of the scientific opinion du jour. It has been ignored and made fun of. It has been used as a cudgel (think the doctrine of a burning hellfire of torment).

However, with all that, it is the most widely published and distributed book of all time, bar none. With much research and comparing of current texts with ancient scrolls as they are unearthed, we find that, by and large, the Bible we have today has remained intact.

People have given their lives to protect the right to own a copy and to read it. They fight in courts around the world for the right to speak with others of it and God and their beliefs. Christians are still being tortured and killed — just in Nigeria alone in 2018 many thousands of Christians, including children, have been burned alive, chopped to bits, raped, beheaded, and otherwise killed — for refusing to give up their belief in the truths it contains.

When we humans read, we read through the lens of our own set of limited knowledge. Those who believe the Bible (example, when it says "the earth hangs upon nothing") over the science of the day (example: The earth is flat and sits on the shoulders of Atlas who is standing on the back of a turtle, etc.), yes, those who believe may be laughed at, but we believe Almighty God because we trust He will not lie to us, and we wait for the information. And sure enough, when scientific ability caught up with the Bible, what did we find? We found the earth hangs upon nothing...just like our Heavenly Father said.

The example of the earth hanging upon nothing is just one way we know the Bible was inspired of God. At the time of that writing humans had no way of going into space and seeing the planet from far away, so we know they did not write that from their personal experience. Therefore, true faith, laughed at and derided and held in contempt, is trusted because of "the assured expectation of realities not yet beheld" based on the promises God has made and the promises He has kept.

Everybody else can believe as they like, but as for me, I will never apologize for believing in a known power higher than myself. Not for me the faceless higher power many today call The Universe.

If my Heavenly Father calls himself a male, then I will believe Him even if it is politically or socially inconvenient to do so. And if His meaning of "father" is one unknown to me and He cares to expand upon it and make it clear at a later date, then I'm good with that, too.

Speaking of the Bible.

There are two scriptures that have always brought me comfort. One is in Genesis 3:19 whereupon Adam is told: "In the sweat of your face you will eat bread until you return to the ground, for out of it you were taken. For dust you are and to dust you will return."

The second is Ecclesiastes 3:19-20, which says: "For there is an eventuality as respects the sons of mankind and an eventuality as respects the beast, and they have the same eventuality. As the one dies, so the other dies; and they all have but one spirit, so that there is no superiority of the man over the beast, for everything is vanity. All are going to one place. They have all come to be from the dust, and they are all returning to the dust."

These have brought me great consolation through the years and have informed my decisions regarding a myriad of choices to be made. For instance, when a bad person is wielding power of me, they always wonder why I smile. Well, I smile because I am imagining them as dust and I am holding the dusting rag and a can of Pledge.[439]

That's right. Eventually these people will become dust again. Never mind that some folks who get embalmed last a long time. If you leave them alone they will become dust. And since animals turn to dust just like humans, then I have to wonder: When I dust my house, just who is it I'm wiping away? I mean, what if...and I'm just spit-balling here...what if the dust is partly Hitler, Pol "Saloth Sar" Pot, Dwight David Eisenhower (who was named at birth David Dwight), the

---

[439] *Pledge* is the brand name of a product made specifically for dusting furniture made of wood. It comes in various configurations (spray, oil, infused disposable cloth wipes, lemon-scented) that when used will protect against dust, moisturize the furniture it is used upon, and make everything all shiny. A water-soaked rag wrung until almost dry does the exact same thing and costs less.

creepy babysitter from when I was six, and Clutch, my dog from when I was thirteen? And that's just one configuration.

The only two I want to visit with are Dwight and Clutch because they cared about the things that mattered for the benefit of mankind. Adolf, Saloth, and creepy babysitter were haters of all that was good and right, so why would I want to hang around with them? In any case, you get my point, right? We don't know who is in our homes, riding around with us in the car, or blowing in the wind.

But dust is not all bad. It purifies the air by removing ozone. It provides a home to microscopic mites that eat the dead skin that drops off us. After it blows across the Atlantic and hits the east coast of South America, it drops fertilizers the Amazon rainforest needs. Cosmic dust gives our horizons a soft-focus effect at dusk and dawn and scatters colors in a never-ending pattern of beauty.

I believe my Heavenly Father knew what he was doing after all, yeah?

Orange Julius, Magic Bullet, and my efforts to help the environment.

My recollection is that the first Orange Julius store in the metro Atlanta area was either at Greenbriar Mall or Stewart Avenue Mall. Memory most strongly favors Greenbriar. We kids were loaded into the VW Bus and hauled over there with the promise that we were going to taste something delicious. This was not a lie, as lips licked by happy tongue will attest.

Then one day, even if to do so meant your soul would be saved, you couldn't find an Orange Julius anywhere in Georgia, and I forgot about the brand and the drink. Years passed. Then my blender broke. My dear friend and fellow crime novelist Linda Sands and I were devastated as our research into Medicinal Margaritas was put on hold until we could find one with industrial strength and start up health examinations again.[440]

To tide me over, I bought this thing called a Magic Bullet in which only one frozen drink can be made per cycle. I make smoothies in my new Magic Bullet. These smoothies feature coconut milk, a little bit of fiber, chia seed, ice, Splenda[441], and fruit. One day not a blueberry or strawberry or peach was to be found in my fridge. But what did I spy? A beautiful juice orange. Hmmmm. Would that work?

Smoothie-making ensued and I put the juicy pulp of the orange with the other ingredients (this time green tea was in there, too) into the Magic Bullet and let her rip. While I cannot

---

[440] The author and Linda are still searching for the perfect blender. In the meantime, they are now studying the health benefits of Skinny Medicinal Margaritas. Conclusions to follow soonish.

[441] Don't say it. The author doesn't want to hear it. Keep your opinion to yourself about what causes cancer. If you want to share an opinion, write your own book but leave her to *hay-ell* alone.

say that what I poured out was exactly like an Orange Julius, I can tell you that it was close enough for government work.

Wow, it was delicious.

But what has any of this got to do with saving the environment? Let me explain. First, you see, my friend who has the Yankee girlfriend[442] told me that Orange Julius had retreated to only a few outlets, but finally made known a national presence again after being bought by Dairy Queen. So, I had been traveling great distances in my car to get my Orange Julius and now that I accidentally discovered a close-enough knockoff version by using the Magic Bullet, I no longer need crank up a fossil-fuel engine and spew pollutants into the air and therefore I have done my bit to save the environment.

But will that make all the P-HWPCLDRSFCs like me?

I think not.

---

[442] See essay "Garden & Gun".

Brownouts vs. Blackouts

When I was a kid there were two things you knew would happen in the summer. One, it was a sure bet you would step your bare foot in a pile of warm dog doo hidden in the grass and it would squish between your toes and you would go *ewww*, and two, rolling brownouts would cross the city.

According to Wikipedia.com, and in this they are right as I can attest, a brownout is "an intentional or unintentional drop in voltage in an electrical power supply system. Intentional brownouts are used for load reduction in an emergency. The reduction lasts for minutes or hours, as opposed to short-term voltage sag."

In other words, when there wasn't enough electricity to go around to keep everybody lit or cooled at full comfort levels, then lights dimmed, making one wonder if one's eyesight was declining. Fan blade rotation slowed until whole families fought for bits of air flow. Those with air conditioners felt beads of sweat pop out on their brow.

Brownouts were a regular occurrence when I was a child and I hadn't thought of them in years until the other day when there was a small brownout. Didn't last but a few minutes, but what happened was that the days had been cool enough that air conditioners had not been running at full peak then **WHAMMO!**, along came a super-hot day and the grid got a bit overloaded, then a brownout occurred, and that's when I said, "Wowzers. A brownout. Why, I haven't experienced one of these since I was a kid."

That got me to wondering and I asked a question on social media: When is the last time you have experienced a "brownout"? Come to find out, many have experienced a "brownout", but not of the electrical kind. I was treated to one comment after the other about poo-purging patterns. Even after I explained it was an electric grid thing, nobody seemed to understand it had nothing to do with poo.

That's when I had two thoughts. One: It sure is nice to have such dependable electric companies that even the word brownout as it applies to electricity is not known. I thank these companies for their service to mankind. Two:

You know…I don't think I have a second thought about this. Can you believe it? Wait one second. I believe I do have a second thought. Let's start it like this:

Speaking of brownouts —

For years after President Ronald Reagan left office and up until Donald "The Hammer" Trump was elected, the Russians and the ChiComs were laughing up their sleeves at those stupid Americans who thought they were free. "Sirree Amewicans. Fwee-dom is on skeed[443]," they whispered to each other at all the CIA cocktail parties. But the CIA bugging technicians thought the Russkies and the Red Army were enjoying a children's cereal and made a note to send them boxes of Trix.[444]

That means from 1989 to 2017, twenty eight years, all presidents of the United States and their various official political representatives who had tea and cocktails at CIA-run parties in other countries did nothing but make a right fine job of sending one clear message: We are wussies, but we'll damn well tell you we aren't, and you better believe what we say. That's right. The RadFems finally managed to push their method claiming strength — via their version of the Helen Reddy song — "I am Woman! Hear me Roar!" which really meant that what they had for balls were macadamias.[445]

---

[443] "Silly Americans. Freedom is on the skids."

[444] These boxes were made with special inks that only children could see so the Politburo leaders in both countries hauled home specially imprinted Capitalist messaging that said, "Ask Dad and Mom for more Trix".

[445] No insult intended to that most delicious nut, especially when it is covered in chocolate.

All this suited the Deep Staters[446] in the U.S. who had been working hand-in-hand with the United Nations[447], Radical Muslims, the ChiComs, and Team Putin[448] to set up a one-world government. Then along came "The Hammer"[449] and blew all that to hell and back, thus causing the biggest brownout[450] in all of history amongst the above-named groups and their followers — duped and otherwise — and newspapers, magazines, and television news programs, causing a run on tissue paper for all occasions except gift wrapping.

And that is the last word I shall make on brownouts.

---

[446] Includes most Democrats, all Republicans in Name Only (RINOs), FBI, DHS, and NSA types with delusions of grandeur, and every apparatchik worried about job security.

[447] The author is not joking.

[448] Includes certain island countries including Cuba, Norths Vietnam and Korea, Venezuela, and California.

[449] A nickname given to Donald Trump by the author based on his days in TV wrestling.

[450] Not the electrical kind.

How to Speak Like a Liberal Newscaster in Three Easy Steps

Oh, for the good ol' days when Walter Cronkite delivered the Liberal Agenda in a voice the Common Man[451] did not barf at upon hearing. Walter's tears were real.[452] His voice was calming, and it was his own. What do I mean by that?

I mean that his style of speaking was not overtly stylized. That is, it was normal. As a child hearing his voice, I felt at peace. If only such a voice could have solved the very real problems in my family, then I would have been over the moon. Alas, while Walter's voice was powerful, it wasn't all-powerful.

Then one day many years later, flipping around the channels, it felt as if I had stepped into an alternate universe. News channels? What? Where am I? The timbre of the voices varied, but the cadence was almost identical. Everything was exaggerated. The pauses were…

…just a touch longer than called for but were identical in length everywhere they were placed. At all times certain words received the same exact inflection. All delivery was pompously humble so that, by design, the listener/viewer would feel stupid and boring and clumsy and would…

…want to tune in another day…

…to be close…

…to such brilliance and truth.

That evening, I went through the channels at least twice, maybe more, doing nothing but listening to the national anchors and stand-up guys and gals and other voiceover

---

[451] Common Man includes females. Get off yer PC high horse, okay?

[452] The announcement of JFK's assassination.

talent…I mean, reporters…as they delivered The News That Matters. My conclusions were correct: They were identical.

By contrast, local reporters are mixed bag. It would be right to say that there was not one voice among my local on-air talent (LOAT) that even came close to being of national quality. Let me make myself perfectly clear here in the paragraph and not in a footnote[453] that the phrase "national quality" in this instance is not a compliment and that by saying my LOATs are not of their quality is a compliment to the local folks.

Look, I wouldn't mind having coffee and a chin wag with my LOATs. As much as they try to script what they say on the air, when they go off-script, they go off-script in such a way that producers (at least in my area) all go bald quickly from pulling out their hair.[454] In other words, unlike the national on-air talent (NOAT), LOATs' off-script is not scripted. No sirree.

But the bigger question is, why can't the NOATs go off-script off the cuff? Because they are Liberals and, even as Tracey Ullman in one of her brilliant sketches so aptly showed, Liberals don't know how to have fun.[455] Even what fun they have has to be scripted. Because they are such bad actors everyone except other NOATs and fellow Liberals can tell they are faking it.

---

[453] Though the author's footnotes always brilliantly add entertainment value to the reader, in this instance she is putting the thought in the paragraph so her local on-air talent will not miss the fact that she is not insulting all of them.

[454] The author can well imagine this cause of baldness is in every market that has LOATs.

[455] The author has written extensively about this subject. She and her good friend and fellow crime novelist Linda Sands have made this a sub-study of their Medicinal Margarita and Medicinal Tequila studies and have found that even with the application of both curatives (tequilas delivered at 100% and in diluted form), Liberals still cannot have fun.

"Angela! You are going around the world to get next door," said my old, old, old but good friend (even if he does have a Yankee girlfriend) upon reading this essay. "Will you please tell the reader how to speak like a Liberal Newscaster?"

To which I said, "Excuse me? Where were you when I just explained all that? Didn't you read the first part of this essay? Oh, can't wait to get back to the Yankee, huh?[456] Shall I review for you?"

"Yes, if you don't mind. Maybe make it a bulleted list?"

To which I responded, "I can do that!" So here is my old, old, old friend's request fulfilled.

How to Speak Like a Liberal Newscaster in 10 Easy Steps:

- Make delivery cadence identical
    - no matter *what* the story is about and…
    - …*EXAGGERATE* everything including
    - …*p a u s e s*…that…
    - …are a touch longer than called for
    - …but are *IDENTICAL* in length.
- Make sure the viewer never hears any trace of a
    - regional dialect
    - or regional accent
    - because the viewer must never know where you are from
    - especially since you are representing a completely homogenous people
    - that would be shocked if they heard their news delivered with any personality.

---

[456] The author admits this was a low blow, but as she is not afraid to speak off-script, nor is she afraid to tell the truth because her old, old, old friend knows she speaks it: He likes pain and Yankee Girl delivers.

- o The NOAT will never laugh or tell a joke.[457]
- At all times use the **same**...
  - o ...exact inflection for the **same**...
  - o ...word while speaking...
  - o [Insert weary and grim expression here] humbl-e-e-...
  - o ...pompous so that the...
- ...listener/viewer...
  - o ...[Insert *BIG SIGH* here]...
  - o ...feels stupid
  - o and boring
  - o and clumsy *yet*...
- ...[hold the pause]...
  - o [ho-o-o-o-old the pause until it is almost painful]...
  - o ...will dupe the viewer
  - o into believing they want...
  - o ...*nay, NEED*...
  - o to tune in another day.
- Have a short memory.[458]

---

[457] This is because their repertoire of jokes is limited, and they are not that good at delivering them. Jokes require timing and, as is well known, most Liberals cannot dance because the lack of timing. But this lack in the NOATs' skill set has been seen as an opportunity by late-night talk show hosts who — all on their own accord, nobody asked them to step up like this — have the show infrastructure to deliver opinion in the form of boring jokes in such a fashion that the audience will applaud thus making it seem that all the cool people agree with the opinion.

The infrastructure consists of: A drummer that knows when to hit the high-hat and or the kettle thus punctuating certain well-known and branded expressions on the show host's face; a bandleader that gives the high sign for the entire band to lead into or exit from the show host's homily that precedes the passing of the ceremonial plate of offering; and a flashing sign that says APPLAUSE! APPLAUSE!

[458] Short memories explain a lot about why Liberals are never disappointed in their leadership.

- [Insert scripted off-script here as you turn your head toward unknown off-camera "crew member". Suggested friendly wisecrack: "I'll see you at the pussy-hat parade, right, Ted? Tomorrow, 6:00 A.M. Sharp. Great. Say hi to your domestic partner, Jerry, for me. (*Wink!*)]
- [Smile at viewer.]
- [Insert personalized branded tagline here.]
- [Insert corporate-approved well-wishes for viewer.]
- [Look away from teleprompter and modestly shuffle papers on desk.]
- [As credits roll, unhook earpiece and let dangle over lapel. Wear weary expression of "Doing my job as serious journalist, ma'am. Dad's on his way home."]
- [At fade to black, push back from desk, take deep breath, finger-tap the desktop with rat-a-tat-tat.]
  459 460

---

459 Admittedly this last step involves a certain amount of acting and timing. Practice is needed.

460 Oh-ho! Soooo, you went back and counted the steps and sub-steps and found out the real facts of this essay do not match what was promised in the headline. Congratulations! You have identified yourself as being a solid thinker who remembers history and can compare what they see with what they thought they read and conclude that maybe something is nasty in the woodshed and confirm for themselves the actual facts, and who then got mad at the writer for being sloppy. You are not a Liberal. The author is ecstatic because **YOU PASSED THE TEST** and she wants to make your acquaintance. Who loves ya, baby?

How to Speak like a Conservative Newscaster

On this page all you will hear is crickets because there is no such thing as a Conservative Newscaster.[461]

However, reports have come to me consisting of the following disclaimer on behalf of certain NOATs[462] who have asked not to have their names mentioned.

> **DISCLAIMER: [NOAT #1] is a conservative, but says he has no say-so in what goes on the teleprompter and is under contract to read it exactly as [Corporate Entities ABCMNS] instructs.**

To which I say: You have sold out to the highest bidder just so you can send the kiddies to the best private schools and keep your well-connected wife who is now out-of-love with you but doesn't mind having you around for now. I say that makes you nothing more than a drunk guard at Treblinka who is only "doing what he was told" by his sadistic masters. You are the worst kind of NOAT. One that wears two faces. A snake with two tongues. Or, as the Laotians say it: ທນບ້າຊິໃຈຄົດ.[463]

---

[461] Some disagree with the author on this and point out the likes of Sean, Rush, et al. Please see the following essay for this type of "newscaster".

[462] You will remember this as "national on-air talent".

[463] The author was told the pronunciation is akin to "nook sahn HOO-wowh" and that when said with a certain push of air from the gut on the HOO and a snarl of the lip with a quick snap of the head forward and back timed to coincide with the *HOO*, one gets the point that Laotians do not like hypocrites, leading the author to believe she must be Laotian.

How to Speak Like a Conservative TV/Radio Pundit

There are no real Conservative Newscasters. There are a lot of seasoned, successful, long-term Conservative[464] on-air talent [COAT] TV/radio pundits, who have successfully stuck to the political facts year in and year out for decades. I made a study of how to talk like one. Each had a distinctive style. I could not quantify any points or styles that are easily duplicatable, assuring a homogenous, standardized delivery to the listener/viewer. But these were the same. COATs all:

- are intense, love freedom, have long memories[465]
- are willing to fight for rights guaranteed in the U.S. Constitution
- love a good joke and love to laugh
- tolerate differences of opinion[466]
- love a good debate they can sink their teeth into[467]
- and believe listeners have a brain.[468]

---

[464] To challenge COATs, Liberals attempt to wear the TV/Radio pundit hat every now and then, but their shows are so boring listeners tire of hearing them beat the same drum and tune out. Advertisers drop out. Proves that NOATs love Capitalism, they just don't want you to know it.

[465] Explains why they get so upset when they are let down yet again.

[466] The author notes this tolerance varies based upon ability of the deliverer of the differing opinion. Tolerance decreases when differing opinion delivered is a mere spouting of banal clichés lacking any facts in support.

[467] The author admits her research shows snips of these "debates" are often played by NOATs and these do not make COATs look good, yet COATs' shows have staying power, higher ratings, and loyal advertisers.

[468] The author notes that it is a given that not all listeners have a brain though most of them do, as opposed to the NOATs who believe — contrary to all evidence — that only they have a brain and viewers are too stupid to think for themselves.

"Romantic"[469] boat trip and "PDA"[470] Alert: Who cares?

Let the reader know that the author does not care who takes a boat trip or kisses their special someone in public and that therefore she is totally unprepared to explain the phenomena of gossip magazines, gossip columns, and gossip shows on broadcast television which peddle visual displays of these things as practiced by British royalty[471], made-for-TV-show actors of drama and comedy[472], and/or actors in movies and other reality shows.[473] But being unprepared has never stopped this brave author, and she will now proceed to step in it.

---

[469] The author has always had a distrust of any advertising campaign that promises a trip will be "romantic". There are reasons for that distrust, but suffice it to say that she has found that those destinations usually include mosquitos, revelries of drunk people she never would associate with in real life, men who want her to go topless just like them, and a hefty price tag that offends her thrifty nature.

[470] "PDA" is the entertainment media's shorthand for "Public Displays of Affection".

[471] No other royalty in the world ever makes it onto gossip shows and if any of them do then it is the exception that proves the rule that nobody cares about any other royalty except the British form.

[472] The group called "actors" includes males and females but no other animals and is here used as a generalization of the job type performed by humans variously described as acting, performing, or singing when accompanied by the attitude of "serious about" and who show they are willing to "hone their craft".

[473] The author recognizes that these "reality" shows are highly scripted and therefore the participants in them could be called actors, but she would equate their talent along the lines of saying they are B-movie quality or less, and therefore not ones who typically "hone their craft".

"Richard Gere, 69, enjoys romantic boat ride with wife, 35" trumpeted the headline. Immediately I said, "Well, of course he enjoyed it. She's 35!" The online article then went on to select 540 words and put them in breathless and titillating phrases, such as:

- Romantic trip
- Met at luxury hotel
- She is *blonde!*
- She went to a fancy *finishing school!*
- *Her daddy was VP of Real Madrid!*
- Gere is her "hero" and "saved her" from her horribly "lost" life
- Now life is the epitome of happiness
- First child *together!*
- Enviable hourglass figure
- Busty
- Soaked up the sun with Hollywood hubby
- Amalfi coast
- Ample cleavage[474]
- Leggy frame
- Boarded the speedboat
- Holidaying in Capri
- Screen icon turned humanitarian activist

---

[474] Yes, the writer of the online article used both *busty* and *ample cleavage* which, at least to the author, seems to be a gratuitous redundancy but one used purposefully to titillate male readers and lesbians, and as a subtle push for plastic surgeons' agenda of bust enhancement for straight women.

[Do lesbians get breast implants? Must research that, though if upon doing so and then reporting the findings the author may very well find herself the subject of a "bitch hunt" which she will not mind if the ensuing drama helps sell books.]

- Best known for *Pretty Woman*[475] [476]
- Was married to another TV royal
- Joined by ex-husband
- 33 years Gere's junior
- Gere is the son of an insurance agent[477]
- She uses a cute nickname for her son, 5
- His son, 18, is Homer[478]

---

[475] The movie was made in 1990 and featured a 40-year-old Gere and 21-year-old Julia Roberts (who is from Marietta, Georgia, just down the road a piece from the author's domicile). That Gere is now 69 and is still only best known for a movie made so long ago, and one that couldn't even begin to be accurately described as groundbreaking or original, simply boggles the author's mind.

[476] The author does not claim to know Julia, nor does she want the reader to believe — falsely! — she has seen the star at the grocery store, though she believes she once saw Eric, her brother, at the Chick-fil-A on North Druid Hills Road in Decatur, Georgia (not the one at the intersection of NDH and Briarcliff, but the one across the street from the Publix and between McDonald's and Checkers and right down the street from the author's domicile).
The man she believes to be Eric Roberts (a star in his own right who is best known for his 1985 movie based on real events called *The Coca-Cola Kid*) was at the walk-up window ordering two chicken biscuits (plus four honey packs), two servings of disc-shaped deep-fried heavenliness called tater tots or hashbrowns (plus only one pack of dipping ketchup), and one coffee (black), which led the author to believe the meal was for him alone and that he was mighty hungry.

[477] And thus, though Gere himself has transcended to royalty, he is from the common stock of citizenry known as serfs. This type of comment makes it seem possible that anybody can become royalty if they just try hard enough and is a particularly insidious form of mind control of the P-HWPCLDRSFCs who claim to want to be classless and make everything equal for everybody but who, when given an opportunity to be more equal than *you*, will take that opportunity every damn time and rub your nose in it, and won't RSVP to *your* party, no sirree.

[478] Because no other explanation can be found for why Gere and Carey Lowell would name their son Homer, it has become speculated the boy was named after **Homer** (Ὅμηρος [hómɛːros]), a blind writer often called legendary, who penned the *Iliad* and the *Odyssey*, poems about the Trojan War that are epic because they are Greek and involved the

The formula for inclusion of the above types of information on these corporate-owned echo chambers was successful for many years. However, print circulation and viewership numbers are down, consistently eroded by two very important factors. One: Education of the masses in Socialist schools, and two: Readers and viewers who announce their lives on social media platforms in small incremental "sound bites", if you will, on their self-promoted echo chambers.

Let's review both types of erosions, beginning with education. From the 1960s onward, the dumbing down of the masses has been the operational motif by which the nationalized system works. I call the system "nationalized" because even though counties and cities believe they have autonomy in how their children are educated, when they seek to exercise that autonomy by improving their local systems and processes, the national teachers' union steps in with threats[479] and slaps down their efforts at reaching all students.

Thus we have what used to be called "Reading, Writing, and Arithmetic" now called "Whole Language Arts and New

---

"no wet work required" murder of readers by boring them to death with cumbersome word arrangements.

Homer was a magnet for drama and, had he lived in our time, would have had his messy second divorce featured on broadcast television gossip shows, and gossip columns in magazines and newspapers would have covered the sale of his perfectly appointed but never-lavish $24.5M now-tony Tribeca area *pied-à-terre* because he was wanting to "simplify his life" which phrase, as we all know, actually means "Can't afford it anymore because sales are down, alimony doesn't stop, and third wife wants a baby."

[Naturally, Meryl Streep would own the unit next door and, seeing her ticket sales plummet due to various famously fatuous statements made on industry awards shows in 2017 and 2018, would soon follow Homer's lead and put her "small apartment" of 3400+ sq.ft. on the market.]

[479] The author has been told by unnamed sources in the teaching community that the exact phrase used to get them to cooperate was "This is not a threat. This is a *promise!*" Fearing a horse's head in the bed and risks to their financial health, cooperation was fast in coming.

Math" which are nothing but [you know which nasty expletive to insert here] hot messes designed to thoroughly make The Maths look incomprehensible so that the child will later seek an Expert Money Manager and will not be able to vet that expert because the child (now an adult) has no clue and cannot get one because they do not understand language and cannot read the terms and conditions of the contract.

Further, the design of the Socialist education system is to separate parents by making it impossible for them to help their children with homework, thereby making parents look more stupid than what children already believe them to be, and by complicating the process will intimidate the child into believing they are too stupid to read. Thus the child will grow up looking to Big Government for all their needs.

This has happened even in private schools. The Soviets sent over to the U.S. certain folks pretending to be disaffected by the Communist way. They acted like they longed for freedom, but their sole aim was to infiltrate and annihilate universities. Much the same way teachers from the Government sector have infiltrated private schools and we see the same dumbing down.[480] Some parents have attempted to stop this erosion with something called "home schooling" which, in most cases, pretty much leaves the child to self-direct its own education.[481]

The second erosion to circulation and viewership numbers is social media. The gorillas[482] in the marketplace are

---

[480] The author is aware private schools will not like what she has said, but she does not back down.

[481] The author is aware that not all parents who advocate for home schooling drop the ball.

[482] The author is not making a racist or prejudiced comment here no matter what tennis fans may think. She is truly thinking of a real gorilla and the strength and power of it that, when it is not controlled, will hurt you bad.

Google (using Google Plus, killed in April 2019 and buried in Google Cemetery, and BlogSpot), Bacefook, and Twitter.

Besides a host of other companies offering the same service but through a paid portal, rounding out that complement of those who will help anybody become their own reality show are a host of wannabe companies who claim they do not collect your information and sell it and will not control the content feed, but who give away the service so you have to wonder if they are telling the truth.

And that is why I do not care. Do you?

Al Jarreau beats Senator John McCain to death.[483]

Given the state of headlines and the copy that follows them in the bodies of the articles, the title of this essay thoroughly explains in a non-political and non-partisan fashion just how screwed up journalism is these days.

The question is why headlines such as this have become more frequent in the last ten years or so. I've got that answer. It's called clickbait. For those reading this in 2118 C.E. or beyond, let me explain the concept of clickbait. Let's break down the headline as it sits.

Without any further information to clarify, the headline is clear: Al murdered John. But do we know who Al is? Do we know who John is? Very few of you in 2118 will know, but in 2018 both of those names are well known.

Al was a Jazz singer and songwriter. John was a senator in the United States. What you in 2118 (and actually, quite a few in 2018) do not know is that Al died in 2017 while John died in 2018. Therefore the "beat" is not as in "Al put the beatdown on John until John died", but rather, Al beat John in the race to death's door.

But those who only read headlines and/or have a short memory — that is, they heard of John dying but forgot or

---

[483] The idea for the title is not original to the author. She freely admits she stole the idea from one Bill Turner of Arizona, who posted it on Bacefook as a serialized joke using a variety of dead entertainers. Oh, that Bill Turner is a funny guy...except when he isn't and that is often. He's a Democrat in Republican clothing who ended up calling the author a really bad name when she logically replied to a statement he made about Christine Blasey Ford, the accuser of now-Associate Justice Brett Kavanaugh, at which time Bill's mask slipped and he showed that it was, indeed, he who was a 300-pound male Russian hacker [insert really bad four-letter C-word here to mean female]. The author had a lot of fun with that lacerated logic.

missed the news about how he died — would be shocked and would click on the hyperlink to take them to the story so they could read about a black Jazz singer beating to death a white senator. But what would they get? A story of how Al Jarreau died the year before Senator John McCain, in three short paragraphs, two of which would mention how much McCain hated President Trump, all of which would be surrounded by a boatload of pop-up ads for Erectile Dysfunction remedies (natural and man-made) and other ads selling a wide variety of products and services, often featuring closeup shots of magnificent cleavage attached to equally magnificent bodies that looked like females and whose breasts looked even bigger as the high camera angle thrust perky pinnacles over hips made to look tiny and legs to look like they could wrap around a man anaconda-like. Rate cards for insurance products were also popular. All of which beckoned viewers to come on in and see as they flashed and wriggled like a digital version of a hawker on a street in front of a New Orleans strip club.

Do you see how clickbait works now? However, the story gets even more nefarious. You see, most of these clickbait ads were bought and paid for through a Google Inc. service called AdWords. Now, Google Inc. was able to micro-control who bought ads, even though they claimed otherwise. I know this because I was blacklisted by Google Inc. as an undesirable when I attempted — but was never successful — in purchasing ads to tell the world about a new intellectual property ownership management service I had called MyDigitalCatalog.com. I've written about this extensively elsewhere and so won't cover it here, but I bring this up simply to point out that while Google was so very helpful to users by providing lots of free stuff[484], they stuffed the pipeline with all these ads that at a penny-or-three per flash-and-wriggle made them a ton of money.

---

[484] Gmail, GDrive, GForms, and more.

I hear you. I understand. "Angela," you ask, "what is wrong with them making money?" Absolutely nothing. But many times these come-on ads when clicked upon would loose the hounds of digital hell upon the computer and every computer it was attached to in a network. These were called viruses, worms, bots, malware, adware, Trojans, and ransomware, each designed to either destroy data, lock your computer, or make your computer dance like a farmer to a drunk cowboy's bullets.

These were all designed in Russia (the former Union of Soviet Socialist Republics) and gave rise to companies purporting to be American (but we all have our doubts as you'll understand momentarily) that said they were the solution to these algorithmic hellhounds. Instead, with each deployment of these antivirus software solutions came even more computer issues along with their own pop-up ads that showed up right there on your computer screen that said "We have successfully blocked 1,235,789,666 attempts to hijack your computer. BUT THERE ARE 35,555,903,666,475 MORE! Please click here to upgrade to our newest version that will keep your computer totally safe!"

The x to shut that notice down often didn't work or was so tiny it couldn't be seen, thus causing savvy computer users to do the three-finger salute[485] with a hope and a prayer that the notice was listed in Programs in Task Manager where they could shut it down and release one corner of their screen from being held hostage. These companies traded on the stock market so millions of stockholders, whose very own computers were being held hostage by these fake American companies, were making money from their own evilness.

---

[485] The "three-finger salute" is when one puts Ring Man and Pointer of the left hand on the Control and Alt keys of the keyboard and holds them down while Tall Man on the right hand hits the Delete key in order to bring up a fancy screen that then allows the user to shut down any open program.

If a computer was not connected to the Internet, there would be none of these clickbait virus Trojan infernal issues, but just try to use one without being connected to the World Wide Web. Even the programs used on the machines rarely come with an installation disk anymore, though you can request it be sent, but then one must wait until it arrives and pray it is the correct one and keep up with the licensing key on a piece of paper.

Which reminds me of Freeware. Freeware is software available for use at no cost and may be used without payment. But it is usually proprietary software, that is, written and/or owned by somebody else who says it can be used but not modified, re-distributed, or reverse-engineered without the author/owner's permission. Which is fine. But how one used to find Freeware was one read computer magazines in print and looked in the back where the Classified Ads were and found the ad that said FREE and you would send a *request to receive* to the address, which would then put you on a mailing list and through the United States Postal Service[486] one would occasionally receive a small catalog listing everybody who had FREE SOFTWARE available.

The catalogs were divided into sections such as Fractal Design, Bookkeeping, Word Processing, Games, and so forth. I could not believe what a nerd I was. If you had put two catalogs side by side, one of frilly girly underwear with things in it designed to please a man and one of FREE SOFTWARE, you know which one I would pick up. The Ex used to watch me walk around the house ooing and aahhing and saying things like "Oh. MY. GOD! I'm getting THAT!" and he'd think I was looking at the frilly girly underwear catalog with things in it designed to please a man and he'd get his hopes all up and say in a sexy hopeful voice, "Whatcha lookin' at,

---

[486] In the United States. The author cannot say how this process was handled in other countries.

Girrrrl?"[487] and I'd say "You will NOT believe this. They have this thing designed to make your own FRACTALS based upon an algorithm of YOUR CHOICE!"

The poor man. Look, I know we are divorced because it's all his fault and you best not make any mistake about that. But I agree that the above situation was simply too much for him as it would be for most men who themselves were not nerds — and by any stretch of the imagination he was not.

I couldn't wait to check the mail because into the mailbox were coming these little 3.5" disks, sometimes 5.25" floppies, that would fit into either my A or B drives and I, without fear of viruses, worms, Trojans, malware, adware, or ransomware, blithely slid those disks in and installed with nary a care in the world. Oh, the happy hours I spent messing around with Freeware. God, the memories. To contact the author of the programs one had to write a letter and send it in the mail. Oh, for the good ol' days.

But do you think I would go online now and download anything called Freeware? Hell no.

---

[487] Actually, The Ex never said stuff like that. This is merely the author wishing he had said things like that, but she knows he was thinking it because of the lascivious lust oozing from his eyes though it wasn't lust for her as much as it was for the model in the catalog. But she wrote the above to at least pretend for a moment that he might have desired her for herself.

Goodbye, PAM®.

Even though I blame her for raising him to expect non-stop coddling[488], I dearly adored my mother-in-law even after the divorce from her son because she introduced me to PAM.[489] You need to understand that before PAM came along, cooks had to jump through major hoops to keep food from sticking to whatever metal or glass pot or pan or sheet they were using to prepare foodstuffs.

Many spread softened butter by hand or stick butter still hard and in its wax paper wrapping whereby one end would be unwrapped thus the hand never touched it. But this was wasteful and messy and never worked as well as it should. Every night across the land one could find many a dishwasher cursing when they had to bring out — yet again — a steel wool pad to scrub those stubborn crusty bits that refused to budge even after soaking for four hours.

Julia Child recommended spreading olive oil by hand, but that was expensive even if, as she said to do, what was left on your hands should be spread on your skin as a softening agent, so that just couldn't be deployed in my household.

It took Arthur Meyerhoff from the mid-1950s until the late 1970s to turn his product into a household name as it became the de facto product to keep food from sticking while cooking. My mother-in-law introduced me to it and for many years it was a staple product on my shelf, and by staple I mean at any one time you could find four cans of it in my pantry. God forbid I should even come close to running out.

---

[488] The author admits that she continued that coddling because she did not have a mother who offered any useful direction when it came to men.

[489] An acronym for Product of Arthur Meyerhoff, who was an ad agency owner and product developer.

This was my modus operandi in the kitchen for years and what a great modus operandi it was. But eight years after turning the coddled son into The Ex and finding myself busy as hell what with doing this and that, I put on my chalkboard grocery list in the kitchen the word Pam[490] when I got down to having only two cans of it in the pantry. The can count went to one, and then that was empty. Busy schedule kept up so much even a quick visit to the grocery store could not be made. What was I going to do to keep food from sticking?

I didn't want to use butter; memories of problems with that were still fresh. Looking around, I saw the olive oil sitting up on the shelf and poured some into a coffee cup and got out the pastry brush and spread it all over the pan and —

It worked great! Julia Child was right. As of this writing, I have not purchased another can of PAM®[491] and do not regret it. ConAgra, who now owns the product, will surely not feel the impact of my lack of use, especially as they roll out new flavors including —

Olive oil!

Speaking of oil, my brother, Michelangelo Darling, called and said, "Angie-Ahhhh! I am lookin' at yer twin as ah speak. I've been tawking ewe up to this woman who is just like you. Here. Imma put her on the phone. Tawk to her."

On the phone comes this woman who proceeds to say the following in the style of a happy machine gun firing flowers:

- OMG! Your brother is so proud of you!
- He's done nothing but talk about you.
- I sure wish I could send you a picture of myself…what?

---

[490] The author did not put the ® symbol on the chalkboard.

[491] The author is including the ® because she does not want to get sued.

- We're going to send you a picture of us!
- It's my friend's birthday and he bought her a drink.
- He is so nice. Bye!

Ding! The picture arrived and sure enough there was a woman who looked almost like me sitting next to my brother. We could've been sisters, but not twins. It was awesome. So I took a picture of myself and sent it to them. Her reply was "I want to be YOU!" My reply back was, "You almost are!" and that is where oil spread on agitated waters was needed because — and this is key — a reply was not forthcoming, and I got to thinking maybe she thought I was insulting her, but I wasn't since she did *almost* look just like me.

But I have a horrible feeling that my reply probably put the kibosh on my brother's opportunity to get to know this woman any better and she's gonna tell people all about the snooty sister that dissed her by text. And all because I answered her logically. Can't win for losing.

But that is much better than the time when I was fifteen and I started singing, "A mind that's weak but a back that's strong" just as Mother's Honey was ending a violent rant around the dinner table. Ability to keep my cool when all those about me were losing theirs' kept me from getting hurt real bad that evening and diverted his attention from the rest of the family thus saving their butts, including Michelangelo Darling's, from the gathering storm, so maybe he will cut me a little slack for ruining his chances with this woman.

Still, how do I make it right with her? I hate to leave things hanging like that. The question that haunts[492] me is, "What if she wasn't insulted and I only thought she was and

---

[492] Yes, the author says she is really haunted by this question and that now you can see why she has so much energy going out all the time and needs two, maybe three, naps per day.

then I go and try to make it right by explaining my logical reply which then will insult her more and she gets her feelings hurt because I thought she was shallow?"

The what-if circle does not stop. I feel like Albert Einstein logically coming up with his theory of relativity only to find he had to answer yet another question and who then came up with another theory thus having to name one "General Theory of Relativity" and the other "Special Theory of Relativity" because he could make a case for both based on three little words: "Well, depending on…" and that is where I am. Depending on her initial response, of which I have no way to observe or find out without affecting her, which, of course, brings into play the Observer Effect and Heisenberg's Uncertainty Principle[493], therefore I don't know what to do. Unlike Heisenberg and Einstein, girly women are much more complicated than their Maths and therefore getting it wrong will affect the universe much worse than chasing a beam of light while riding Timothy Leary's astral plane.

"But, Angela," you ask and rightly so, "why do you have such a hard time reading social interaction clues?"

This is covered in the next essay: "Women vs. Girly Girls: No wonder guys are so confused."

---

[493] For a full discussion of these, please see the last essay in the book: "Gilding the Lily".

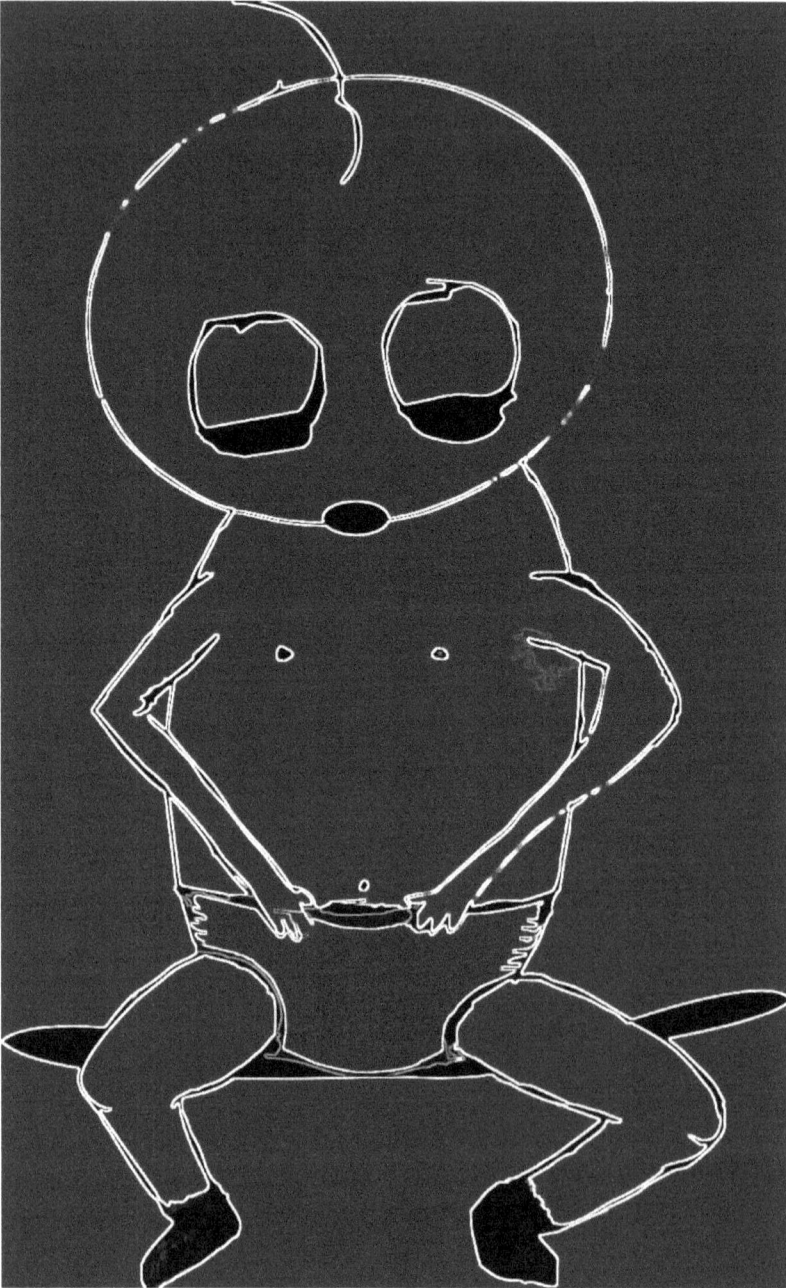

Women vs. Girly Girls: No wonder guys are so confused.

In another essay, "Goodbye, PAM®", readers asked why I have such a hard time reading social interaction clues. This essay attempts to explain it.

About four years after Kevin[494], my now-ex son-in-law, married my daughter, he came into my kitchen shaking his head and laughing. "Mother-in-Law," he chuckled, "Father-in-Law[495] is the woman in your marriage. You are the man."

That's right. The Ex was in the living room watching the Lifetime channel and crying over some sad and silly rerun of a cookie-cutter Movie of the Week that ran four hours because of all the commercials featuring empowering messaging, hugs, sensitivity, birth control, and tampons[496],

---

[494] Truth! This is his real name.

[495] The author is not lying. This is what Son-in-Law called us.

[496] In 2016, Adage.com reported that "new analysis drawn from neuroscience-based testing shows that overall, women have higher levels of engagement with advertising than men." The author could have told them that and saved them a bunch of money.
In the U.S., most 2015 Super Bowl ads were
- gender neutral
- women reacted 35% better than men when viewing
- many men liked ads aimed at women

The author has always thought a sizable portion of male Super Bowl viewers are pussy-whipped and looking to guys for how to grow a pair and, if one looks, one can find these same men wearing pussy hats while marching beside their pussy-hat wearing girly girl and/or lesbian best friends. Given that, Adage suggested marketers should:
- have women front of mind
- make messaging sensitive
- include perceptiveness
- tell a story that involves relationships
- be authentic
- show an empowered woman

which is why I was in the kitchen beating a steak to death and thinking of movies and books featuring guns, torture, death, blood, and intrigue, all while running through every level of three Super Mario Brothers games, move by move, wondering if I had missed any score/time-increasing tricks in getting to and defeating The Boss.[497]

In any case, Son-in-Law[498] was correct. Mother-in-Law is a Female Guy[499]. No, I was not and am not a lesbian, nor did I have surgery to give me girl parts. I am 100% woman.

I've never had a girly-girl thought in my life except once and that was an anomaly, a glitch in the hard-wiring, though it did cause major upset with The Ex because he got all confused and didn't know what to do.[500] I told him it must be his time of the month. Yes, Son-in-Law laughed. Son-in-Law's timing was never good, but he was a guy and that's why I like him so much.

Though I do not expect to do as good a job as Dave Barry did with explaining the difference between Men and Guys, I shall attempt to explain the difference between Women and Girly Girls.

---

[497] The author reports that she had uncovered and used every single one and that she was the first — and most probably the only — mother in the subdivision to do so as the other mothers were such girly girls.

[498] After their divorce, the author now calls him Now-Ex Son-in-Law and he calls her Angela.

[499] "Guy" as defined by Dave Barry in his guy-generation-shaping work *dave barry's complete guide to guys* of which the author concurred with all the way through because Dave's research was thorough and complete.

[500] The same thing happened when The Ex acted like a guy one day and the author just stared at him and he said, "What? What? You are never happy! Wah! Boo-hoo!" The author is not exaggerating.

SITUATION	GIRLY-GIRL RESPONSE	WOMAN RESPONSE
You see a spider.	SCREAM while running wildly, then faint.	SPLAT!
You are at a funeral. A hug is required.	You cry, moan, wail, and beat your breasts in agony as you cling to the bereaved while repeating ad nauseum, "I know. I know. You will miss [dead loved one] so much. How will you go on?"	A quick hug, but preferably a gentle squeeze of the hand as you murmur "I'm so sorry for your loss." You move on.
Another female kisses you on the lips without your wanting or asking them.	SCREAM and say, "Ooooo, I've always been *curious*, hahhahahaha!"	Draw back quickly and threaten to bitch-slap the drunk ho saying, "What the *hayle*?"
You see a cat.	"Oh, how beautiful! What's her name? Here, kitty-kitty-kitty. That's a good kitty."	"You wanna die, Cat? Just come one step closer. Come on. Double-dawg dare ya."
Your ungrateful male-of-choice and/or your children ask what's for dinner.	"What do you want, baby? I'll fix whatever you want. Pizza? KFC? Sketty?" Pancakes? Lasagna? Tell me."	"Fud. Cat fud." (Evil grin.)
Your teenage son informs you that doing laundry is "woman's work".	You do his laundry.	You drag him to the laundry room whereupon you instruct him in the ways of laundry and then inform him that, furthermore, he will be doing the dishes every day until he leaves home.

Your teenage daughter informs you she is running away because you are a terrible mother.	You cry and beg her not to leave and tell her you'll do anything — *anything!* — to keep her home.	You help her pack, take away keys to *your* car she is using, take away cellphone *you pay for.* **Wave goodbye and holler "take care".**
Your husband agrees The Boy does not have to do his own laundry.	You agree and promise to get The Boy's laundry done in time for school the next day.	You withhold all nookie until he changes his mind.
Your husband agrees you are a bad mother and the teenage daughter has every reason to run away.	You agree and promise to change your bad ways and ask them to pretty please make a list of things you should work on.	You withhold all nookie until he changes his mind.
Your husband marks his territory in the bathroom with a generous spray.	You clean it up every day.	You rub his nose in it and threaten to "go Lorena" on him if he ever sprays again in the house.
You are out of food and must go to the grocery.	You get in your car and into the GPS plug the address of the grocery store down the street and do not move the vehicle until it tells you to go.	You go.
You think you might need new panties.	You peruse malls, specialty stores and catalogs for eighteen months until you find the perfect pair.	You examine your "drawers" and realize they will last for another seven years. You then go rub your husband's nose in his spray.

See? Real women are basically guys but with much more cleanliness and smarts and logic who, in point of fact that cannot be denied by any lover of truth, accomplish real things and contribute to the efficient running of the world. Without real women even dictatorships tend to fall apart. We know this because any dictator that kills his wife or concubines after saying "You sure are getting uppity!" inevitably finds himself assassinated. Never fails.

And think about pro golfers and presidents of countries, all of whom are pussy hounds. When their real-women wives find out, they proceed to put the beatdown on their husbands, some publicly like Tiger Woods' wife did so spectacularly. But others quietly, like in the case with presidents, but we can always tell because all of a sudden they get all aggressive and such and go and start a war.[501]

---

[501] I would continue with this essay except that, as I write, I realize this might be evidence for a larger study that would be a perfect fit for the medicinal studies my really good friend and fellow crime novelist Linda Sands and I continue to refine.

Speaking of Conversations in Hyperreality...

I've written about these phenomena extensively in my unpublished novel series *The Dance Floor Wars*[502] though, if memory serves, this particular story about a conversation in hyperreality was never used as a plot mechanism.

I happened to remember it when my real good friend and fellow crime novelist Linda Sands and I were doing more Medicinal Margarita field research one evening at the 2018 AJC Decatur Book Festival in controversy-filled Downtown Decatur.

I say it is filled with controversy, but maybe I'm dragging the controversial story out longer than need be[503] because at the 2017 AJC Decatur Book Festival I, astute as I am, saw the looming controversy four months away when these two self-righteous white women did not check their *white privilege* but still tried to act *woke* and proceeded to swing by my book-selling station in a virtuous huff assuming I would agree with them, which I did not because — as soon as they handed me the glossy oversized postcard with a picture of a monument that must come down or else the po' black chillens of 2017, no mattah where theyze be found around the world, no suh!,

---

[502] The author wants the reader to note these titles are, in order: *Dispatches from the Front*; *Lucinda's People*; *Collisions*; and one more of which she is still toying with the title. Further, if any agent or publisher with moxie and vision wants to see these, please be advised she can supply the finished manuscripts...unless she beats you to the publishing punch.

[503] In fact, the story made the news and therefore the author thought the women got their way and the monument came down. She should've known the story was spun by the fake news media.

---

feelz da put down be oooPONE dem[504] — I groaned and said, "Oh, crap."[505]

Where was I? Oh, yeah: 2018 AJC Decatur Book Festival. Medicinal Margarita research. Got it.

So there I was with Linda at the AJC DBF[506] and we were collecting more research data and there we were at the VIP Author Event[507] totally meeting by accident and spent about an hour schmoozing with movers and shakers and such until finally I said, "Linda, we must get on with our research!" and we took our medicine and went to sit at an empty table where we could compare research notes.

Well, one thing led to another and then we found ourselves back at her room where she was going to give me a fifty-pound box of books to haul to Florida for her for the 2018 Bouchercon and as she lifted the box to my soon-to-be-bent shoulders I said, "Hey, Linda! This reminds me of a funny story."

What happened was this: There was this guy who asked me to dance the waltz. The evening was early and the floor was empty, so it was a perfect time to do that. I've waltzed with several men, but never as perfectly as this one. We were flawlessness itself and the man simply could not speak for

---

[504] The reader may assume post-modern irony in the use of this appropriated cultural language and should not read into it any racial bias.

[505] The women started in on the author trying to "school her" so that she would also become "woke" like them, but the author just waved her hand and made little go-away motions.

[506] The author hopes she does not have to explain this acronym, but she will if she is sent money.

[507] The reader may remember how the author stole one ticket for this event from Linda's purse in 2017 and pretended to be surprised to see her at the event. The author did the same thing this year and acted like it was a TOTAL COINCIDENCE that she ran into her really good friend and fellow crime writer at the 2018 VIP event.

---

some time after. Then he said, "That was the most perfect dance ever. You are the best dancer I've ever had the privilege of escorting around the dance floor."

I know you will think I'm bragging, but it is the truth: It was the best and I was the best, too.

What the man didn't know was what I knew. You see, my first dances tend to always be absolutely great. It's the second ones where the men have the problem.

So I took the compliment with my ego fully in check because I knew he would be back and would expect the exact same result: Perfection.

You see, it's all about expectations. And you know what they say about expectations, don't you? They are nothing more than anticipations making one wait and go crazy.

So this man went crazy all week thinking about repeating his perfection and having the absolute knowledge that he'd found *The Woman* of his dreams, and back he comes and there I was sitting in my same spot in the corner at the bar and off we go to be alone again on the dance floor and within two seconds I knew it was not going to be good.

The man had frozen up. He was second-guessing every single move he made and was not leading worth a flip. Naturally, I stumbled and fell against his chest and he stomped my toe and fell onto the stage whereupon he proceeded to lay his arms out like a supplicant and start whining.

"What's wrong with you? What happened to you?"

I straddled him and leaned over, placing my hands on either side of his body. It was time to give him the big boy speech.

"Wrong with me?"

"Yeah! You were so graceful last week."

"And you could lead last week. But let's just stop and ask ourselves a little question right now, shall we?"

His eyes opened wide and he nodded.

"Which person is laying on the stage right now complaining that a woman knocked her soft girly parts up against him? And which person laying on the stage right now hasn't had this much girl action in several years? Hmmmm?"

The man started laughing and said, "Yeah. That's right. Let's dance." And we finished that dance.

But we never danced again because, you see, expectations got the better of him. From that point forward, he showed up with mousy women who could barely move. More his speed.

And that was just too sad.

The History of The Dark Web

If you read or watch anything produced by mainstream media on the subject of the Dark Web, it is likely that you, as a law-abiding citizen, got very scared unless you are a guy.

Let me be clear about the use of the word "guy" in this essay. By "guy" I do not mean a male claiming to be a man, a female claiming to be a male, a female who had surgery to look like a male but hasn't claimed anything (they just want you to guess), or any non-female who does not eat meat and prefers salads.

"Guy" as used in this essay is based on the early yet germinal work of one Dave Barry[508], a humor writer from way back when my children were small and the world had not gotten all serious and such, and when a person could make money from writing humor that was definitely politically incorrect and therefore really funny. Dave explains how to identify a guy. A guy:

- Cannot speak or think when they see breasts on anything, including cows.[509]
- Never stops scratching his personal private parts even in public.[510]
- Will spit even if he does not have loogie to hock.[511]

---

[508] Namely the book entitled *dave barry's complete guide to guys* [exact punctuation as shown on the cover of his book].

[509] Which explains why non-female farmers are so quiet at milking time and when baling hay.

[510] Guys do not scratch other males' private parts even in private.

[511] But gives himself a great big ATTABOY when loogie does fly.

- Believes best time to tell joke about guy who had Alzheimer's and died of cancer is at a funeral.[512]

There are more bulleted points I could lift from Dave Barry's book called *dave barry's complete guide to guys*[513], but I've reached the limit of what could rightly be called "not yet plagiarism" and would prefer not to hear from Dave's attorneys so I will stop at four bulleted points and get on with this essay about why the Dark Web got started in the first place.

We've heard the Dark Web has something called the Silk Road and it is a bad, bad thing because it sells drugs and people and children[514] and peddles and shows other nasty and illegal and immoral and just plain bad stuff. But the Silk Road is only a small portion of the Dark Web, and those activities are not why the Dark Web got started.

See, here's what happened. Guys were going to work like they always did. They would arrive and, spying a fellow employee, would say something like, "Well, hello, Susan.[515] My, your hair looks nice today. Have you lost weight?" And Susan would stop and say, "Oh, my. You noticed. I wish my husband would notice, but he's just a sumbitch." And then the guy would say, "A woman like you should not be married to a sumbitch." And then they would have a flaming affair, the guy would dump her, and she would run back to the sumbitch because now, comparing him to that guy from work, the sumbitch wasn't that bad after all.

---

[512] The author was shocked at the public nature of this admission, but thanks Dave Barry for sharing even the most egregious fact.

[513] This is proper "guy punctuation", so do not blame this author.

[514] The author says, "These are bad things, for real, and that is not a joke."

[515] This is a placeholder name. They could have just as easily said Martha or Jane or Sheniqua or Jilly.

You see how guys help marriages? It is amazing. Of course there was all that time they spent telling jokes nonstop. They told them in meetings with the manager. They told them at lunch. They told them at the company picnics where little guys[516] could overhear them. And on the road going on sales calls. And delivering freight. Anywhere they were with other guys these jokes were the grease of social discourse that kept things moving nicely.

But then Radical Feminists started in on the guys and the guys gave it back as good as they got making all other guys laugh and so the Radical Feminists[517] began suing companies for employing nonstop-joke-telling and women-flattering guys and when the insurance companies had to make payments[518] to these harassed women then the joke-telling went underground.

All this started just as something called The Internet came into popular use and extremely expensive computational devices could be had for the home. As Dave Barry so aptly points out in his important and seminal book *dave barry's complete guide to guys,* guys thought no amount of money was too much to spend on this new toy. Oh, to be able to access the AOL Joke Forum via a dial-up modem![519] But the RadFems' reach was long and they said it wasn't fair that the guys could still tell jokes where RadFems and girly girls and their pussy-whipped men could see them.

---

[516] Also known as male children.

[517] Also called RadFems.

[518] Also called "hush money" but the Radical Feminists didn't get that memo because, just like Stormy Daniels, they have not shut up.

[519] Yes, we are talking quaint technology.

So somebody, nobody knows who though he went by the name The Dread Pirate Roberts[520], started the Dark Web, a place where RadFems and girly girls and their pussy-whipped men never go and who, if they did try to go there, would be sucked into a vortex of practical jokes and pranks from which they could not exit. You want an example?

Okay. I will give you one.

Of course, you are wondering, what with me being a 100% woman, how it is I can give you such an example and it be true without having gone there myself? Well, I have gone there because I do not identify as a girly girl. I am a 100% woman. You see, a girly girl is usually politically correct and wants to make sure nobody mistakes her for a male woman though she will honor the so-called gender.

A 100% woman pays no nevermind to any of that sh!t and can go on the Dark Web. Let's get back to the example.

An example of a prank-slash-practical joke played on interlopers on the Dark Web would be that a solid blue color would appear on their computer screen with the little characters and symbols in white which say, "Windows Error 45/7-+p>u^n~k:e@d< PLEASE REBOOT OR ALL IS LOST!"[521]

Hahahahahahaha.

That.

Is.

So.

FUNNY.

Hahahahhahaha.

But to keep guys from telling jokes at work and further stirring the shallow pots of RadFems, the FBI, NSA, DHS[522],

---

[520] So chosen because of being in the movie *The Princess Bride,* which was nothing but one guy joke after another.

[521] This would also show up on Apple Macintosh computers, causing even more fear and not a little bit of paranoia.

[522] The FBI, NSA, DHS.

and other alphabetized acronymed agencies[523] have declared war on the Dark Web thus assuring its success for years to come. Especially since — and this is very important — most of the field agents working for the A. A. A.s are guys who like their jokes and they know where to find them and how to divert attention from those sites so that their clueless RadFem and girly-girl bosses and their equally clueless pussy-whipped congressional oversite committee members will never know where to find them.

But something even better is happening that threatens the Dark Web and could, if left unchecked, crumble the very foundation upon which it was built.

Guys are telling RadFem- and HR-disapproved jokes again. That means guys are rediscovering their balls and I don't mean the ones they scratch all the time because they have never forgotten those. Yes, I mean the metaphorical balls that give a guy a spine and make him say things like, "Woman, I've got a joke to tell you and you can say *ewwww* all you want, I don't care, I'm speaking to *you*, Woman!"

If this trend continues then the Dark Web could be a thing of the past and that makes me sad because the Dark Web was like this really exclusive club into which only the really cool kids can get except it was for the nerds and to them I say, "Talk nerdy to me one more time!"

---

[523] The A. A. A. is Alphabetized Acronymed Agencies. The author is very proud of her use of "apt alliterations artful aid" in her book.

"Carmel woman drives to police station during road rage incident."[524]

All the best stuff is buried then unearthed, like Thousand-Year Eggs. This headline appeared way down in the feed on MSN's home page where I found it and then remembered some funny stories about my road rage incidents. When I say "my" I do not mean to implicate myself, for twas not I what got all raged-up[525] and acted the fool.

The story goes that this woman didn't let a man merge into traffic and he got all mad and started honking and so she, like an idiot, stuck her hand out the window and proceeded to give him a fistful of feathers[526] and he took exception to that and, being a man who must have issues with women, proceeded to follow her all the way to the police station while honking. He veered away when he realized where he was.

Anyway, I thought to myself that this woman was just plain stupid. She ought to know better than to antagonize a strange man like that. I have better, more non-violent ways to antagoni-…errr…I mean, control the situation. I shall tell you of a few methods that have worked over the years…at least for me…but I bet they will work for you, too, if you are a woman.[527]

---

[524] This is a real headline. The author did not make this up. She could have if she wanted to, but when something is handed to one on a silver plate then one takes it as the gift it was intended to be.

[525] In this section the author seems to be reverting to speech favored by her brother, Michelangelo Darlin', and many other North Georgia mountain folk. She asks your forbearance as she gets control of herself.

[526] That is, she shot the man a whole "bird". If you have to ask…

[527] DO NOT TRY THESE METHODS IF YOU ARE A MAN. No matter if the road-raging idiot is a male or female, IF YOU ARE A MAN I BEG YOU NOT TO DO THESE. The effect will not be the same. YOU HAVE BEEN WARNED.

The first time I experienced road rage directed at me was when I was married and it was from my husband who was screaming that I was a horrible driver. I know, I know. You are saying, "Angela, you said you are going to tell us about strangers. Your husband is not a stranger, so why are you including him in our learning session?"

Glad you asked. As always, I am happy to give clarification. At that moment in that car with that man, he was a stranger because I didn't know who he was. It so upset me that I took my hands off the wheel, raised them high, and said, "HERE! YOU DRIVE!", at which point he got calm and asked me to pretty please continue driving on Interstate 75 during rush hour and the problem was solved. Took maybe two seconds max, but he didn't say another word.

I do not recommend this technique, however, because for the rest of our marriage when he allowed me to drive when he was in the car, he showed himself to be an…you know what? This essay is not about my marriage. Let's get back to the stranger danger.

The next time a man got mad at me while I was driving he was behind me in a car and I was not moving fast enough for him. But, see, the light was red and while turning right on a red is allowed and the man was turning right, I was not turning right and so could not go. But did he care? He did not. I saw what his mouth was saying and it was not nice. The longer I sat and stared through the rearview, the worse became his antics.

First thing he did was the horn. Honk! Honk-honk. He followed that with a Tall Man[528], then a double Tall Man with honking via his knee. [529] He soon added the dirty words

---

[528] Those with children know of which finger the author speaks.

[529] The author admits she did not see this man's knee, but assumes it was a knee and not any other member of his body that became rigidly prehensile and honked the horn while his hands were busy waving in the air.

strung into sentences and whole paragraphs. To all that he added bouncing around in his seat, fisting the dashboard, and shaking his head violently.

I couldn't take my eyes off the man. It was a spectacle and I was a witness to it. Like John or Ezekiel were witnesses to the vision given them by God they then reported in their famous Bible books of Revelation and Ezekiel. But, after a while I thought *Oh, that poor man. He needs a mama to tell him to shut up*. And, since I are a mama, I told him to hush. Yes, I did. I quickly put an index finger to my pursed lips, then raised that index finger in the fashion that all children know means "Get a grip, child!" and lo and behold if the man didn't stop his tantrum right that second, nod a *Yes ma'am*, and sit back and wait patiently.

See? That Carmel woman has a lot to learn, though it is clear she isn't a mother. Or she might be a mother but also a Liberal which, of course, would explain everything including the fact that upon reading this essay she would be more concerned about the use of the words Bible and Man instead of Universe and Person.

But I have other incidences. Each is different. There was this other time a man behind me was thoroughly pissed off but I could tell this guy must have had a bad day and that he was a lover of yoga[530] and so I looked in the rearview mirror and caught his eye. Holding up my hands and making the circle of meditation with both, I briefly closed my eyes, and said *ooooohhhhmmmm*. The man calmed down, assumed the position, and smiled.

See? Stress relieved. Rage dissipated.

Then there was this other time. Hahahahaha! There I was sitting in traffic, again at a red light, in my 2002 Pontiac

---

[530] The author is aware some readers are disbelieving her that a practitioner of yoga would "lose it". To that she says, "You have answered your own question. Obviously the man was a *practitioner*, not a perfect disciple."

Bonneville[531] that I've owned since that year and behind me was a guy in a brand-spanking-new, low-slung Maserati. The man looked to be in his early sixties but dressed up like he was in his early partying forties. His face seemed to have had "work" done on it, thus pushing the illusion he was younger than he was. It was obvious to me, The Most Brilliant Woman In The World Who Is Also The Most Astute, that this man was furious at having to spend all that money on his own body to attract the young hot women when all he had to do was spend it on a vehicle that cost a lot.

And let me tell you, he was furious. Then who should be rubbing his nose in it and right in front of him but a woman, in what he knew to be an old vehicle, impeding his progress. And here he started with the honking and the Tall Man dancing and the parenthetical pronouncements of prissiness. Again, I could not take my eyes off him. His orange tan was turning red and purple he was so mad. If he only knew how many wrinkles showed up when he did that, he would be humiliated.

At this particular light in Buckhead[532] the traffic pattern is quite complicated and so what with one light after another changing in a pattern nobody has yet to figure out, the man was behind me for quite some time. Which meant I had ample opportunity to stare at him. I took that opportunity. That only made him madder.

But see, the man needed me to push his buttons because, like a child throwing a tantrum who then says "I'll show Mama!" and then holds her breath and the mother watches in quiet amusement while the child turns blue and faints, hitting the floor, and only then catching her breath and learning a

---

[531] As of this writing in 2019, the author is still driving Baby Doll and proudly brags about the vehicle on social media every chance she gets.

[532] This was in the tony part of Buckhead, not the seedier part where the author's 2002 Pontiac Bonneville would have made her look like a well-established drug-pushing madam.

valuable lesson the hard way, this man needed me to teach him a lesson the hard way because the hard way is the only way such men learn their lessons.[533]

And so I began seeing how it was that I could deliver such a lesson the hard way. First, as soon as a little bit of space opened up in front of me, the man laid on with the antics even more, trying to get me to move five feet. I remained where I was, foot firmly on brake. In fact, to tease him, I let up on the brake pedal in a random staccato fashion to make him think I was going to take up slack but then Baby Doll didn't move because…why is that, boys and girls?

Because I had set the parking brake, that's why.

Oh, the look of triumph on his face when he thought he had forced me to his will, but then nothing happened. Hahahahahaha! I told you I was The Most Brilliant Woman In The World, didn't I? Didn't I? Hahahahaha.

Next on his face was a little smile that said, "Slut, you might have won this battle, but I shall win the war." Then a spot opened up to my right and he gunned the engine and made the tires smoke and moved into the spot next to me which, as we all know, simply made him equal to (not better than) me. He turned his head and gave me a shit-eating grin and then he made both his Tall Men dance again and then I…

…gave him a feather.[534]

He blinked. He was confused. He did not understand. What was this slut-woman in an old car doing raising a pinky finger to him? This form of "signaling" was unfamiliar in his limited world and he chose to deal with it by rolling down his

---

[533] It is this type of man that often employs the services of a dominatrix skilled in the use of psychological torture. The author is not admitting to being a dominatrix though she has been accused of it by more than a few.

[534] A "feather" is also known as Pinky. So by raising Pinky instead of Tall Man one is saying the receiver is only worth a feather, not a whole bird.

window and yelling and making movements commanding me to roll down my window. I mouthed, "Ya think I be stoopid?"[535], then shook my head like "You poor sap".

The light had still not turned green, but finally it did and the man floored it and whipped past then in front of me then back into the other lane to prove some point of his. We weren't down the street two blocks when another light turned red and he had moved into a right-turn-only lane that did not allow right turns on red.

The signs were there big as life. DO NOT TURN ON RED. It's not like he could miss them. My lane began moving and I began passing him, by which time I was dying laughing and waving buh-bye while he sat slumped in his seat staring after me. I have many more examples. For instance, I've said to mad men:

Hey! Wait your turn!

Say please! That's better.

Mind your manners, Boy.

Does a widdle boy got a boo-boo he needs kissin'?

[And my favorite] *Wanna see my gun?*

The problem with the Carmel woman — and other women like her who make one aggressive move but then start shaking when the rubber meets the road — was that she acted like a victim. As if she had no power. See, what these men in a rage on the road need is a strong woman, a no-nonsense mama if you will, to tell them what to do, make them do it, and not apologize for it.

Unfortunately, most women don't know how to be a no-nonsense mama these days. They've been indoctrinated into the pussy-whipped approach to childrearing and

---

[535] The author used "street vernacular" to allow the man to continue with his opinion of her.

manhandling. This concept seems alien as you think mother = female = vagina = pussy, so how can a female be pussy-whipped if she has one? Well, she can be if by pussy-whipped we mean that the concept of teaching a lesson by force of will is ignored, which in the matters of teaching lessons to children and men is the approach of childrearing and manhandling that says feelings matter more than facts and the fact is that, just like children often do, men need a good verbal (and sometime physical) beating to help reorient them to their manners.[536]

These are facts. I know these things. I will not back down from truth.

Even with my now-ex-husband. He learned his lesson fast when I simply took my hands off the wheel and said, "HERE! YOU DRIVE!" He learned lessons the hard way, too.

Just like his father, so said his mother and she should know. Poor woman. She didn't know how to teach lessons the hard way either, and I ended up marrying her coddled child. I'm not saying anymore about it.

---

[536] The author doesn't want to hear from anybody about this subject if that person disagrees as they will have self-identified as pussy-whipped.

The Vagina Wars

DATELINE: TODAY

CLOCK: SOMETIME THIS MORNING

WHERE: ATLANTA-ISH, GEORGIA

Nut graph:

Mr. Lou-Lou Frakkakhan is working hand in hand with pussy-hat wearers who oppose the famous and witty play *The Vagina Monologues*[537] written by Eve Ensler.

Main body of arrrrtickle:

While Lou-Lou (as he would prefer to be known) chants "DEATH TO AMERICA AND JEWS!", Socialist haters chant "CHANGE THE SCRIPT OR SHUT IT DOWN!"

Frakkakhan and an anonymous androgynous ambisexual gender fluid studies leader issued a joint press release at a live event on some stairs in front of a government building somewhere suitably evocative of the struggle, wherein they confirmed their joint goal of annihilation of common enemies by any means.

"We stand before you today," Frakkakhan boomed into fawning FLOTSAM microphones. "And because we stand here YOU. MUST. TAKE. US. SERIOUSLY. Hold your questions while my fellow opposition leader speaks."

The anonymous androgynous ambisexual gender fluid studies leader then moved to the bank of microphones and waited for the cameras to stop making that racket so she could be heard clearly. "Good afternoon, evening, morning,

---

[537] The author saw this play under duress as she thought it was going to be stupid. She was wrong and her friends were right — it was well worth seeing. It was akin to the book *Passages* by Gail Sheehy only funnier, shorter, easier to understand, and superbly wonderful.

or whatever time of day you decide it is. We are inclusive of all time-counting methods and opinions except for Drumpf's because he is wrong all the time. Please! Please! Hold your questions AND YOUR APPLAUSE. Not really. Just hold your questions."

Frakkakhan was forced to jump in.

"Death to FLOTSAM[538] if you don't shut up and let my esteemed colleague speak!" FLOTSAM shut the hell up because as good little Socialists, they know a real threat when their friends issue it. Frakkakhan continued, "That's better. As you were saying, Dear 'anonymous androgynous ambisexual gender fluid studies' Leader?"

"Thank you, Lou-Lou. We need to talk about your shoes later. Niiiice. I assume they are not real leather?...Oh, they are OLD leather. How old...Never mind. It's okay. But let me finish with my statement: We stand before you today. In all our fluid genders. EXCEPT...except for actual females because they are trying to steal the thunder of Lou-Lou and our transgender friends who do not have a real vagina and who hate America and Jews. But basically what I want to say is: 'What he said'."

Members of the fawning press corps were left holding mics, shoulder-mounted cameras, and unasked questions as the anonymous androgynous ambisexual gender fluid studies leader and Lou-Lou, surrounded by armed guards that looked 100% male (Lawzuh MURZEE!), left in an armor-plated limo owned by The Little People LLC, a non-profit organization that serves to keep all children safe except for the ones who stubbornly insist they are 100% of a single gender/sex, also known as what God called male and female.

---

[538] **FLOTSAM:** For Liberal Opinion That is Serious and Actually Matters.

Post-Apocalyptic Movies

Too much of a good thing is never enough. Except when it comes to post-apocalyptic movies, because they are too much. What brought this up was the release of a movie wherein the world gets all blown up — again. So naturally, with all infrastructure gone, all the major cities of the world proceeded to build whole cities that float in the sky and on the ocean and roll across what land is left.

Let me just tell you, such movies as that are pure fantasy. I know this for several reasons. The first is that their cosmetic application is superb. Plus, eyeliner never smears until a strategically emotional moment and upon that smearing comes the knowledge the character is in deep doo-doo, has just gotten out of deep doo-doo, or has just had awesome sweaty sex just before deep doo-doo hits the fan.

Secondly, or is it thirdly? Whatever. Besides cities made of metals floating in the air and on the water, and airborne cars, their technology never fails, which right there makes the whole thing a fantasy. You know how much has to go right to make a city float on air? Even the laws of nature must change, and that's not going to happen.

So spare me the computer graphics overload and get on with the damn story. Sheesh.

Commas be gone.

It is my intention to write this entire essay without the use of a comma. Neither shall I use a semicolon since part of it is made from the comma. Don't get me wrong. I love commas. We are besties. A well-placed comma can turn a convoluted sentence into a thing of beauty.

Why am I writing this essay without a comma? It is simple. I love a challenge. Writers often get their kicks in the most esoteric of fashions that totally confuse the rest of the world. But the other reason I'm avoiding commas is this:

Commas are so misused and misunderstood as to be ridiculous. To start a fight in a bar all one need do is say "Anyone not using the Oxford Comma is a pussy!" I've done this. The fight lasted two hours and involved many men drinking lots of beer and wine and pounding on the bar while hollering "You don't believe in the Oxford Comma? YOU SUMBITCH! Ain't that right? Angela? He's a sumbitch. Ain't that right?" After which I hollered back. "That's right! Baby! Sock 'em a good one for me. Baby! You hear me? Sock 'em. Sock 'em good!"

The place hadn't seen such madness before or since. Which totally surprised me because we were in Decatur, neighbor to and northeast of Atlanta by a skosh. Atlanta/Decatur is home to certain institutions of higher learning who say they value punctuation. Agnes Scott. Emory. Georgia Tech. Georgia State. And one seminary who clings to a certain comma because without it they would have to change their doctrine and that's all I'm gonna say about that. Wouldn't you think that with these four university-slash-colleges in such proximity that surely to heaven a fight over commas in a bar would have already broken out? Then again…we are talking Decatur where the men vote Blue and are genteel and learned and practice the art of disagreement by writing a paper and getting it published and the women are lesbians even if they married a self-identified male and have children by those men.[539] Not for them the fisticuffs of drunken comma fights. No way. No how.[540]

Let me say this another way my readers in Red states might understand better: Decatur is not a place you would ever find Dave Barry hanging out.

At this very same bar is where I had my first encounter with a lesbian couple who liked threesomes. I kept turning around trying to see who they were looking at behind me. Then I realized it was me they had spied with their little roving eyes. Oh! *Hayle* no. I wrinkled my brow and shook my head and made the gesture of slitting my throat in the biggest negatory ever. That's when they turned around to see who I was turning down. They were so disappointed.

But back to the fight in the bar. Maybe it took the introduction of a real woman[541] into the mix to get the men's dander up.

---

[539] The author sort of exaggerates here though she has it on good authority inseminations are done in a sterile lab.

[540] Does the reader see how smooth the author was in the avoidance of the use of a comma in the last two sentences? Damn. She is good.

When interviewed about the entire paragraph she was quoted thusly: "The breaking up of the clichéd comment into two short but whole sentences caused a major upping of the power of the thought thus rendering the cliché as a new art form that writers would do well to study. Please be advised that Linda Sands and I are available to teach a three-day seminar on this topic as well as the bonus topic of *Medicinal Margaritas and Their Proper Place in a Writer's Life* at any foreign port of call.

"Our fee is $5,000,000. Half due upfront as a deposit. Travel and hotel expenses extra. We take credit cards and PayPal transfer payments at ***PayPal.me/AngelaKDurden***. Receipt will be sent via email."

[541] By that the author means heterosexual. She hopes she does not hear any whining from the LGBTQ-Z1-?-Curios because this is a book of humor and she hopes the reader has learned how to laugh already.

The owners still flinch when I walk in with a book. I was once headed off at the door and told this was not a good evening for me to be there.[542]

The misuse of commas these days is out of control. Many years ago I edited a manuscript that had sentence after sentence with six or more commas in each. I went insane looking for the story in what he thought were brilliant incomplete clause-laden sentences broken apart by commas thrown in like ammo coming from a machine gun wielded by a meth head jonesin' for his next hit. Holy Frickin' Moley.

This comma thing got me to thinking. Those who have no respect for commas must be P-HWPCLDRSFCs.[543] Let me explain. These folks believe several things.

One: Rules do not apply to them.

Two: Rules can be broken willy-nilly.

Three: Rules can be ignored when one doesn't like them.

Four: New rules can be made up on the spot.

Five: Those new rules only apply to you and not to them.

Sounds a lot like a Socialist Ruling-Class Wannabe to me. We are having a lot of those pop out of the woodwork these days. One example is the 2018 Midterm Elections in the United States wherein the Georgia Secretary of State was running for governor. His name is Brian Kemp. His opponent was one Stacey Abrams.[544] Abrams crisscrossed the U.S.

---

[542] This is a total lie. What they actually said was "Look. You can come in. But...do not bring up punctuation tonight. You understand? We just got through painting the walls from last time you were here. Promise you won't mention commas tonight. You promise?"

[543] In case you've forgotten: Pussy-Hat Wearing Politically Correct Liberal Democrat RINO Socialist Fascist Commies.

[544] The author writes this in October 2018: She predicts Stacey Abrams will lose. We will check in after the election to determine if she is correct. AFTER ELECTION RESULTS: SHE IS CORRECT.

looking for funding and went up and down the state registering what she called "disenfranchised voters".

She and her non-profit's employees did it all wrong — almost twenty five thousand times.

Many of those they registered were flagged because they were either non-existent or names and other legally identifying information on the voter registration forms did not match state driver's licenses and/or Social Security numbers assigned by the Feds.

That's right! People spelled their own names incorrectly and Abrams' helpers did not think to confirm the spellings. These people also forgot their Socials. How does one do that?[545] One registered as Jesus Christ of Heavenly Lane. No Social Security number or driver's permit or photo ID. And no ZIP.[546] But Stacey Abrams' people found him and signed him up and then whined when his application was completely rejected. So what did Abrams do? The next step was logical. She went on the offensive. She and her minions[547] deployed a huge campaign accusing Kemp of voter registration tampering to keep her from being governor.

---

[545] Actually, it happens all the time. Just ask anybody who has to read a resumé or job application.

[546] He lived in Blue Ridge. This is deep in the foothills of the Appalachian Mountains. So...that 'splains a lot.

[547] This includes local mainstream media.

But the author cannot fault local media too badly. They dug up a picture of Abrams from the Atlanta Journal-Constitution showing her burning the state flag and proceeded to run front and center with it for several days.

But just exactly how did the mainstream media and the Atlanta Journal-Constitution find out about that picture from 1992? It wasn't because of research. No way. No how. Abrams' preacher mother was out stumping for her daughter and told an admiring crowd all about it. She then said: "Bet y'all didn't know about that?" At which point a reporter snarked: "*NOW* WE DO!" Then Abrams' mom went: "Oh. Shoot."

That's right! Abrams pretty much said all those stupid people and illegals deserved to vote no matter whether they could prove who they were or where they lived. But who was the stupid one in this instance? You're right![548]

Abrams manufactured this so-called crisis by claiming Kemp himself was manipulating the system. The truth of the matter was different. Flagging was done by county registrars doing their duty to confirm voter information was correct.

There is also an interesting thing happening as I write this. There is a growing walking caravan of migrants coming up from Honduras and Ecuador and Guatemala[549] with the stated intent of invad-…errrrr…I mean…crossing the border into the United States without having the legal right to do so. Mexican police unsuccessfully tried to stop them but were beaten up for their troubles and decided to "escort" the caravan instead. Fifteen hundred dropped out and applied to stay in Mexico and Mexico took them.

I am not surprised at Mexico. It is my understanding Mexican police work for the drug cartels and so are only used to shooting unarmed Mexican citizens. They aren't used to having to deal with well-funded multi-national gangs… errrr…I mean poor people seeking a better life. Nor are they used to having the bright light of international media shining on them in a highly politicized situation. No wonder their police got their asses whupped. But there was another reason bloody police pictures were all over the Internet. To warn

---

[548] The author leaves this up to the reader to answer.

[549] This group initially consisted of entire families. Yes. Children were included. They were leaving conditions so horrible that walking the 1800+ miles through Mexico to "freedom" was a better alternative and they were there to demand asylum — or so the mainstream media reported. By the time the caravan reached Mexico's border hardly any "families" remained. U.S. flags were being covered in swastikas and burnt. Flags from their countries were being waved. They even got their chant wrong. Instead of saying "Yes we can!" they said "Yes we could!"

President Trump that he should be mighty skeert[550] of the righteous caravan.

That's right! Trump better open that border or else he was going to have a can of whup-...Hang on just a second. I must take this posted update on the situation from that most favored of real-news curators and fake-news-stopping social media giant Bacefook. Seems relevant and important and so I must not ignore it.

"Honduran…"

[Huh. Peruse and Scroll.]

"Migrants push north…"

[Venezuela is south. So. No, duh. Peruse and Scroll.]

"Five myths debunked…"

[Sure they are. Peruse and Scroll.]

"Trump holding back aid…"

[It's Hammer Time! Peruse and Scroll.]

"Anybody who votes for…"

[Huh? Peruse and Scroll.]

"Bitch! You're not a woman. You are a 300-pound Russian male hacker, you c—."[551]

[Whoa! Does your mama let you kiss her with that mouth?]

---

[550] This is a Southern American phrase which means scared to the point of being a yella-belly and maybe pissing one's pants as one views the trouble coming one's way.

[551] The author was actually called this on Bacefook by someone purporting to be a man but who seemed to be confused about what a woman is. Real men are never confused about that. The C-word is not a nice word. Are you still scratching your heads because you cannot figure out the word? In alphabetical sequence the letters in the word are: C. N. T. U. The author leaves the sorting to you.

My reply: "Hey, dude, now you're just flirting."[552]

I thank you for your patience.

Now we can get back to the reason for this essay.

The mainstream media is not mentioning anything about how this group is managing to carry nothing with them but is somehow totally getting fed and keeping clean and hydrated or that their "big walk" is timed to coincide with the "most important midterm elections in our lifetimes" in the United States. Nor have they mentioned how they hope like hell that the military will act under Trump's orders and kill all those poor migrant folks at the U.S.-Mexican border so they can get their Democrat Socialist candidates elected and be able to say na-na-na-boo-boo to those big bad Republicans who hate children and pussy hats and gender-queer-curious vegan tree-hugging union members.[553]

I seem to have gotten off track here. Look. It is difficult to write on a good day. But you try not using commas and see how the pressure mounts.

Look, I'm under a lot of pressure here…No…I will not stop using apostrophes or ellipses…What?!?…Now you're just tying my hands…Dude?…Oh. So now you hate me because…

---

[552] The author does not count these comma usages as going against her stated goal of not using commas in this essay because she is quoting from a published source that used the punctuation mark and could not take it out without getting permission.

[553] The author is the first to admit this sentence mightily pushed the boundaries of "Commas Be Gone" usage. But she makes no apologies and simply says for the reader to "deal with it and put on yer big-girl panties and stop whining!"

I know you are. But what am I?...Dude. Sticks and stones. **Sticks and stones!**...I will not stop using quote marks or colons...You shut up first...Oh! Well then. It's on...

Oh yeah? Yer mama![554]

Where was I? No commas. Migrant caravan. Pussy-hat...Oh yeah. I'm back on track. So the pussy-hat Socialists cannot get enough votes from citizens. What do they do? They go out and illegally register non-citizens to vote thinking nobody is going to notice them breaking the law of the land. Then — and here we've come full circle — they whine like a *gurrrly-mahn*[555] when somebody notices they broke voter and election laws and won't let them get away with it.

I hate *gurrrly-mahn* whining. Do you see me whining about not getting to use any commas? You do not see me whining because I'm not a *gurrrly-mahn*. That may not be the best argument as to why I don't whine, but heck, it's the best I've got after writing this entire thing without com-...oops, my bad.

---

[554] The author hates it when certain readers get rude and interrupt reading.

[555] It is imperative the reader imagine an Arnold Schwarzenegger accent to get the full flavor of just how pitiful *gurrrly-mahn* types can whine.

The Nature of the Crave: Part Three

There are two things I adore more than anything: Justice and Loyalty.[556] I capitalize these here because to me they aren't hollow words. They are ideals. Justice, if we want it to be lasting, must be rendered by God…and it will be in His good time. Otherwise we get small justices that bring partial justice, but never healing. Religious doctrinal opinion with quoted scriptural support and discussions about judicial systems' wide variance of application of due process of law are for another essay at another time.

Loyalty, on the other hand. I know my Heavenly Father has been loyal to me, but that is often not seen until years later and looking back. A daily dose of it, though, is something I believed could be had from ordinary humans, one to one, in the moment. It wouldn't be easy, but surely people of integrity would just be that, right? Wouldn't they see the bigger picture and be willing to sacrifice themselves for loyalty to a cause, or even to a person?

I believe I am wrong in this.

Being loyal is defined as faithful adherence to a cause, ideal, practice, custom, or person. Having loyalty means the absence of subversive tendencies or liaisons. One can even be loyal in their opposition if that opposition is for constructive purposes.

---

[556] The author begs the reader not to worry about her too much. This essay was written during yet another long damn night when the author was having more dark thoughts and believed suicide was a viable option. She wrote this footnote come the morning when she awoke after a mere three hours of sleep. Feeling the coming rain carried on the cool air through her open windows, she contemplated that maybe, just maybe, it was time for a second profligate morning full of tea bags used only once. She now proceeds to the tea, then her balcony.

Yet what I find more and more to be the case is that loyalty from one person to another is not as widespread as I thought.

Then again, maybe it's always been the case and I am just now seeing it. Maybe loyalty is not as dogged as I had always assumed it to be. Maybe I have an overactive loyalty meter toward others. Maybe I have a fanciful and romantic vision of what loyalty should be and therefore I am always disappointed when the reality of it slaps me in the face.

I write this in the early morning hours after a long month of back-to-back episodes of having those I am loyal to not being loyal back. Insulting me. Spreading rumors about me. Undermining projects I'm working on. Pretending not to know I asked for assistance. Refusing assistance with vague excuses of being sick or busy. Not getting things they promised to me in a timely enough fashion thereby throwing me under the bus.

The problem for me is that most of what I do is creative in nature. I know a lot of creative people in various industries. Creatives tend to form what look and sound like friendships so that the line between business and personal becomes blurred. I know I have a difficult time with that separation myself, but to me loyalty is loyalty. If someone is worth being loyal to in one part of your life, why not in all parts?

Like I said, this last month had multiple opportunities in it for people to be disloyal. The thing is, this is not a new situation for me. My mother was not loyal to me. My sister and one brother were not loyal. My stepfather wasn't loyal to me. I was the one who was always loyal to them, no matter what, sacrificing myself to them, for them. Was it returned?

Never.

Granted, homes with abusive parents are not places where one expects to find loyalty. But my marriage was not any better. At a business event one time where I was shining as a bright, smart, beneficial addition to the proceedings, a man said to my husband that he must be proud to have such a smart, beautiful, and good-natured woman for a wife. My husband did not know I was walking up behind him, but I clearly heard him say dismissively — and disloyally, "She isn't anything like that. She's not smart. She's just…" He shrugged like I was a piece of trash. The man was shocked and felt badly that I heard. Stopping dead in my tracks, I turned and walked away quietly.

I never said anything to my husband about that. Why didn't I? Probably because I knew how he felt since he had been passive-aggressive like that for a long time. He was disloyal, too, in other ways; surely you can guess what I mean. I put up with it until I couldn't. But he can never say that I wasn't loyal to him through it all.

Was I stupid to keep showing loyalty to him for so long? On this dark night every instance of disloyalty screams for attention. "Me, too! Me, too! Hahahaha! See how people care so little? Hahahaha!"

But this last month was particularly hard because I put myself out for so many to help them accomplish what I thought were mutually beneficial goals in shared projects, only to find out, publicly even, that I was just their tool. When it came time to do their part for me, it was never going to happen because I was not worth having my name associated publicly with them.

I make vows, here, now, as I wipe tears and blow into tissues and wonder if I have enough pills to stop my heart, that I will never again tag them in a social media post or take another beautifully arranged picture of them or post or send that picture or mention them on my blog or write reviews of their books or help when they call unless they pay me first.

I crave loyalty so much it isn't even funny. When I don't get it, I feel the loss keenly. But can I say that my keen craving should be the standard against which I measure all others' responses? Is the nature of my crave based solely on the need to feed my ego, and as such, am I only setting myself up for the fall? Am I that self-centered?

I don't think so, but could I be fooling myself? Could the two things I value above all else — Justice and Loyalty — be two sides of the same coin? After all, isn't disloyalty only another form of injustice and that, somehow, conflating the absolute with the makeshift makes me more disloyal to myself than anyone? I no longer know. Even after I've reconciled myself to waiting on Justice, the crave for Loyalty hounds me every damn day.

Disloyalty is everywhere I turn. They say that wherever you go, there you are. They say that if something continues to happen to you everywhere you go, then it isn't them, it's you. But how could I be inviting disloyalty? How? Tell me if you know, for I do not. Am I missing what loyalties are shown to me, inaccurately defining them as what they always seem to turn out to be: Temporary ways to use Angela to their advantage by pretending to have her best interests at heart?

Or am I correct in my initial woe-is-me conclusions?

Frankly, I am tired of the sacrifices I make for others only to have them thrown in my face — or altogether forgotten. I'm tired of the internal and external guilt trips laid upon me by myself and others when I speak up for me. I would rather spend time alone and slog through the mud of life on my belly than go through the disappointment again of being told that others matter so much more and that I am not worth the mattering when if for Angela to matter means an inconvenience must be borne by another and that is just too-too annoying for them.

The words to follow are part of a song I wrote a few years ago called "Black Roses Hang (It's the Way of the World)"[557] that I hadn't much thought of it since, but they popped into my head and would not go away a few days before writing this essay.

---

[557] Reprinted with permission of Angela K. Durden.

Dead eyes. Broke heart. Slammed door. Car starts.

She says to no one at all,

"Not good. Must go. Pain so slow"

burns her skin, she falls.

Time

doesn't ease the pain.

No. No.

Yeah, it's the way of the world.

In sleep I am aware.

Is that why I dream?

Perception is reality.

Is that why I scream?

Tell me why I am here.

Identity is strange.

Faith is not truth.

Black roses hang.

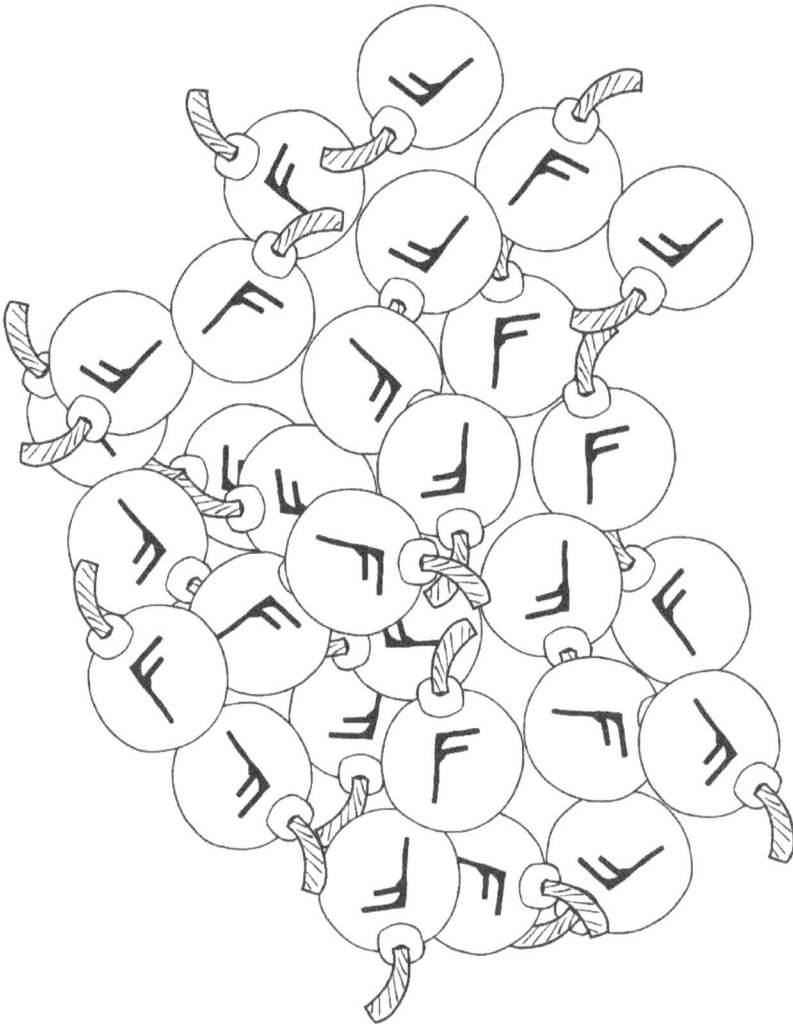

Funnier on Paper

People who write aren't usually as fluent, smooth, and slick in person as they are on paper. It is the rare person who can deliver joke setups and punchlines live. Not even all comedians can do it as is evidenced by so much use of the F-word. I will prove to you why the F-bombers use that word in their routines: It's easy. Read the follow paragraph:

They bomb the fuck out of the fucking audience until they fucking can't take it the fuck anymore. It's true! Comedians hurling fucking F-bombs are fucking everywhere you look. They breed like fucking rabbits.

Now read this paragraph and compare the two paragraphs:

Comedians bomb the hell out of the paying audience until their ears and brains are so scarred they can't take the assault any longer. It's true!

Comedians indiscriminately hurling F-bombs are literally everywhere you look. They breed like rabbits.

The edit made seven F-words go away and, in their places, came words that painted a picture. A woman once asked me to read her book and tell her what I thought of it. The F-word was fuc—...errrrr...I mean, absolutely everywhere, yet it only belonged once in the book. I pointed out that one place and why that placement in particular was so strong and that all the other F-words destroyed the power of the story, hiding all the good things she was trying to say.

She did not like my opinion. In fact, her exact words were, "I use fuck to prove how tough the woman [main character] is. I do not like your fucking opinion. You are a fucking moron. Fuck you, bitch."

Like it or not, I was still correct.

Another time at a songwriters meetup that I run, a man got up and sang what could have been an absolutely heartbreakingly beautiful song with deep meaning but who chose instead to sing the F-word to talk about:

- He [effing] loved the woman
- How [effing] she broke his heart
- How [effing] he [effing] hated her
- How much she is [effing] hated
- How [effing] badly his [effing] heart was [effing] broken
- How [effing] much the [effing] woman was [effing] loved
- How much he [effing] misses [effing] her

The club members began talking about it, but twas only I who had the courage to say, "Man, if only you hadn't said the F-word so much." Oh, the catcalls from other club members and the look of anger on the songwriter's face.

"You're just a prude, Angela!"

"Hey, Angela, lots of people use that word all the time."

"Wow, Angela, you are so behind the times."

I stood my ground and proceeded to make my case for how much better his song could've been if only he had told us instead of making us guess.

- He loved the woman with an absoluteness that only the warmth of the sun in deep space could bring.
- His heart was destroyed worse than if an atom bomb had dropped on it.

- Hate for her now equals the love he felt before and that was huge.

- There is no way he can love her again even if she should come begging and jiggling soft girly parts in his face.

- The poets say "we are strongest in the broken places" and he will survive, damn it.

- Oh, she threw away his worship and adoration like it was nothing but an empty Dairy Queen ice cream cone.

- He misses her love more than the trees would miss the sun, the grass the rain, the poets the rhyme, and the cooks the thyme.

You see what I mean? Where is the poetry in "effing"?

I will spare you the rest of the gory details, but after the meetup was over, a few club members came up and whispered privately, "I agreed with you about the F-word!"

Oh, really?

Then where the *hay-ell* were you when I was being attacked and dissed? That's right. They were trying to be invisible. *When they came for the good songwriters, I did not speak up…*

And that is how evil begins to take over.

Playing Strip Poker Like a Boss

When men marry women and vice versa[558], it never fails that one of them will want sex when the other does not. The reasons for this are multitudinous and I will not belabor those here as each will simply lead to the axiom that in this instance the Nays will always rule. Instead, I will focus on one negotiation for changing the Nay to an Aye that happened between The Ex when he was still The Husband and myself.

The children were in grades K and 2. They were asleep. Their father and I were in bed. He reached for a part of me he liked. I threw his hand back onto his side of the bed. That went on for a bit until finally he said, "Let's play strip poker. If I win, we do it. If you win, we don't."

I laughed and said, "You will lose."

He affirmed he would not and pretty much said, "Well, then, put your panties where your mouth is, Woman."

And so a deck of cards was brought to the bed and we got ourselves dressed in multiple layers of our *chips* of choice, equal by count. The deck was shuffled, cut, and dealt. Five-card stud. Nothing wild. He won the first hand. I handed over one piece of clothing. He could taste the victory. He won the second hand and another piece of my clothes joined the pile beside him.

Then *click!* I could feel it. That thing that happens in my brain when I play poker. Which is why I don't play it. The *click* is not a good click. Years after this incident that I have not quite finished relating, my married daughter was grown and we went with her to visit some of their friends up at a

---

[558] If the reader is whining by saying the author is leaving out LGBTQ+/-1~AZ*T1² people by saying males marry females and vice versa, the author has authorized this footnote to say, "Shut up with the whining and keep reading. Jesus, you people are just sucking the life out of everything."

swanky lake house. The guy had poker tables set up and wanted to play Texas Hold 'Em. I'd never heard of the game, and that's when he thought he could detect an easy win.

My husband and I were invited up to the game room to play with my daughter, son-in-law, and a couple of other people. I kept telling the guy I really didn't want to play, but he just had to keep on pushing the issue. Even my daughter didn't want me to play, but again, the man could taste an easy victory. "I'll teach you," he said helpfully.

My husband said he preferred to stay downstairs and help with making the coffee and talking with the other women…ummm…I mean our hostess and her friend. I sighed and followed the crowd up the stairs. The rules were explained to me, chips were passed out, hands were dealt… and the guy won two hands. You know what? Let me get back to the strip poker story.

So, there my husband was. Having won two hands and *click* went my brain and faster than you can say **Boom Shakalaka**, he was sitting sad and naked on the bed and I was laughing and covered in clothes. But he would not give up. "Okay. I tell you what. Let's play one more hand. Double or nothing."

"What does *double or nothing* mean? I have everything already. You have nothing."

"Look. Please…double…or…nothing."

"Okay. If you win, we do it. If I win we don't do it tonight or tomorrow night. That will make it fair since I've got all your clothes, right?"

He agreed and…**Boom Shakalaka.**

No nookie for two nights.

Back to the guy at the lake house. I didn't like his smarmy attitude. He was whooping my son-in-law's ass in the game and rubbing his nose in it, too. The other two people did not fare well, either. My daughter knew when to fold and so her chip pile was not going down as fast. Now, this guy was king of his castle and I never did like bearding a lion in his own den, but damn it all to hell, when he started getting snarky and full of himself, *click* went my brain and my daughter saw it and she said to the guy, "Get ready to lose."

But did he believe her? He did not. I said *Deal* and before you could say **Boom Shakalaka**, I had all that boy's chips and everybody at that table was screaming in pure happiness that he had the beatdown put on him. One of the kids watching ran down the stairs screaming, "Mama! Mama! That woman beat Daddy!"

My husband did not come up the stairs because he knew who "that woman" was. But the wife came flying up because she did not believe it. We had four adult witnesses plus the kid to attest to how fast he lost to "that woman" who hadn't ever played Texas Hold 'Em until that night. Besides, all the chips were in front of me and the guy was saying that I cheated somehow and, of course, I had to give him the cold dead-eye stare and call him a name. I believe it was *whining pussy* but I could be misremembering. I know he wanted to kill me, but he didn't quite know how to get away with it.

The thing is, though, that when *click* happens, it doesn't feel good. I don't like it. So I don't like to play poker or play with people who are hell-bent on winning. When we were newly married, it was the first time I ever played Hearts. My husband and I teamed up against his sister and her husband. I told them I didn't know how to play[559] and didn't want to.

But they just had to get snarky, see. And she had to keep making fun of her brother — my new husband, damn it! — and me who were losing and…*click!* **Boom Shakalaka!** At least no clothes were involved, though they never wanted to play with me again. And they kept calling me a liar. But I wasn't lying. I cannot help it that my brain goes *click!*

---

[559] The author is willing to swear on a stack of Bibles that she is not lying here and wants to remind the reader that truth is stranger than fiction.

The same *click* happens when I meet certain people. For instance, there was this man I met a few years ago at a business event. *Click* went his "little brain" when he saw me and a couple of months later (after hiring me to do a project), he's telling me he broke up with a woman he was about to propose to because he knew I was The One. No. No, no, no. NO! When I met him my brain also went *click* because I knew he was going to do something stupid like that and I tried so very hard to keep it on a professional footing, but his "little brain" just kept on *clicking*, if you get my drift. I mean, I'll take his money for a job well done, but I did not want to marry him.

After being forced to hurt his feelings on the subject just to get him to stop with trying to convince me otherwise, I finally see on Bacefook that he has proposed to the love of his life. "She is The One," he said, this time correctly. Yes, the same woman he threw over in an instant after meeting me.

But my *click* also told me that this man and I were poles apart when it came to principles of governance. After watching his posts for several years now, I can tell you my *click* was on the money once again. His latest post came as I was writing this book. On October 26, 2018, he wrote:

I was going to wait until Election Day to vote. Call me naive, sentimental, patriotic or something uglier, but I like the idea of the nation waking up on the morning of the first Tuesday after the first Monday in November to make our voices known.

This morning I woke to another of the President's middle of the night tweets, and then a mid-morning tweet followed: I couldn't get out the door fast enough. If the dog catcher had a D by its name, he/she/it got my vote.

Did you read what he said? "If the dog catcher had a D by its name, he/she/it got my vote." So the man has said he votes on passion, not logic. The man is overly emotional and does not use his brain to think. See? *Click!* This is a man who would whine about losing at a fair game of strip poker when the stakes are nookie. To such a man I would have to say, "Well, if it's a man part that starts with a D, then it doesn't get my support."

I'm being snarky. But more importantly is that the Left completely hates their presidents to tweet "in the middle of the night". It isn't presidential, you see. So President Trump "should be acting presidential and be asleep".[560] I am not making any of this up and future historians best believe what I'm saying.

You see, Trump had been hotfooting it between devastated areas over multiple states caused by two hurricanes on different coasts. These were bad storms, too. Plus there were all the meetings at the White House to determine how to handle the "Kavanaugh Thing" and the caravan of immigrants marching up from Honduras. He was also going to various states where he headlined as Cheerleader-in-Chief at massive conventions attended by Conservatives where he told them, in so many words, "We need your help in kicking some Democrat proverbial butt at the polls in this most important of midterm elections. Do not fall for their tricks."

Now, what happened was that the Democrats continued whining about Trump's tweets and speeches beginning from the day he announced his candidacy. The height of the stupidity came when one columnist complained that in his latest speech Trump didn't say anything bad about the Democrats at all. That's right. ***Trump let the Democrats down once again!***

---

[560] The lack of logic is amazing.

So what did the Dems do? They lined up a convenient patsy (the press would name him the MAGA Bomber[561]) and sent mail bombs to each other that were designed not to ever explode. The press followed the FBI running around the country trying to find the MAGA Bomber while — I am not making this up — certain broadcast organizations and politicians whined when they did not receive a mail bomb.

Husband to the presidential candidate who got her butt whupped at the polls in the 2016 election, former president Bill Clinton, was seen in one popular meme complaining to another former president, Barack Obama: "I thought you said her bomb would explode!"

Oh, the Internet fairly blew up with jokes about the Dems sending mail bombs to themselves the second the first one was "discovered". Ah, yes. The wisdom of the crowd spoke; the Democrats went insane and doubled down until even actor Robert de Niro received a bomb.

It's called *inclusiveness*, see.

The FBI found the MAGA Bomber within three days which is a miracle seeing as how it took 150 full-time task force agents over twenty years to find the Unabomber.

See?

Click went the crowd when they saw the obvious setup.

---

[561] **MAGA: Make America Great Again.** A slogan Donald Trump used in his bid for the White House. The framed bomber was named this even before they claimed they knew who he was. But when found, his van's windows were covered in pro-Trump and anti-Hillary stickers.

Never mind that the man lived in Florida and had his van parked in the sun, those stickers were in the absolutely most perfect rows you ever did see, never overlapping each other, and not a one of them was faded. They were all brilliantly clear and fresh as could be. Why, one could say they were almost "fresh from the shelf". As someone who is a graphic designer familiar with designing content to fit a predefined space, the author knows a good layout when she sees one.

Anyway, back to me. Do you see how I avoided a lot of years of pussyfooting around another man's fragile ego? I learned my lesson the first time the hard way. I was young and stupid when I married. Now, I listen when my *click* is screaming. Back when I first met The Ex, my *big click* was screaming for me to run, but my *little click* told the *big click* to shut up, and now the *big click* takes great joy in saying "I told you so, but did you listen? You. Did. Not. You gonna listen now? Yes. You. Will."

And boy oh boy do I ever listen now. Which is why I will never again play strip poker[562] unless it is truly in the spirit in which it was invented:

Purely for fun and games.

---

[562] At the rate things are going, the author will never get to play strip poker again...unless she meets Dave Barry as he collects new stories for his next book, *dave barry's complete guide to guys — **updated** for genX, genY, and the new retro millennial.*

"Gilding the lily."

It is with great pleasure I write this final essay for this book. Upon the reading, certain of my pre-readers said, "Angela, Angela, Angela. You need not have written it as now you are merely gilding the lily." So I changed the title of this from Afterword to the title you see above. Hey, when a reader is brilliant, they are brilliant.

However, by the use of that phrase they accuse' me of writing better in this section than in any other of this book. It is not for me to agree with the reader or dissuade him from his opinion, although I may if I so choose; in any case, I mustn't tell the reader in case they be the type of person who turns into a stalking fan and will knock on my door one late, dark, and stormy night asking to read something of mine that is unpublished. If however, as I attempted to do in this book, I have trained the reader well, then it is almost a given they will come to this opinion about the last chapter but — *and I mean this seriously and stress it strenuously* — you may disagree and believe it to be the worst I've ever written and yet I still will not attempt to dissuade you from it though I may have my say in my heart upon my bed while keeping silent about it[563] as I dissuade myself from sinning against the reader that did not like it.

But after I have dissuaded myself from sinning against you with, oh…say…real murder, I may put you in one of my books and have you killed off anyway. Much like I did with the bad guy in my novel *Whitfield, Nebraska,* in whose mouth I put a bunch of the stupid things The Ex said and in which the bad guy dies because he needed to die.

See? Bible admonition followed.

No laws broken. Prison time avoided.

---

[563] Bible scholars recognize this as not an original writing from the author, but where she quotes the Israelites' second king, David, in Psalm 4:4.

But my opinion about your opinion matters not since language is a living, breathing thing that adheres to the Observer Effect[564], often confused with Heisenberg's Uncertainty Principle though they are close cousins.[565]

You see, by you reading my words that, on purpose, do not *tell* you what to think (the destination) but instead tell you *why* I think what I do (the journey), my words have put you on a journey and isn't that what life is all about, the journey?

I do not even provide the path because that is the telling of you where to go. I provide the forest and hidden within

---

[564] Basically, the Observer Effect means that once you start watching something and trying to measure it, then the measurements are not accurate and the movements of the object will change based on the fact that it knows it is being watched. As an example: A man goes out dancing. He feels the need to rearrange his "package" for maximum effect on the female. Females are watching, but he does not yet know it, therefore the observer can see the real man and from that can deduce about his personality.

But, once the man knows he is being observed, his actions change as do the actions of the observer, thus the Observer Effect is in play, bringing into the mix Heisenberg's Uncertainty Principle.

[565] Heisenberg's Uncertainty Principle is a bit more difficult while being more simple. Using the man in the footnote above, it works like this:

The man enters the room. His vibes, or quantum waves of manliness also known as waves of quantum manliness, precede him across the room, hitting all other humans. However, based upon factors beyond his control, the man cannot know for certain who will be favorably impacted by those waves and thereby notice the adjustment of his "package".

His belief in the favorable quotient is merely his opinion and will not inform the actual results of whether that package adjustment is likely to be enjoyed by or make him unpopular with any one observer and, if he is like all men, will in both instances say something stupid to the female like, "I saw ewww wuz a-lookin' at my ginormous package."

And thus the uncertainty principle is in play, and if you are like me, you write a series of novels exploring Heinsenberg's Uncertainty Principle coupled with the Observer Effect, bringing them to their most logical conclusions: Marriage and Murder or Experimentation and Execution? Happy Ever After or Artful Misery?

that forest are opportunities for readers to forge a path of their own. It may run concurrent with another's. It may not. It doesn't matter because I have done what all writers should do but often do not: Provide opportunity for you to talk to another fellow traveler and, if you mind your manners, maybe find someone to hold hands with on that journey.

Umberto Eco said, "A narrator should not supply interpretations of his work; otherwise he would not have written a novel, which is a machine for generating interpretations." I add to that statement that the writer can do the same thing with non-fiction works of humor and opinion and thus I leave you to your interpretations of my words in this last essay.

But let me get back to this last essay so that you, too, can see how the lily was gilded and what has caused such a ruckus in the literary world.

In the literary world, an author must answer tough questions. At this juncture I am not discussing the questions asked of agents and publishers because, as we all know these days, there aren't enough to go around for all the writers who would like to have one or more of each. And agents and publishers that do remain —

- do not understand sales[566],
- promise, at most, one year of exceptionally minimal effort to push one's book[567],

---

[566] The Big Five have laid off many, if not most, of their in-house editors and publishers. These corporate apparatchiks then go to Wordpress.com, Wix.com, or GoDaddy.com to build a website wherein they claim their new "boutique" agency or publishing house is looking for things they've never seen before, but when approached with what "they've never seen before" promptly turn it down because it does not "fit their agency" which is patterned after the now-losing-money company they used to work for.

[567] Laid-off Editors-cum-Agents do not do anything for you after placement with a publisher. Publishers, should they even deign to sign you, want

- couldn't find a reader if one was laying on the floor in front of them and a big ol' neon arrow was pointed at their feet[568],
- and disdain the writer who sweated and slaved for the reader.

Let's talk about that sweat and the slaving. What do they smell and look like? The smell is awfully bad. Think about it. Writers sit at their computers for hours at a time, day after day, their arms in one position: Elbows firmly bent and tucked in tight to the waist as fingers fly over keyboards. What would anybody's pits smell like if they were never aired for hours on end? Exactly! Bad.

As honest as Umberto Eco was about the writing process, this is one thing even he did not have the courage to mention: Writing is a dirty business from the get-go.

Then there is the slaving. Why, you ask — and rightly so! — would a person spend years of their lives with such little payoff? I agree. The odds of making it big as a writer are worse than winning at shooting dice in a back alley and

---

you to provide to them a comprehensive marketing plan, effectively having the author do their job for them. In any case, should the author supply such, the publisher will ignore it and not have the books available for signing when the author shows up to bookstores for an ego-beating...errrr...I mean a signing with eager readers.

[568] In this the author does not completely blame the agent or publisher because even bookstores and online retailers of books don't know where the readers are. This inability to find a reader started a long time ago (in the late 1990s), but she says the reason readers are hard to find is because publishers are doing a piss-poor job of bringing interesting stuff to the reader. Instead, publishers choose low-hanging fruit of authors' pens and continue to publish the same stories year after year.
For some reason, publishers cannot understand that the reader is not stupid and will only purchase so many of an author's works when they realize the plot is identical and only the names have changed before they stop buying.

walking away from the strangers with your earnings. That makes we writers slaves. But slaves to what?

We all know getting published is a crapshoot at best, so why do we do it? Well, for some, they have nothing better to do.[569]

For a few select others, they have no choice but.

Since childhood they have been the slave of words and will always write, honing their craft each day, and when they see others misuse the power inherent in words and the punctuation that supplies meaning, they go stark raving mad and can often be seen standing on street corners near writing conferences as they hold up disgusting examples of that misuse and tear at the pages while their teeth gnash in agony and they scream "The end of publishing is near. Rewrite while ye still have the time!"

When invited to schools to talk to the little kiddies about "being an author" the children run from the room crying at the horror of such a life and the teachers complain to their principal about the author and how I...errr...I mean...how that author was not nice to the kids. And when that principal confronts the author, the author will say, "It's called *tough love*, you sumbitch. Ever hear of it? I just saved these children from years of addiction and *you* are calling *me* crazy? Hahahaha! Hahahaha!" Sobbing soon follows as the author runs out the door to my...errrr...their vehicle.

---

[569] You will find these people to be retired from one profession or another and who are looking for something to do that will allow them to travel and which will engage their minds so that they will not die early. These people write science fiction, historical romance, cozy murder mysteries, and paranormal romance, among other genres, whose main character just happens to do what the author did in real life (not that there's anything wrong with that).
They engage in publishing deals they do not want to talk about, but they go to all the writing conferences for their genre held in exotic ports of call and post pictures of themselves "meeting" famous writers they just adore (but which famous folks never post pictures vice versa).

While becoming a published author is easy these days what with the re-emergence of the time-honored endeavor called Self-Publishing[570], I hope I have made it clear that being a real writer is tough work and not for the faint of heart even if that real writer decides to invest in his effort by publishing it himself because the rest of the publishing world is so damn blinkered and dogmatic.

I keep harking back to Umberto Eco (may he rest in peace) because the man had to have read my mind except that he was much older than me and wrote a lot of things long before I did, but there must have been a metaphysical tap into my brain[571] when I was a mere child and had a purity of thought because it is amazing how and what he writes is *just like me*.

For instance, Eco says "A title must muddle the reader's ideas, not regiment them." Well, that is what I have totally been doing since I was a child and teachers would say, "What does this title mean?" and I would say "That is for you to figure out! What does it mean to *you*?" and they would say "But...but... Angela...aaaaahhh."

Then there are the times I am asked, "Which character in your books or stories do you most identify with?" Nobody likes the answer when I say, "None of them. I don't like this character and that one I would never date though he might be fun at a party." They don't like the answer because the questioner wants to get to know me the easy way and thinks I am such a limited writer that I must base my characters on myself.

---

[570] The author chooses not to delve deeply into this subject at this time because so many do it so badly that it depresses the author and that while she is here in this essay gilding the lily she prefers not to be so depressed.

[571] The author reminds the reader of how such a tap would work when she refers to the popular song "Radar Love" which calls such communication a "wave in the air".

What an insult.[572]

How would they like it if I asked them…

You know, I would never ask these people anything because they have nothing interesting to tell me, which is, I guess, why I spend so much time alone with words. Now, words are interesting as hell. If I was stranded on a desert island, all I ask is that I have a Bible and a dictionary and a fishhook and some distilled water and Strike-Anywhere-Anytime matches and I'm good to go. See? Simple needs.

Umberto Eco says that nothing ever comes from a flash of inspiration as if it came from nowhere. In this he is correct because inspiration is 99% sweat followed by 1% genius, and it is that 1% genius that is the sparking energy to the sweat because, as we all know, sweat of and by itself, even by the gallon, produces nothing but salty, icky, stinky *ewwww*.

For instance, I once had a song come to me in a flash. I've written about this in other works and won't tell the story here as it would take too long, but this song did not come out of the blue. After I wrote down the song lyrics and chord progression in a fixed format for copyright-proving purposes, I asked myself how it is I could be listening to Kris Kristofferson one minute and getting flash-banged the next with this wonderful song?

I traced the roots of that *flash* to a moment one year previous wherein a man said to me one simple sentence. But that sentence itself only held meaning because of a journey I had been on my whole life that led me to a point of dread. So, you see, that flash which birthed a song only did so because the seed had been planted, not because it was dumped into my brain willy-nilly by an alien looking to snatch a body.

But here is another important point to remember: Just because that song (or story, as the case may be) means much

---

[572] The author says of such readers "Screw them!"

to me and others appreciate it, does not of and by itself prove it is better than any other.

You know this is true if you've ever watched the Oscar or Grammy shows and/or literary prize awards ceremonies. I mean, really? "What were these people thinking?"[573] is a question you've asked yourself many times.

I was having coffee the other day with a criminal defense attorney[574], one Jason B. Sheffield of Decatur, Georgia. We were having a robust conversation about the topic assigned to us: Writing About Women's Issues. What a boring title. One surely designed to inhibit interest in anything we had to say, but what could we do? The topic was chosen for us. As a criminal defense attorney who wrote a book about a female criminal defense attorney[575], and me as a woman, somebody thought we could opine about that subject. So there we are in our planning meeting inside the Starbucks having a rip-roaring old time and otherwise entertaining and shocking the patrons with language that was at once accurate, enlightened, and provocative in its political incorrectness.[576]

---

[573] The author would not turn down any award either organization presented to her because then she would have hope that maybe, just maybe, their ability to discern high quality from low would be improving.

[574] The author notes they were prepping to be on a panel together and that she was not in need of his services.

[575] Sheffield wrote **Son of a Bitch!** which featured his real-life criminal defense attorney mother in the title role of bitch and him as another character.

[576] The author was hoping one of the patrons would say something like, "Oh, my God! You two are such weirdos!" at which point the author would have deployed the art of the snappy comeback by saying, "I know you are, but what am I?" and then would thoroughly document for the reader what would occur. But nobody in that place had any courage to stand up for their Liberal beliefs. Unless! Unless nobody in there was a Liberal. There is hope after all.

Because the conversation was so good[577], we found ourselves exploring other topics and went from women's issues to the craft of writing, at which time I told Jason about two characters, Gordon and Lucinda, in my series called *The Dance Floor Wars*. The first book, *Dispatches From the Front*, is written first-person by Gordon, a war correspondent and journalist. I told Jason that, after having written the first book, naturally I should write the second from the viewpoint of Gordon's love, Lucinda. [578]

The problem I ran into in the first chapter of the second book, *Lucinda's People*, is that, while Gordon is a hell of a writer, Lucinda can't even get out one chapter without boring the reader and making a thorough botch of it. Lucinda couldn't write a whole book!

Jason laughed loudly and threw himself back into his chair raising his arms and yelling, "What? How can that be? Aren't you the author?"

And this is where we get to another point, and one that Umberto Eco pointed out so well: "Characters are obliged to act according to the laws of the world in which they live" thus making the writer "a prisoner of his own premises".

Gordon and Lucinda inhabited a world of my making. The world is not so alien that regular folks cannot identify with the plot and characters, but Gordon made his living writing and therefore, it followed, he better be damn good at it[579], whereas Lucinda had a job as a regular employee doing stuff we never learn about at a company that is never named because it doesn't matter for the purposes of anything the reader need know. Lucinda is a great gal. She had to be, or

---

[577] The author says, "It was better than sex!"

[578] As of 2019 this series is yet to be published.

[579] Gordon was always getting in trouble for his truthful writing which tended to be straightforwardly honest, sparing none, but his newspaper printed it anyway because he was that good.

else Gordon would never have fallen in love with her. But she was not only not a writer, she was not even self-aware. Writers that are self-aware make better sentences and paragraphs and Gordon was self-aware out the wazoo.

Which is why I, who put these two people in the first book to make them do as they did, did as they did because I made the world in which they existed and I was true to them, but it wasn't until I started the second book that I found out just how bad a writer Lucinda was, and how limited she was in understanding herself. The chapter I wrote from Lucinda's POV was scrapped in its entirety. And why? Because Lucinda didn't have a POV, or at least one she could verbalize with any clarity. Her journey was tough.

What was I to do? Was I to forget about this second book? No! *Lucinda's People* had stories to tell. Important stories. Necessary stories. And am I ever glad that Lucinda was a terrible writer because once I was forced to tell the stories using the omniscient narrator's (O.N.) voice, now we could learn the truth about Lucinda and what motivates her. You see, the O.N. is not inhibited by anything because he can read minds and hearts and motivations of all characters and never has to explain one tiny bit how he knows because he is above it all. All-knowing, all-seeing, uncaring what the reader thinks of him, with nothing to prove because he has no pony in this race.

Whereas first-person is limited in the telling as first-person can tell the truth about others only as they know it, can prove it, and then the writer has to explain how that happened. The writer cannot just drop in information from the first-person narrator because the reader will want to know who told him, what was the reason, when was he told, where was he told, why was he told, and what that has to do with the storyline.

An O.N. certainly can drop in facts from any number of places or people and we believe him because he is omniscient. This does not mean continuity of character or plot lines are sacrificed when the O.N. makes his report. If anything, these must be tighter because there is so much more information. Which is why so many stories are written in first-person.

In any case, it is binding upon the author to train the reader in how to navigate this new world. Too many "authors"[580] take courses on how to write thinking if they only apply the approved rules that their story will advance from pedestrian to horse-race exciting. This is not true and is a fairy tale sold by those who teach such courses at places like Full Sail, Emory, Agnes Scott, SCAD, and other so-called schools of higher learning across the land.

Words are funny little animals. They live wild in the woods and in the city and in the country and are like rats and termites and roaches and ants: They will not be controlled in any meaningful fashion by experts who claim to have them figured out and believe them to be controllable. Words wait — no, they *long* — for someone to come along who respects them, much like many husbands who want respect and who don't care whether they are *understood*.

The novelist or humorist that writes according to an arbitrary set of rules has already lost his ability to train his reader and, frankly, will not benefit them at all because he cannot expand the readers' horizons beyond what even the writer could have imagined. Here we get back to the Observer Effect and Heisenberg's Uncertainty Principle in all their glorious effects and affects.

Though we know there is really nothing new under the sun, there are a lot of people who haven't seen everything and so when a writer plans something "new" he does so with the explicit understanding that he has a lot of work to do and much of that work will include — according to Eco, with whom I concur — becoming a philosopher who "wants to reveal to his public what it *should* want, even if it does not

---

[580] The author of this essay has put this word in quotes to indicate irony, or sarcasm if you prefer.

know it. He wants to reveal the reader to himself." And the writer does so without having to personally know the reader.

But the writer who approaches a new[581] form or method of delivery of thought has a steep climb in getting eyes on his works. The reason is usually because these do not have the familiar flash-bang which greets the reader on the typical bookstore shelf. The Big Five in publishing have done a great job of training the public to purchase their books based solely on flashy covers, one- or two-word titles made from verbs or strong nouns, and the printing of Best Seller on the cover without the offering of any evidentiary proof of that status.

Eco understood this in the American reader and knew it held him back from penetrating the market here, whereas in Europe the sensibilities of the reader have been trained differently and his fight for sales there was not nearly as fierce while much more profitable.

In the U.S. there seems to be this belief among readers that somehow it is the novelist's and humorist's job to lead one to a conclusion that is agreed upon by experts and other readers, so that they can meet to discuss those pre-approved conclusions knowing that no argument will break out and that no debate will be entertained. A literary feel-good group hug, if you will.

He who understands that pressure turns coal to diamonds and irritation turns grains of sand to pearls and that the conflict between tectonic plates is what makes mountains to climb is a better writer than those who feed overcooked words to toothless readers for them to gum.

The novelist who is not afraid of conflict and who trains the reader how to properly appreciate his words is much like the familiar "bad boy" that trains a series of girlfriends to like

---

[581] New as in not known by the current batch of buying readers.

the beating she's gonna get when he arrives.[582] In other words, the reader will love getting mistreated and otherwise tortured, and will show appreciation by begging for more.

The novelist must lead the reader while not leading at the same time. Is it really such a bad thing if the reader gets to the end of the book and finds out that the journey was better than the destination — or that there was no destination at all?

As I write this I realize that there will be many readers who will be lost, confused, and unable to figure out what the hell I'm writing about. This should not cause the reader any anguish and does not mean they are stupid. In fact, whoever reads this and then proceeds to make commentary upon it to "explain" it will be viewed by me as a faker, a poser, an impostor, and a fraud. And if they do so by charging a fee from gullible audiences, I call them a charlatan.[583]

Still, though, while the reader may be confused, they cannot help but see that this essay truly does "gild the lily" and will freely admit and spread the word that I am The Most Brilliant Woman In The World.

Of course, as I write these words I do so with the full knowledge that there will be readers who will not get my humor and will come to an opinion that by my naming myself these dazzling titles and talking myself up that I am a bitch who does not know her place. I have been told this to my face, so it is not out of the realm of possibility that a random reader or two would have the same thought. To these, by way of answer, I point to me playing "My Heart Weeps for Thee" on the world's smallest violin.[584]

---

[582] Not really. That's just the author having a little bit of sick fun and she does not want to hear from anybody about her insensitivity when all she is doing is making a parallel of thought to get a point across.

[583] Unless they have made a licensing agreement with the author, at which time the author takes back everything she just said and will call them brilliant.

[584] This should be accompanied by a visual, namely, an index finger lightly rubbing its accompanying thumb to simulate violin playing.

Folks like that also believe all headlines the mainstream media puts out. As Eco said, "There is always someone who takes ironic discourse seriously."

My heroes are Mark Twain and Will Rogers after him, and Dave Barry and Victor Borge, none of whom took themselves seriously. They talked themselves up in an over-the-top fashion, making fun of themselves while, at the same time, not apologizing for their skill. What they did was break down the barriers that "serious" artists and musicians built between themselves and their audiences, the general public. Through satiric commentary coupled with sarcasm and not a little bit of wit, these humorists granted All-Access passes to those who didn't give one whit about the opinion of the hoity-toity intelligentsia who couldn't recognize irony if it was their mother at a family reunion.

Those hoity-toity, intelligentsia-built barriers are bigger than ever these days. Laughter has been outlawed unless a Deep State committee has approved the subject matter. One only must look at certain television talk shows where contrary discourse is not allowed, if it is brought up it will often be shouted down by bully hosts, and in which only those things dear to the hearts of regular folks in flyover country are made fun of.

Deep State-regulated humor is a deceptive and treacherous cancer upon the psyche of nations. We know this because it has accompanied the dumbing down of the populace through state-funded means. Need I mention the USSR, Cambodia, North Vietnam, China, North Korea, a slew of African nations, several island nations, Iran, Iraq, and soon to follow if we don't fight it, the U.S.?

The novelist and humorist who understands all this, and who wants to help their fellow, has huge opportunity these days to say, "Come on. Laugh with me! Open your closed little mind."

The novelist and humorist who bucks the system also appreciates that to do so means they will paint a big target on their chest. They understand they must constantly "check their ego at the door" while seemingly not doing that very thing. They must confuse and clarify, muddle and mandate, cause panic and bring calm, elicit terror and provide refuge for the reader who seeks without knowing they are blinded. Ella Wheeler Wilcox said in her poem *The Winds of Fate:*

One ship drives east and another drives west
With the selfsame winds that blow.
Tis the set of the sails
And not the gales
Which tells us the way to go.
Like the winds of the seas are the ways of fate,
As we voyage along through the life:
Tis the set of a soul
That decides its goal,
And not the calm or the strife.

Novelists and humorists being true to their art form are the captains of their ships making way on politically storm-tossed oceans. They do not let the prevailing winds of political correctness tell their ship where to go. They control the set of their sails, not knowing in which harbor they will find protection. They worry not about their own protection because their worry is for others. By doing so, novelists and humorists give Morpheus-like succor to those who are caught in The Matrix and who feel something is wrong but cannot figure out what it is.

Novelists and humorists, if they are any good, are realists. As we await God's purpose to be fulfilled, we are the last defense against Satan's crafty, cunning, and underhanded treachery against the innocent. We are the last defense because, though we don't like it, we understand treachery. We can smell cunning coming our way three miles out. We can grapple with evil in dark places favored by the wicked and walk away scratched but intact.

We eschew the popularly accepted and applaud the extraordinary. We are behind the times because it is in the historical we find the answers to the future.

We yearn for gratitude and thanks for our sacrifice but know it will not ever be ours in our lifetime. And we are good with that because we have been called never to be satisfied with the pretty façade and always to question and poke and prod the bones and guts of the systems under which we live and of those who attempt to control.

We exist to spark conversations in hyperreality.

— AND WE END ONLY TO BEGIN AGAIN —

BOOKS BY ANGELA K. DURDEN

BUSINESS
Nine Stupid Things People Do to Mess Up
Their Resumés (2000)

MEN! K.I.S.S. Your Resumé and Say Hello
to a Better Job (2013)
Also available from Audible

LADIES! K.I.S.S. Your Resumé and Say
Hello to a Better Job (2013)

Opportunity Meets Motivation (2010)

Navigating the New Music Business as a
DIY and Indie: Coming Clean with the
Down and Dirty (2015)

Music Business Survival Manual (2019)

CHILDREN'S
A Mike and His Grandpa Series:
Heroes Need Practice, Too! (2006)
The Balloon That Would Not Pop! (2012)

HUMOR
Dancing at the Waffle House
and other stories Neal Boortz wishes he had told
(2018)

OTHER
Eloise Forgets How to Laugh (2010)
Twinkle, a memoir (2015)
First Time for Everything (2018)
Do Not Mistake This Smile (2018)

FICTION by DURDEN KELL
Whitfield, Nebraska (2015)

TWO NOVEL SERIES IN DEVELOPMENT
The Case Files of Smith and Jones:
The Case of the Cotton Fiber Snuff Tape
The Case of the Cat-Loving Killer
The Case of the Angelic Assassin

The Dance Floor Wars:
Dispatches from the Front
Lucinda's People
Collisions
Life Cycle of a Fling

EXECUTIVE/DEVELOPMENTAL EDITOR and PUBLISHER for
I AM ISRAEL: Lions and Lambs of the Land
by Jedwin Smith (2018)

Rock Around The Block
by Alan Ray White (2019)

PUBLISHER
Imprints
WRITER for HIRE! Press
Second Bight Publishing
Blue Room Books

CONVERSATIONS IN HYPERREALITY
and Other Thoughts Umberto Eco
and Dave Barry Never Had

9780985462376

BLUE ROOM BOOKS
DECATUR, GA

www.ingramcontent.com/pod-product-compliance
Lightning Source LLC
Chambersburg PA
CBHW080658110426
42739CB00034B/3325